BUT YOU MADE
THE FRONT PAGE!

Wonderama,

Wars, *and a*

Whole Bunch of Life

SONNY FOX

Paperback ISBN 9780786754182

Produced by Marcovaldo Productions, Inc.
Book Design by Backstory Design

Distributed by Argo Navis Author Services

Distributed by
Argo Navis Author Services
www.argonavisdigital.com

To all my "kids," now in their fifties and sixties who grew up watching my children's shows in the '50s and '60s, and who constantly integrate those experiences into their lives today. The bond of trust we built between us has always resonated as the most satisfying experience I have had in television.

You have encouraged me to explore and learn about that unique class of humanity we call children.

You continue to astonish me with the vividness of your memories.

Thank you.

Contents

CONTENTS

Foreword

In 1977, when I was Vice President of NBC Children's Programs, there was one of those bloodbaths at NBC when they decided they had to get rid of three hundred people. Every department had to cut. Somebody noticed that I was working without a contract and that they could absorb Children's programs into Daytime. Next thing I know, I'm told that they're canceling the position. Six weeks and I'm out. The following day the *New York Post* runs a big front-page story: "Bloodbath at NBC." Then there are the names of the people who have been axed, like a list of victims of an airline disaster, and, like Abu Ben Adhem, my name led the list. It was the only name that was on the front page; the rest were a carry-over. I'm balefully looking at this newspaper at my desk when my assistant says, "Your mother's on the phone."

"Hi, Gittel."

"Congratulations!"

"What about?"

"I read the article in the *Post*."

"Ma, it says I got fired!"

"Yes, but you made the front page!"

In a life filled with successes and some failures, my Mother's ability to flip disappointment into a semblance of triumph—of not allowing a failing to become failure—suggested an appropriate title for this book.

In my more than eight decades of life, I have been a prisoner of war in Germany and a war correspondent in Korea. I have taped TV shows in Portugal, Denmark, Finland, Bolivia and Israel. I have played the part of Papa Noel in Guayaquil, Ecuador and watched Jawaharlal Nehru in the nascent Indian parliament. I have ascended the heights of the television industry as a Vice President of NBC-TV and Chairman of the Board of the Academy of Television Arts and Sciences, and I have been plunged into its nether regions when fired as host of the number one show in the country, The $64,000 Challenge. I have gotten to know Senator Robert Kennedy, done a program with Harry Truman, and been hit with a pie in the face by Bob Hope.

When writing a memoir, one does rely on decades of memory, and memory is an interesting storage space in our brain cells. There were times, in writing about my early childhood in Brooklyn, when the sense memory of the streets and the games and the humiliations were more vibrant than much more recent events. But memories can also be vagrant and elusive and not always unembellished. It was Gore Vidal who said, "the last time we speak of a past event, it is not the event we are recalling, but the last time we described it." If one were to embellish or change the events a bit, with each retelling, the final outcome might be rather skewed.

The experience of writing this book has taken me on the most complex and unexpected journey of my life—a journey into a time warp of memories, encounters, convergences, and interventions that finally brought me to the realization that my entire professional life seems to have been lived at the intersection of the impossible and the inevitable. I was born when Calvin Coolidge was president, grew up during the great depression, careened through WWII, started in radio and participated in the growth of the television industry from its earliest days, and today I am involved with the production of a digital soap opera.

I have lived one third of the history of this country.

FOREWORD

This is my personal Baedeker.

As you read this book you will not find a lot of self-examination and introspective musings, since I was not brought up that way, nor am I inclined to examine my emotions too closely even today. But in this book perhaps you will find a reflection, a memory, an insight that may refract through the prism of your own life.

CHAPTER 1

December 28, 1944.
Bad Orb, Germany

Name?
Irwin Fox.
Rank?
Sergeant.
Serial Number?
42022375.

It was late afternoon when they finally let us out of the boxcar that had been our prison for seven days—with no food or water. The air was freezing cold, the sky was gray and the snow stood in waist-high drifts. There were German soldiers everywhere; posted in watchtowers, barbed wire all around. As I waited in a long line, two things became clear—I was a long way from Brooklyn and there was no getting out of here. Alongside the tracks the Germans had set up some desks where clerks signed us in. I was hungry and exhausted. We all were. The line moved slowly as the clerks took our information and processed it carefully. Goddamn German efficiency. Finally, I got to the front of the line and was facing another convergence. Instead of a German, I was looking at an American who had preceded us into this camp and had been designated by the Germans to assist in the checking in process.

"Division?"

The Germans already knew that they were going to be attacking the 28th Division when they kicked off the onslaught that became known as the Battle of the Bulge. Anyway, the red keystone patch on the shoulder of my combat jacket gave it away.

"Company E, 110th Regiment, 28th Division."

"Father's Name?"

"I'm only supposed to give name, rank, and serial number."

"Listen, kid, if you don't answer these questions they're going to make you stand in the snow until you do."

After what we'd just been through, I just wanted to get into a warm place, anywhere, and lie down. And get some food. So the idea of standing in the snow for a few hours definitely did not appeal. I figured they're not going to win the war if I tell them my father's name.

"Julius Fox."

"Occupation?"

"Textile converter."

"Religion?"

So here I am, a Jewish prisoner of war behind Nazi lines, being asked my religion. In December 1944, in the snow at Bad Orb, I had not thought of hearing that question. I had not planned on being a POW.

"Religion?" the clerk repeated.

Who was that gangly, 19-year-old person being confronted with that question? What was he carrying within him that would shape that answer?

𝒥𝑅

It was a brutally hot July afternoon in 1938 as my bare feet shifted to try to keep them from frying on the scorching sand of Brighton Beach, on the Atlantic shore of the United States—the part called

Brooklyn. I didn't care about anything except that a major swing orchestra, Shep Fields and his Rippling Rhythm, was playing and my eyes were trained on the bandleader. Nothing mattered, except the moment when Shep Fields would give the gang a wave. That's what I was waiting for. And the whole gang was waiting with me. I knew it would come, because Freddy Feldman, Shep's kid brother, was standing there, right next to me, on the hot sand at Brighton Beach. I waited for Shep Fields to turn around and give us his benediction.

Suddenly, there it was. Shep looked straight at our gang and WINKED. I saw it first and grabbed Freddy, "See that?!" I was grinning from ear to ear. This was like a blessing from the Pope! Shep Fields was in that glittering, glamorous, untouchable world called "show biz." A champagne and limousine and swimming pool world, a million miles from East Ninth Street and textile converters like my father.

In the 1930s, Brooklyn was for the most part, an interesting place to grow up. For one thing, there was a great sense of neighborhood and extended family in Brooklyn. Norman Unger, Freddie Feldman and Alan Levine and some of the others served as my extended family. Being part of the 9th Street gang was important to me.

There were always rites of initiation upon arriving on the block as the new kid.

"Ever played 'Fire in the Church'?" the kids had asked me when we first moved there.

"No."

"Bring a handkerchief and meet us at the lumber yard."

The lumber yard was an abandoned lot that ran between Ninth and Tenth streets along Ave. H. There were piles of what looked like railroad ties. In the middle was a hut of galvanized tin with no door or windows. Always anxious to become a member of the gang, I showed up at the appointed hour with a nicely folded handkerchief, ready to play "Fire in the Church." The guys, perhaps six or seven of them, made a circle.

"Okay, put your handkerchief down there." One of the guys indicated the ground in the middle of the circle. I did as I was told.

"Fire in the church! Fire in the church!" they cried.

They unbuttoned their flies, and proceeded to "extinguish" the imaginary blaze with streams of piss onto my neat handkerchief. Much laughter ensued. I am not sure if I laughed or stood there, stunned. But I had passed through the portals of membership as a kid on East Ninth Street—at least the Jewish part.

We all lived in Flatbush, but East Ninth Street was our neighborhood. Actually, it wasn't all of East Ninth Street; it was *our* half of East Ninth Street. The other half was Italian. The Italian houses were one-family homes with trees. The Jewish part of the block was mostly four-story apartment buildings with a lot of pavement.

We all went to the same school, PS 217, but there were the Italian kids and the Jewish kids. We never hung out together. Once, an Italian girl in our class died. We knew we had to make a house call so a few of us went into the Italian part of the street, all sort of helping each other along. When we got to the house it was dark, with people in dark clothing, crucifixes on the wall and the body in the back. It felt as though we had stumbled into an Egyptian burial chamber. We mumbled something appropriate and ran like crazy till we were back on our half of Ninth Street. That was when I started breathing again.

On East Eighth Street, where I had lived before, there had been no other Jewish kids on the block. Anti-Semitic taunts were hurled my way from time to time and I was the subject of bullying by other kids. Carrying my violin case to my lessons didn't help. I was also a lot smaller than the other kids and not disposed toward fighting. A Jewish wimp made a pretty good target.

One evening, this led to a lecture from my mild-mannered father on the need to stand up for one's rights. I was not to back down. I had to let the kids know they could not push me around. It was Henry V at Agincourt. I could feel the POWER growing within me. I could feel my father's strength transmogrifying into my sinews. So the next day, I was riding my bike on the street—and rode right through a game the kids were playing. One of them told me to get out. But this was not the wimp he thought he knew. This was the new, brave and dauntless Sonny, cloaked in the powers vested in me by my father. I leapt off my bike and charged toward my considerably larger adversary.

Next thing I knew, I was on the pavement looking up.

The following day, my father hauled me over to the home of the winner of this short fight. My father exhibited my black eye as evidence of the evil lurking in the other man's son. This visit was a bit confusing. I had picked the fight. I had been decked. Now my father, who yesterday was urging me on, was copping a plea.

Soon we moved to East Ninth Street.

One of the ways we survived the Depression was by moving a lot. We would move into an apartment, Dad would sign a year's lease and get two months "concession," which meant he got the first two months free. He'd pay rent for the next eight months, then stop paying when the last two months were due and get a "dispossess" notice. That was how he managed to pay only eight months rent and got a year out of it. But it meant we moved a lot. Bensonhurst. Manhattan Beach. East Eighth Street Foster Ave. East Ninth Street Sheepshead Bay. So I was always going to new PS's, and always the new kid on the block. And the youngest in the crowd.

That had occurred because in the early grades, every time the teacher would say, "Sonny's not working up to his capacity," my pushy mother would answer, "Of course. He's bored. Skip him." And they did; three times between the third and fifth grades. My mother pushed me a year and a half ahead of myself, which ended up meaning I was sort of bewildered about a lot of things. Like long division. And girls.

When it came time to choose up sides, I was the kid picked last—the leftover when the choices had been made. I learned to not let them see I was hurt. My age and size led, ultimately, to a series of humiliations for which I had to develop coping skills. I learned to guard against anyone knowing how I felt. I developed a place deep inside of me that no one was going to reach—the part that kept me from crying. The part that, years later, when I was very publicly replaced as the host on the number one TV show in the country, kept me standing upright and continuing to present myself as a successful performer.

This resource was sorely tested as I tried to keep up with my older buddies.

"I bet you don't even know where babies come out," sneered one of my buddies.

I didn't, but I was certainly not going to confess that. "I do so," I declared, with a quiver of uncertainty in my voice.

"Yeah—where?"

I desperately thought of what cavity in the body would be big enough for a baby to come through and finally announced:

"From where you make BM!"

Gales of derisive laughter told me I had screwed this up too.

My sex education took place largely on the street. One of our favorite hangouts was the cut along Ave. H where, down a hillside, an occasional Long Island Railroad freight train would rumble through. It was on this hillside we would often repair to roast "mickeys"—baking potatoes taken from the small supply of food we had in our homes. It was here I saw my first pornographic, crudely drawn, but anatomically correct comic books. I finally saw how sex worked in these raw, but graphic presentations. It was here, and in Prospect Park to which we would ride our bikes—probably three miles—that I first experimented with smoking cigarettes and a pipe. Perhaps I started as early as 13.

My sex education at home came when I was 16. I was drying dishes and Dad was alongside me. Without facing me he said, "So you are dating now."

"Yeah."

"Do you know how to protect yourself?"

"Yeah."

"Good."

That was it, folks. The truth was I was so hapless with the girls I never had to concern myself with "protection" until I returned from WWII.

The attitude toward schools and teachers, at least in my part of the world, was very different than it is today. Teachers were in a special class and only had last names. I recall the day I heard one teacher hail another one as they left the school. "George," he called. George! He had a first name. I later discovered teachers also had children. But through much of my life, whether they were good or inadequate, they were TEACHERS. But in the ascending order to Godhead, none was higher than Principal. To be sent to the Principal's office for dereliction of decorum was probably close to being on the tumbrel on the way to the guillotine. I would sit outside her (yes, they all seemed to be 'hers') office awaiting her stern lecture as if awaiting the governor's response to a plea for clemency. In retrospect, the admonishments almost always ended in a promise by me to reform my ways, and then I was allowed to return to the classroom.

And they were pretty smart in handling those of us who were the most fractious. Our gang at PS 217 had been marked by the pedagogical mafia as a disturbing influence in many small ways. The principal, Mrs. Lieberman, was a woman of ample girth and an uncanny ability to deal with these lower middle-class kids. She co-opted us. She deputized us to become crossing guards. We were given AAA white Sam Browne belts and, voila, we were now members of the establishment. We were given assignments to control students at street crossings near the school and make certain no one crossed against a traffic signal.

Smart lady.

Most of education in those days emphasized rote learning. You repeated and repeated until whatever stuff you were supposed to learn was drilled into you. In thinking back to the songs we were taught, I am startled by the contrast between the students, who were first or second generation from Italy or Eastern Europe, and the songs we were taught to sing:

Do you ken John Peel at the break of the day
Do you ken John Peel with his coat so gray
Do you ken John Peel when he's far, far away
With his hounds and his hares in the morning
Oh his view halloo would awaken the dead

What the hell was a view halloo? What was ken? What was an English fox-hunting song doing at PS 217 in the middle of Flatbush?

But I remember the words and I can still sing it—though there are few requests lately for that gem.

There wasn't just education at school. There was religious education, Services. I trained for my Bar Mitzvah at the Young Israel of Flatbush. The process of memorizing the portion of the Torah I was to read was tortuous for me. One is looking at the ancient Aramaic symbols with none of the diacritical markers indicating the vowels. The only marks, other than the words, indicate how your voice should chant at each point. Somehow, after many weeks of practice and tears, I managed to get through this important ceremony.

In today's societies, there are huge and very expensive dinner/swim parties and more to celebrate such an event. In 1938, our celebration was in our small backyard between the house and the garage. Unfortunately, my ability to squeak through the chanting on that day, led to a painful experience for my proud Grandpa.

Zayda (grandpa), my mother's father, had come to this country in late 1905 and spent five years making enough money to bring the rest of the family over from their Shtetl in Austria-Hungary. He had worked hard as a pants cutter, but his true delight was to be the president of a shul. It did not matter how large or important a shul, just so he was president. If the members of one shul did not agree with him, he left and started another shul. I remembered walking along the streets of Brooklyn with him as I carried a sacred torah to yet another storefront that was going to be his new place of worship. Naturally, he was to be its president.

On Friday nights, we would go to my grandparents' house for the Sabbath dinner. The glow of the candles, the wonderful Challah and the warmth of the family made up for my Grandma Goldberg's horrible cooking. I remember when Zayda would come home from shul with his cohorts—the Chasidim—with their black garments, their love curls and their black felt hats, their teeth stained yellow by the nicotine of their ever-present cigarettes. They exuded an energy that filled the small house. Best of all, I remember when the music would start; how the Chassidim would sing songs of joy, with fervor and laughter, banging on the table to keep time.

And I remember the day I had shamed my Zayda, a few months after my Bar Mitzvah, when I was attending a Saturday service at his shul. When the reading of the Torah started and I heard my Hebrew name called, "Yitzhak ben Yehuda, (Irwin, son of Julius)."

There was my grandfather, beckoning me from the Beemah, proudly awaiting the moment when he was going to show the congregation how his grandson, Yitzhak, would chant the passage from today's portion of the scroll. I could feel my dread grow as I mounted the steps to the center of his world.

It had taken more than six months of practice to master my Bar Mitzvah. It had been a severe trial, full of frustration and tears and this was an entirely different portion. My Zayde smiled proudly at me as the dreaded moment came. The Rabbi pointed to the beginning of the portion on the un-scrolled torah with a silver pointer, shaped like a hand at the end of a dowel. I was to read from there.

The shapes swam before me. I stared at them but none of them made any sense to me. I tried to speak but nothing came out. I am sure that eyes were rolling in the heads of the sages around my Zayda but I couldn't say anything. I tried not to look at my Zayda when, finally, the Rabbi stepped in and chanted the portion.

When it was over, and the blessing given, I descended into the congregation feeling like I'd shoved a dagger into Zayde's heart. I wanted to flee from the shul and pretend it had never happened.

⚜

Religion?

The clerk was waiting impatiently. I didn't want to be here. But I was. I took a breath and said,

"Jewish."

The clerk looked up from the form, stared at me for a moment and said, "Protestant."

At first I thought he hadn't heard me. Then I understood what he was trying to do. Why place yourself in peril? I was a Jew in Germany. It was enough that I had already surrendered, physically. Now they wanted me to surrender morally? I wasn't going to do it.

"Jewish," I repeated.

This time I don't even think the clerk looked up.

"Protestant!" He could not be bothered to spend any more time with a putz who did not appreciate the gift he was being given.

Then he indicated for me to move on. Which I did, gladly. I was cold. I was hungry. I was exhausted. Maybe that's why I was willing to spout out my incriminating answer. I was too tired to be devious. I was too hungry to stand outside in the snow and refuse to answer their questions. Maybe that's why people who are given the third-degree or worse confess to crimes they didn't commit—you get to the point where you just want it to be over.

I left the desk and proceeded into the camp, Stalag 9B. I was one of several thousand American prisoners, privates and non-coms, in the camp. There were prisoners of all nationalities—American, Russian, French, African, British—each with their own compound. 240 prisoners were jammed into each one-story wood and tar paper barracks. All were in a state of disrepair: roofs leaked, windows were broken. Each building was infested with bedbugs, lice and fleas. Washroom facilities consisted of one cold water tap and one latrine hole. Each of the barracks contained a stove with enough firewood to provide heat for a few hours a day. We were always hungry. Breakfast was weak tea. Lunch was a thin soup (sometimes with bugs in it). Dinner was a piece of ersatz bread—made from some wheat and some sawdust.

Two or three weeks after I got there, the German Hauptman (Captain) and his staff came through and called the names of the Jewish POW's from a list—or anyone with a name that might be Jewish. It turned out that Stalag 9B was the only POW camp in WWII where they segregated Jewish prisoners and sent them to work in a slave labor camp. Of those Jewish POWs sent to work in a salt mine in Berga, about 80 never returned. My name was not called. It was the luck of the draw that I had gotten a clerk who had apparently written "Protestant" on my papers. The process of selection went on for maybe fifteen minutes. I said nothing. I wore a dog tag with an "H" for Hebrew, but they didn't ask to see it. This was my second moral crisis in a couple of weeks. I had declared myself to be Jewish to the clerk. Now do I step forward and join my co-religionists to share whatever fate was to befall them, or do I remain mute and allow the selection process to finish without me?

I remained mute. Outside, I rationalized, I had options. Taken away, it was clear the danger substantially increased. I felt angry and relieved—and confused.

That night, after the Jewish prisoners had been taken away, I lay on a bunk in the barracks, trying to get some sleep. That's when I heard the other GI's, thinking that there were no more Jews around, start hurling jokes about the Jews—about living in a Jew-free zone—into the dark.

The Germans did not have a lock on anti-Semitism.

Things settled down to what passed for a routine and as the dark, cold days passed, my thoughts dwelled on home—my family—and the food.

CHAPTER 2

Origin of this Species

It was a tough time for everybody in the Depression, but I never felt I had it worse than the other guys. There was always music in my house and we always had enough to eat. My mother, Gertrude (or Gittel, the Hebrew equivalent), was a wonderful cook. She would cut up hot dogs, carrots, cabbage, potatoes, cook them for hours and announce that tonight we were dining on Veal Paprika. The next night it would be called "Irish Stew." Sundays, it was called Hungarian Goulash. I never knew that meat came in one piece until I was fifteen, the first time I saw steak. But I never felt deprived. Everyone around us was in the same shape, and, somehow, Dad always managed to have a car.

One summer, when I was fourteen, four of us had gotten our parents to spring for $12.50 apiece to rent a locker at Brighton Beach, a swath of beach fronting the Atlantic Ocean just north of Coney Island. On the way home from the beach we collected bottles. We needed them to get into the moo'm pitchers. That's what we called the moving pictures in Brooklyn—moo'm pitchers. We went to the movies on Saturdays, at a theatre called "The Leader," on Newkirk and Coney Island Avenue. It cost fifteen cents and we got the money by collecting milk and coke bottles. Sunday afternoons on the beach were a goldmine for us. We were "recycling" long before the environmentalists of today. Since empty milk bottles were worth three cents and coke bottles were five cents, we only needed three milk bottles and two coke bottles to get into the theatre. By the end of an afternoon we had more than enough. We turned those bottles in at the store, got fifteen cents and went to the moo'm pitchers.

The show at the Leader on Coney Island Ave on Saturdays would start at one o'clock. There would be two cartoons and two serial dramas—Tom Mix or Dick Tracy—then there would be the Pathe News, then two features. I would stagger out at six o'clock with a splitting headache, but boy, was I happy. It was an escape from a lot of pain of adolescence. Of not hitting the ball two sewers (the measure by which strength was measured on our streets. I rarely hit it one sewer). While in the movie theater I could lose myself in a Dick Tracy serial or the Northwest frontier of Gunga Din or the insanities of the Marx brothers.

Growing up, radio was omnipresent in my life. Many years later, in the TV age, my children said, "Dad, there was no TV then right?"

"Right."

"So, what did you watch?"

"I watched radio." This was greeted with incredulous looks. I explained that when a show was on, I would stare at the Majestic radio console, the opening of which was shaped somewhat like Gothic version of the Radio City Music Hall stage—but much less grand. As the radio story unfolded, I peopled that stage with the characters as I could envision them. Radio, along with books, gave us the audio clues as well as the words to engage with these creatures—and their adventures. Years later, when I was involved with "Candid Microphone" and then "Candid Camera," I had the opportunity to compare radio versions of episodes with their TV counterparts. Both were funny. I still preferred the radio versions. The addition of the visual locked one into a very specific experience. The radio version gave each listener the chance to create his or her own reality.

Then there was Uncle Don. He was on a New York radio station every weekday at 5:30 PM. He sang songs like, "The Green Grass Grew

All Around," told lucky kids where they could find their birthday gift—behind the third cushion on the sofa—and did commercials for the Dime Savings Bank. Even after more than 75 years I can still sing his theme song. I dragged my Mother down to Hearn's Department Store on 14th Street for one of his personal appearances. When, in later years, I was making personal appearances, I could always relate to the scene from the child's, and the mother's, point of view.

Uncle Don, according to the announcer at the start of each show, would arrive in his "puddle-jumper," which I imagined looked like an auto-gyro, and would be down in the studio in a moment. What we later discovered was that Uncle Don did more than a bit of tippling, and while they played some music, the staff was desperately trying to sober up Uncle Don. Uncle Don's career came to an abrupt end when, after he signed off for the week, and not realizing that the mike was still hot, said, "That should hold the little bastards till Monday."

That took care of Uncle Don for life.

When I was in bed with pneumonia for the two and a half months, my constant companions were the daytime soaps, "Myrt and Marge," "Mary Noble, Backstage Wife" (can a simple girl from a mining town find happiness married to a star?) and "Just Plain Bill." Then, in the afternoon, would come the adventures for kids. Jack Armstrong, the All-American Boy. I can recall that theme song—"Wave the flag for Hudson High boys, Show them how we stand…" And Buck Rogers in the 25th Century. I may be one of the few people around who knows how he got into the 25th century. Since you ask…Buck Rogers was working in a coal mine. When there was a large explosion, Rogers was trapped in a bubble of gas that put him into a state of "suspended animation." When he finally awoke, it was the 25th century. Of course I accepted that premise. When I first heard this show I was about five years old. Anything was possible.

As teenagers, we loved to listen to the spooky shows at night like "Lights Out." We would sit around a table and join hands and enter to the dark and eerie world of the drama. Today, we would never sit around a table, join hands and watch even the eeriest TV drama. All eyes would be transfixed on the screen and each viewer would be experiencing the drama fully. Around our table, listening to radio, each of us was creating our own production.

On warm summer nights, when the baseball season was in full swing, we would saunter around the corner to the soda parlor to await the "bull-dog" edition of the *Daily News*. We knew that on its uniquely pink back page would be the box scores of that day's games. The bundles of *News* would hit the pavement about 8:30 PM. While waiting, we would buy Pepsi Colas, the new drink that promised twelve full ounces for five cents. We would then engage in a "greppsing" contest to see who could produce the most belches. That kept us reasonably occupied until the newspapers arrived. After scanning the scores, and exploits, such as home runs and no-hitters, we would repair back to the block for discourse.

Usually, the session would take place on my stoop. ("Stoop" is a Dutch word and, like Brooklyn [Brueklen], is a residue from the time New York was Nieuw Amsterdam.) The whitewashed steps of my stoop seemed to be a good place to lounge as we examined the relative merits of the Dodgers, Giants and Yankees. The arguments would grow more intense when it came to comparing the merits of players in similar positions. Discussions went on until mothers started calling out of the windows that it was time to come home. The only statistics mothers knew were things like eight hours of sleep and the five building blocks to good health.

The summer I turned fifteen, I decided it was time to put away the childish activities of Brighton Beach and go to WORK. I wanted to taste the grown up world of commerce. I also wanted to put a few bucks into my wallet. I raised the matter with Dad, who agreed to help me in my pursuit. The result was a job as shipping clerk at a nurse's uniform loft factory on 18th street in Manhattan. Five and a half days a week. Ten bucks.

The walk to the Sheepshead Bay subway station took about fifteen minutes. The ride to my stop was about forty-five minute. The walk to the loft took another ten minutes. The trains were not air-conditioned. Neither was the factory.

I found out about work. I found out about those young women whose lives were filled with sitting at rows of sewing machines turning out the shiny white uniforms. I made friends with one pale looking woman of eighteen. She had a gaunt face that looked like she had lived a lot longer than that. She had a growth on her back. I discovered that she liked to write poetry. I liked to write poetry. Our bag lunches on the fire escape became a time when we shared our poems with each other. For a number of weeks, she was probably my closest friend. When I left, I never saw her again. To this day, when I see the countless men and women scurrying up from the subway tunnels to their unsung jobs, I am reminded of her and the others I spent those weeks with. In "A Chorus Line," when the "gypsies," those unsung members of the chorus in the musical theater, come out in their gold costumes with their canes and high hats and have their moment in the spotlight, I tend to cry. To me they, and that young lady at the nurses uniform factory, and the countless other people who are working with drug addicts, or terminally ill patients or making nurse's uniforms, are heroes. They manage day after day, to slog through a difficult life, unnoticed, unsung, uncelebrated. They get the job done.

They don't even get Warhol's 15 minutes.

CHAPTER 3

My Father and Gittel

I graduated PS 217 in 1938 with no particular distinction and started high school at Erasmus High. Hold on. I just found my autograph book from January 25, 1938. It is a worn brown faux suede covered book with a clasp, part of which is broken off. The spine is partly worn away. I open it. Oh my God. There are the dumb rhymes and old adages passed down from class to class. What catches my eye on this page is the salutation: "To my best friend, Irwin." It's signed by Alan Levine. Here's what startles me. That anyone would write "best friend." In looking back, I knew I was part of a posse, but I never thought of having a friend. I never had anyone I could share my doubts and anxieties with—not in the family and not among my companions. Alan was as close as any of my group.

Did I really have a "best friend"?

I remember being lonely. One Easter Sunday, I arose early and took the subway to Radio City Music Hall to attend a Sunrise Service. I loved the Music Hall with its curved, capacious ceiling and its marble bathrooms and the ushers in striped trousers and jackets with epaulettes. I was curious about this romantic-sounding and somewhat mystical ceremony, Sunrise Services.

And I was lonely.

That's why I would go, alone, to Radio City—the RCA building—

and attend a radio sitcom broadcast—alone. And subway to the new public library on Eastern Parkway, at the northern end of Prospect Park. It wasn't just the books. With its murals and marble and endless catalog drawers, it could function as another country in my lonely world.

What other memories of more than seventy years ago are kicked into life? Some pages are torn in half in an irregular way that speaks to someone ripping these pages with anger fueled energy. My older sister Shirley? Why? I have no idea now, but I do know she would be the only member of my family who would do something like that. Or maybe the half torn memories should lie with the missing part of the pages.

Dad's contribution to the book is, I think, the most striking because it reminds me of one of the legacies of his life. "*The greatest asset you can maintain is to tell others what they would like to hear*" was what he wrote; a carryover from his Willy Loman days as a salesman working on commissions. There was more than a bit of Willy Loman in Dad. As a man who did not finish high school, he also had the desire at all times to appear dignified and educated. Notice the use of the word "maintain." It is an odd choice, but to Dad, I suspect, it sounded upscale.

Dad was the sweet, accepting part of the parenting duumvirate. Not always, but mostly. He was one of thirteen—count 'em—thirteen children, eleven of whom grew into adulthood. Though Dad shared some of the values he had learned growing up in that crowded tenement on the lower East Side, the act of marrying Gertrude Goldberg meant a major renovation project was at hand.

By his own admission, Dad did not function well with babies. We had to get to the talking-walking stage for Dad to really take an interest. But then he really enjoyed being with his children. It was Dad who took me to my first baseball game at Ebbets Field. And my first Broadway show. Because Dad played the violin I decided to study the violin.

It was Dad who gave me the only strapping of my life. I had broken a 78-rpm shellac record. Not wanting to face the uncertain consequences, I cleverly buried the two halves in a rubber plant in the living room! Somehow Dad determined I was the culprit. I have always harbored the notion that my older sister Shirley ratted on me. Be that as it may, when Dad confronted me with the evidence of this malfeasance, I compounded the sin by denying I had anything to do with it. That's when the strap came out and a few lashes were dealt to my bottom.

I suspect the result of this was to make me a more skillful liar.

For most of his life, Dad was a textile converter. For those of you who have to know, a textile converter contracts to buy greige (pronounced "gray") goods from the mill and has it printed to the specifications of the customers who used the resulting output for shirts, dresses, curtains, etc. The converter never actually sees the cloth. It is all done with paperwork. Thus Dad could work out of a tiny office in Manhattan with space for him and a secretary. I guess Dad was good at his work. But Dad's real pleasure came from other sources.

Dad loved to find something political or social to rant about. One of his favorite plaints had to do with the green line painted down Fifth Avenue every March in time for the St. Patrick's Day parade. He felt that all that paint and all that manpower was a misuse of his tax dollars. Each spring, as surely as the blooming of the Iris or Hyacinth, Dad would start his grumbling a couple of weeks before the parade and carry it to a crescendo the day of the parade. Of course the day after, with all those wonderful photos of the event, his frenzy hit another peak.

One day, perusing the *New York Times*, I happened on a story about that very line. It seems that, with all the traffic, the line down the middle of the avenue had to be re-painted four times a year. When they did the spring repainting, they added "forty dollars worth of pigment." I eagerly took this data to my Dad and explained to him that all his ranting about what it was costing the taxpayers apparently boiled down to $40 a year. The next spring, right on cue, the outrage about the line down the middle of Fifth Avenue started again, and soon Dad was in full voice.

My father never allowed facts to cloud his mind.

Dad loved writing angry letters to important personages. One day, after complaining about it for some years, my father sat at the Underwood and pecked out a letter to the New York Philharmonic. Why, he inquired, do we, who have paid to hear a concert, have to sit through the raucous noise of the orchestra tuning up on stage? I paid to hear a concert, was his reasoning, why can't you tune up in the wings before coming on? He received a page and a half reply from the conductor Antal Dorati, both explaining the reasons for waiting to get on the stage before making this critical last-minute adjustment, and being a bit sardonic. It read in part:

"Concerning the tune-up of the orchestra, this is an inevitable procedure before each concert. If you found the sounds ugly played by a well-tuned orchestra, can you imagine how terrible it would have been if they had not been in tune with each other."

I don't know that Dad got the sardonic part, but at least he did get the personal attention from the conductor. I think that impressed us all. But I truly believe Dad's favorite time was the hours spent in Small Claims Court having a go at some of America's largest corporations. He took on Sears Roebuck for a chipped sink and won. He took on Railway Express (that generation's FedEx) and won. And my all time favorite: JA Fox Vs. John David.

Dad, having grown up in dire circumstances, always insisted on observing a formal dress code to prove he really was a man of some distinction. He wore suits, ties and a homburg. Even when visiting me in Connecticut or my sisters in New Jersey or Middletown, N.Y., Dad tended to dress as though he were going to work in New York City. His idea of a really informal outfit was to leave off the homburg. So it was that my sisters Shirley and Phoebe and I decided to pool our money and get Dad a gift certificate at John David, a chain of men's clothing stores, one father's day. There was one a few feet from his office building on Thirty-Second Street and Broadway. We presented his gift with specific instruction that it was meant for a pair of SPORTS slacks.

Dad dutifully went to the John David men's store and told them he wanted sports slacks. They agreed on the color and style. Then, Dad added, "The slacks have to be twenty inches wide at the bottom." The salesman whipped out his tape measure and discovered that the slacks were 18 inches wide.

"Won't do," stated JA.

The salesman discovered that none of the slacks they carried was wider than 18 inches at the cuff. They called other nearby John David stores. Same answer.

"I'm afraid we do not have any slacks that are made that wide at the bottom, Mr. Fox.

"But," he continued, "May I ask why they have to be twenty inches?"

"When I get up in the morning," Dad explained patiently, "I put my left sock on first. Then I put my right sock on. Then I put my left shoe on. Then I put my right shoe on. Then I put on my pants. If the opening is not 20 inches wide, the pants will not go over the shoes."

"Mr. Fox," the salesman asked, "would it not be easy just to put your pants on BEFORE the shoes?"

"Each morning, for over sixty years, I start the day by putting my left sock on first. Then my right sock. Then my left shoe. Then my right shoe. Then my pants. I do not intend to change a lifetime habit to suit your needs. You do not have what I need so I will take the money and find the pants elsewhere."

"Oh, I'm afraid we cannot give you money. This is a gift certificate and can only be used for merchandise. You can pick anything in the store which is covered by the amount, but we will not give you cash."

"My children specifically want me to have sports slacks. You have none that meet my needs so I will go elsewhere to buy them. Please give me the money so I can fulfill their desires."

The salesman remained true to the code of the chain and refused to give my father the face amount of the certificate.

Bad move on the part of the John David empire. Into small claims court.

It is many weeks—or months—later. I am in Connecticut to join my buddies for our weekly poker game. My host for the evening informs me that a friend of his, a lawyer, is sitting in at tonight's game. When the newcomer arrives I am introduced to him.

"Is your father JA Fox?" he asks.

"Yes."

"Is he a lawyer?"

I explain that he is actually a textile converter. "Why do you ask?"

"Today I served as an arbitrator for some cases in small claims court and a case came up involving you father as the plaintiff."

Enough time had passed for me not to be sure which case was now occupying my Dad's attention. "Who was he going after?"

"It involved the John David store chain and a gift certificate."

"Aha! And how did it go?"

"Well, when I asked him to explain his side of the case he said, 'Each morning when I get dressed I put my left sock on first. Then I put on my right sock. Then I put on my left shoe and then my right shoe. And then I put on my pants'."

"And how did you find?"

"I gave him the money."

Maybe Dad should have been a lawyer.

In later years, after my divorce, when I came into New York from L.A. on business, I would stay at my parents' apartment for two good reasons. Their rates were terrific and their apartment on Riverside Drive most pleasant. One morning, when I got to the kitchen to have breakfast, there was Dad, as usual, reading the newspaper. After a bit, he lowered the *Times* and asked, "So, what time did you get home last night?"

I was a man in his fifties, with four grown children. Here was my Dad still acting as though I was a teenager. And the schmuck answered, "2 AM." And I lied. I had gotten home at 3 AM.

I have learned, as a son and as a father, the roles go on forever—if you are lucky. A parent finds it very hard to stop parenting. The minute I crossed my parents' threshold, part of me reverted to my role of a child. So it is that when a second parent dies, we cry not only for the lost parent, but because one is now an orphan.

GITTEL

You can't read my story without you should hear about my mother.

My mother, Gittel Goldenberg, came over here in 1909, when she was ten years old, from Austria-Hungary. Or what was then Austria-Hungary because sometimes it was Poland and sometimes it was Russia. Her family lived on Hester Street on the lower East Side. When she was in school, the teacher looked at Goldenberg and told her, "Nobody in America has a name that long. It's Goldberg." So my mom went home and said our name is Goldberg. And her parents said, "Okay," because they wanted to be Yankees.

My mother's name became Gertrude Goldberg. She went to school for maybe three years before her father said, "Okay, now go out and work." But she refused to be what she should've become – a lower East Side yenta with three years of education. That was never good enough for her. Limitations would not be something my mother ever bought into. As a result, she reinvented herself several times in her life. When she married my dad, she became Gertrude Fox. She was a very strong and willful person and she shaped our family. Dad was gentler, more accepting and more limited.

My mother was quite beautiful and quite vain. My dad was also good-looking. They made a great couple but it was a tempestuous marriage. My sisters and I used to play the game, "Who are you going with when they split up?" Gertrude was a big talker and my father was very concerned about her time on the phone and the resulting bills. Once, in anger, he ripped the phone out of the wall in the middle of her conversation. He had very specific expectations about the kind of family he should have. When he came home at night, the kids were to be in bed and dinner would be on the table. So my mother would come rushing into the house from her club meetings, knowing that dinner had to be on the table in a half-hour. Stuff would start happening. With her hat still on, she would stand at the sink with her feet crossed because she had to go to the bathroom but couldn't take the time. It was like a cartoon. She would be at the sink and things would start flying—the meat, the bread, the table settings. In half an hour it was all done. When my father came home, the table was set and dinner ready. She could've been home all day as far as he knew. Meanwhile, we were in bed when all the other kids were still playing out on the street. I could hear them from my bedroom. But there I was, put down at 5:30 because Dad was coming home.

Despite her limited schooling, my mother wrote exquisite letters and had wonderful diction. Having decided that she was not going to be defined by where she grew up, it was clear that I was not going to be defined by where I grew up. Meaning Flatbush. So she had me taking elocution lessons when I was eleven. Added to my violin case it was like I had a bull's-eye painted on my back.

Most teens think about suicide at some time. I actually think I tried it twice. To this day I am not sure if I was serious or trying to elicit sympathy and attention. In my family, we were not encouraged to deal with real issues in our lives. The unwritten motto was, "Got a problem—wash your face, brush your hair and get on with it"; whatever the "it" was.

The first time I moved toward actually trying suicide I was on the sill of the second story of our rented house, my feet dangling out the window. My mother happened along at that moment, (did I know she would be there at that time?) walking down the sidewalk and spotted me.

"If you jump from there you will only break your leg and run up doctor bills. Find a higher place to jump from."

That was not the reaction I had anticipated, so I withdrew from that attempt. Some months later I shut the doors to the kitchen and turned on the gas jets. This time it was a closer call. When my mother pushed into the room, I was almost asleep.

"Gas is expensive," she said as she shut the jets. "Find a cheaper way."

End of suicide attempts. I wish I could understand now what actually led me to those two episodes. I know I was not having a successful puberty. I had almost no self-esteem. Interestingly, in neither case did Mom or Dad ask why I was trying to commit suicide. I don't think the matter was ever brought up. Certainly the idea of counseling was never mentioned, though in the 1940s that was not very common—at least not among lower socio-economic Jewish families.

Mom was fifty-two when she apprenticed herself to a theatre party agent in New York, spent three years learning how it's done, then opened her own business. She became the second or third largest agency in New York. She was very successful at it. I used to call her "Broadway Gert."

Later, when Mom was in her seventies, we were having lunch at Sardi's and I was trying to convince her to retire. Dad was already sort of retired. I wanted her to move out to L.A. and stop fighting New York winters. "You should slow down," I said. I tried to convince her how good it would be for her to be near my sister and me. But she wasn't buying it.

"That's crazy. All my friends are here. I can take a bus or a taxi. If I go out there I'm a prisoner. I have to wait for someone to take me places."

"You know what? You're right. But you've got to make this deal with me. The only place you can die is in the lobby of the Booth Theatre or at Sardi's. Those are the only two places where you're allowed to die."

"Okay," she said. "But your part of the deal is you've got to do my eulogy."

I agreed and we sealed that deal at Sardi's. She didn't keep her end of the bargain but I kept mine.

She got cancer late in her life. Up until that time, when she was eighty-four and a half, she was still heading down to the office every day. In L.A., I would learn of a 'snow emergency in New York' so I would call her to see if she was all right. No answer. I'd call the office and she'd answer.

"Ma, what are you doing there?"

"It was boring, staying home."

"Did you take a cab?"

"No, you can't get a cab. I took the bus."

Eighty-four and a half. She was a great entertainer and her hospitality was legendary. There was always room, always a meal if anybody dropped in. When she got older, every Passover at the house there'd be strangers. If I asked where she met them, she'd give me the same answer—"Well, when I passed out on fifty-third street, in the gutter, he/she picked me up."

The last twenty-five years of her life she walked around with a tumor in her head. It was nonmalignant but it was pressing against the pituitary gland and optic nerve. They treated it as much as much as they could, until she couldn't take any more radiation. She never stopped working, even when she had no peripheral vision. But she did have a tendency to pass out. So people were always picking her up. And she was always inviting them over for Passover. That was how we met a lot of interesting people.

When she died of cancer, no one in the family was with her. They were all in Los Angeles for the wedding of my daughter. The hospice called to tell me, "We knew your mother loved the theatre, so the Sister who has a guitar was at her bedside singing 'Give My Regards to Broadway' as she passed away."

CHAPTER 4

The Day My World Changed

We moved, once again, from 9th Street in 1939. Leaving Erasmus High in 1939 after three terms, and moving on to James Madison had meant starting all over to meet new friends. But this time we moved because Dad had finally done well enough to buy our first house, an attached brick building on Avenue Y at the extreme Southern end of Brooklyn.

The FHA made it possible for people like Dad to actually realize their dream of being a homeowner. The three-story house sold for $7,000 with a 4 ¾% mortgage. It was also the model house, so it was furnished. Dad offered $500 for all the furnishings and it was a deal. It was like moving into the Versailles Palace.

One month before graduation, on Dec. 7, 1941, I was standing in the kitchen of that house on Sunday afternoon, drying dishes and listening to the broadcast of the New York Philharmonic from Carnegie Hall, when the news bulletin announced an attack on Pearl Harbor. I did not know where Pearl Harbor was, but I sensed that my world was about to change. It was going to change for everyone.

I had followed the developing scenario since I was eight years old and

Hitler took power. I listened to the radio avidly as the Anschluss took place in 1936 and the Germans took over Austria. In 1937, after Kristallnacht, President Roosevelt called his ambassador home to show his dismay. My father gave each of us one dollar to write the President a letter of our approval. Then came the 1938 Sudeten crisis and HV Kaltenborn, with his clipped, no-nonsense delivery, nightly pronouncing how history was being created before my very ears. The rest of my studies and conversations seemed unimportant as I was enthralled by this darkly developing and increasingly unstoppable slide into another world war. Only this time, I felt a part of it. This was not the WWI books I had so carefully read and whose pictures both dismayed and excited me. This time the Jews were at the center of the ugliness that was the Third Reich. This time, I felt, somehow, I would be a part of this incredible story.

After the declaration of war, in December of 1941, people started worrying about the Huns storming the beaches of New York. The Army dug machine gun nests into the sand at Coney Island. Anti-aircraft guns appeared in parks. Nobody quite understood that the Germans were incapable of landing on our shores. As it turned out they couldn't even cross the English Channel.

As we sat in our seats on graduation day, January of 1942, listening to the Principal's speech, all the guys in the senior class knew we were going into the military when we turned eighteen. Since I wouldn't turn eighteen for a year and half, first I was going to matriculate at North Carolina State, the premiere school for textiles. My uncle had gone there. Through the years Dad had watched as one big firm after another hired his wife's brother, all because he had a degree. That degree, my dad concluded, made the difference between being a textile converter like him, and becoming management material. If my father couldn't attain the extra prestige and money, I would. So my getting a degree from North Carolina State was the logical step in the unspoken assumption that I was going into his business.

I applied and was accepted. There was just one problem—North Carolina State didn't allow one to enter until September. Six months is an eternity when you're sixteen-and-a-half. More than an eternity when you know that when you turn eighteen, you're going to be drafted. So here is an example of the convergences that have shaped my life. If I had graduated in June, I would have gone directly to NC State. If that school allowed a freshman to enter in February, I would have gone to NC State. If the war hadn't broken out, perhaps I might have waited until September to start college. Because none of this happened, my entire life changed.

I decided to start at NYU in January. I figured I could transfer credits from the courses I took there to North Carolina when I started that next September. While I was there I found out that they had radio writing and production courses. They sounded interesting so I enrolled in them, too.

At NYU the radio classes met in the East building, a very primitive place in 1942. It might have been the only building in New York where the old elevator went as much from side to side as up and down. The radio classes were mostly production-oriented but some involved a good bit of writing. As I got more involved in the classes, I discovered that writing and producing radio was something I was good at. Gradually I came to realize I didn't want to go into textiles—I wanted to go into radio. Up until then, studying radio had been fun and exciting. It had never even occurred to me that this could be a serious life choice. But I had made my decision.

There I was, my father's heir, his only son, expected to go into his business. It was what I had been born into, what I had been raised to expect. Only now I'd decided otherwise. I had to tell my father, had to deal with the unspoken commitment between us. Besides, he was paying my tuition. My loins girded, I went to talk to him.

I told him how much I loved studying radio. "Good," he answered unsuspectingly, and went back to his newspaper. I told him how good it made me feel to do something I loved. How studying radio had made me realize what I really wanted to do. My father looked up with a puzzled frown. I swallowed hard.

"Dad," I said, "I want to go into radio. Not textiles."

My father looked at me in silence for a moment. I waited for lightning to strike me; for the earth to quake. But nothing happened, except that my father listened kindly as I explained my request. He was patient as I waxed poetic about the future of this industry, about my love for writing and producing radio, about how much I wanted to pursue this. He clearly didn't know what to make of radio as a profession but he saw my determination.

If he was disappointed, he didn't show it. If he was worried about my choice, he didn't show that, either. After we'd talked for a while, all he said was, "Let's talk to someone in the business and see what he thinks." Then he went back to his paper and I went back to school.

Mom knew someone who'd gone into "the business." Dad thought we should go talk to him. My mother and that "someone's" mother were best friends. A few years older than me, he had been a hot-blooded enfant terrible in the advertising world, becoming an account executive at twenty-three. He was currently producing a radio game show called Ladies Be Seated. When he was younger, he, too, had been known as "Sonny." Now he went by his given name—Alan. Alan Funt.

Mom talked to Paula Funt and Paula Funt talked to Alan and word came back that Alan would talk to us. So Dad and I went off to talk with him. Alan asked about my studies at NYU. I told him how excited I was about radio. He asked what I liked best. I talked with enthusiasm about my love for production, writing, for all aspects of radio. Dad asked Alan practical questions about the business. Alan was very encouraging about its potential. To my father's credit, he listened and saw that this was a legitimate way to make a living. A couple of days later, it was agreed. I could stay at NYU and major in radio production. I was on top of the world. I was going to be a radio producer! Just being in the milieu of the radio department was exciting. In fact, it was the most fun I'd ever had in my life.

Going to school in New York had several advantages. Living at home meant that the dent on Dad's wallet was reduced substantially. As it was, he had difficulty getting the money for each semester. Being in New York also allowed me to indulge my love for the theater. Dad had taken me to my first play when I was about thirteen. It was a silly comedy starring Constance Cummings, but it was magic to me. Later, my sister, Shirley, and I would go into the city and see plays on our own.

I stayed at NYU for a year and a half, taking every radio course I could, checking coats to see plays for free, working at part-time jobs such as a shipping clerk in a company that published racy books like "The Bedside Companion." And when I turned eighteen, on June 17, 1943, I registered for the draft. I loved having that draft card in my wallet because I was dating by then, pretending to be the same age as the other kids in my class. Since the girls I dated thought I was eighteen, like them, it was getting more and more difficult to explain why I was still not in the Army. I certainly did not want to inform an eighteen-year-old lovely that her date was still seventeen. That draft card helped my story a lot.

But most of all, the draft card would be my ticket out of a restricted life in the outer edge of Brooklyn into, what seemed to me, the grandest adventure I could hope for. I would be entering an entirely different world, a place where, when I arrived, I had no past. No one would know I was a wuss at sports. No one would care that I couldn't lick any other kid in a fist fight. Part of me wanted to feel what being the midst of combat would be like. I wanted to be tested. I was scheduled to be inducted in October 1943. The fact that I scored well on their test gave me a choice of several special programs I chose the A.S.T.P., the Army Specialized Training Program for college students with high IQ's. It was designed to return college students to school after thirteen weeks of basic training.

CHAPTER 5

This Is the Army, Mr. Fox

On October 23, 1943, I said good-bye to my parents without a hint of dread. I was excited. In 1943, in the middle of the war, everybody felt one hundred percent American. But our good-bye was painful for my parents so my uncle took the long walk to the BMT station with me. Then I disappeared down into the hole and took the train to Penn Station, where I joined other draftees for the trip to Camp Upton on Long Island. Most of them were my age, eighteen, and a number were from my draft board: #143.

After two weeks of sorting out whether I was to be in an A.S.T.P. unit, I was finally put into one. We boarded a troop train and headed down to Fort Benning, Georgia, for basic training. Fort Benning was a big place, with a hundred thousand men. And the pimply-face, scrawny corporals were waiting for us. They were especially waiting for kids from a big city like New York. They got even more delighted if you had a Jewish name. The jackpot would be a New York Jew who was very fat. Bingo!

All their lack of self-esteem and education and sophistication could be balanced by indulging in humiliation and little acts of cruelty. Just learning how to execute the commands from these crackers was tough. Leading the instruction in the art of proper turning was a scrawny red-faced, red-haired, red-neck corporal with a thick southern accent. He bawled out, "When you make a left turn, you turn on the ball of your left foot with the 'sissance' of your right. When you make a right turn, you turn on the ball of your right foot with the 'sissance' of your left." As I struggled with the execution he was illustrating, I was also struggling with which part of my foot was the "sissance." It took a couple of days to understand that he thought he was saying "assistance."

We definitely were not in Greenwich Village anymore.

I learned that soldiering wasn't only firing guns; it was keeping your footlocker organized in a precisely designated manner. If one thing was out of position-if there was a fleck of dust in your rifle or if a quarter would not bounce on your blanket—you were gigged at inspection. That meant a punishment—usually being confined to base on the weekend. I piled up quite a few gigs and spent many a weekend on base. The nearest town, Columbus, Georgia, wasn't that much anyway and had no buddy to spend time with so I did not miss it that much. When I did go into town, I would sometimes attend a Christian service just to hear music.

I think the greatest shock was the Deep South itself. This was 1943. First there were the black and white water fountains, then the restaurants and hotels that the black soldiers could not get into. But the reality and stupidity of all this struck home most tellingly when I first encountered the restricted buses. These were U.S. army buses taking American soldiers into town for some R&R. There were buses for white solders that a black soldier would not be allowed to get on. The Great War to save democracy was being fought by a totally segregated U.S. military.

I kept telling myself only a few more weeks, and then it's back to the campus. You can do it, I said to myself. You can put up with the red clay mud of Georgia. You can put up with the sadistic crackers who enjoyed pushing the smart-ass New York kids around. It's only for thirteen weeks.

Then, just as we were completing the thirteen-week cycle, we were informed that the army was abolishing A.S.T.P. The program was dropped as battlefield losses mounted. Having lived through the hell of basic training, buoyed by the thought that I was college bound, I found myself in the infantry for the duration. My first thought was, "Oh, shit." But part of me, the adventurous part, re-awakened and was not too unhappy about going. Anyway, I figured I had passed through the worst of it by now.

So here is another convergence. At the very moment I was going to return to college and ride out the war far from any action, someone in DC decided to abolish the program and, once again, changed my life totally! No A.S.T.P. We were now in the U.S. Infantry for the duration. So it was on to Camp Alexandria, in the middle of Louisiana, to join the 86th division. Six more months of war games and old latrines and exploring the glories of the South. Halfway through the tour, the army decided it was time to give some of us a couple of weeks off. We were assembled in the base theater for instructions before we left. The Army was concerned about the consequences of releasing two thousand virile young men filled with ardor and testosterone. To take the necessary precautions, the army presented us with what seemed to me an appropriate combination of the ideal and the practical approaches to safe sex.

First the chaplain stood before us and advised us to "keep it zipped." He spoke of wives and children in the future and our responsibilities to them. He was very effective. When he left the stage, the top sergeant came on and advised us to heed what the pastor had said.

"However," he added, "in case you can't..."

At this point, a very large wooden phallus was wheeled stage center, and instructions on how to put a condom on were graphically acted out. On the way out of the theater we were each handed a kit with condoms, medication and cleansing agents. So, here is proof that government agencies can act intelligently every once in a while.

On June 6, 1944, I heard about our landings in Omaha and Utah

Beaches in France. "Damn," I thought, "the war will be over before I can catch up with it." I continued to train in Alexandria for another three months, until I was shipped to England. Almost one year after I'd joined up, I was going to catch up to the war.

I took my first North Atlantic cruise and it was on the Queen Elizabeth I. She sailed unescorted through the war. Her speed enabled her to outrun the Nazi submarine packs. In peacetime, the luxury liner had carried two thousand passengers. Now, she was carrying 20,000 U.S. personnel. We were "double loaded," meaning we could sleep in the cabin every other night and on deck the remaining time. In what would have been a cabin for two, there were now triple tiers of bunks for 18 men. After one night in the cabin, I chose to stay on deck for the rest of the voyage. There were so many of us on board that they could only serve two meals a day. Having tasted the food, twice a day was enough. I bought cartons of Hershey's with almonds from the ship's store and settled back to enjoy my first North Atlantic cruise. We talked, played poker, and watched the stars. Since we were sailing on our own, we made the crossing in five days.

The British would not risk the QE sailing into a port near the French Coast, so we sailed up the beautiful Firth of Clyde, Scotland, where we were to be loaded onto smaller boats. First to go was the USO troop, which was off to entertain the troops. As he looked up at our huge vessel from their small boat, a baritone with the troupe saw fifteen balconies of fans leaning over the side. The performer understood that he might never again have this setting and this size audience. He seized the opportunity, stood up, and as we all looked on, and began to sing, a capella, "Wagon Wheels, Wagon Wheels, Keep on a-Turnin', Wagon Wheels."

I think I shall never forget that scene. In Scotland, in this beautiful setting, looking down from the promenade deck of the Queen Elizabeth, in the middle of World War Two... What a moment!

On to Crewe, England. Crewe is a transportation hub in the midlands. We were clearly passing through on the way to the front, so when it was suggested we get our hair cut short, I decided to have mine shaved. Hell, I wasn't going to bump into anyone I knew and was surely not going on a date. A few days later an officer arrived in our barracks and announced that on Saturday night some GIs would be going into town for a dance. Each barracks could send but two soldiers, to be decided by drawing from a deck of cards; the two high cards would be selected.

I, who never wins at such drawings, drew an ace and was therefore one of the chosen, shaved head notwithstanding. Saturday evening, we were loaded on to trucks and driven into Birmingham. This is an industrial city, but with the brown outs, it looked even bleaker than normal. At the dance I met a comely, young British woman, also in uniform. We had a few lovely dances—she was soft and pliable and seemed about my age. The critical moment came at the end of the dance when the orchestra struck up God Save the Queen and we were expected to remove our hats. I quickly stepped behind her swept my hat off and replace it before reemerging into her line of sight.

We left the dance and headed back to the rendezvous point with the busses. In the few minutes before we had to re-board, this young, lovely female person and I snuggled and kissed and pledged to meet right back there the following Saturday night. There was a glimmer of hope that Pvt. Fox might actually lose his virginity before getting killed. Of course a couple of days later we shipped out and I never kept the date. For a long while I nurtured this fantasy that every Saturday night, an older, but still youthful looking woman, would appear in the square and wait for her Yank—who never came.

We sailed across the channel to Omaha Beach, on D-Day plus about 90. We started our journey to the front aboard the famous Forty and Eights so named because in WWI they carried either 40 soldiers or 8 horses. As we neared Paris, we switched to 6x6 trucks which were the main component of the U.S. supply line.

While racing through the country-side the trucks did not make comfort stops. One Sunday, while going through some recently liberated parts of Belgium, I decided I could not wait to relieve my bladder. I clambered to the tailgate of the truck, put one foot over, zipped open my fly and started the process. Since I was looking out the rear of the truck, I could not see that the convoy had just started roaring through a village.

All the families, who had been at their Sunday dinners, came running out to cheer us on. There I was, hanging off the back of the truck, frozen by the sight of these families, seemingly applauding my efforts to relieve myself. I fell back into the truck, embarrassed. I still harbor the notion that to commemorate the occasion, there is a fountain in the center of that town where a GI, carved in stone, is the source of the water.

Oct. 23. 1944

Dearest Folks,

I'm sitting right now on Belgian soil (and my own posterior) under a shelter of pine limbs, next to a warm fire, in the coals of which are roasting some potatoes. I've just finished a good hot meal, augmented substantially by one of the occasional cow or deer which "accidentally" strayed in the line of fire of one of the men. Of course, if someone should say I could go home, there would be a puff of dust and a flash of speed and Brooklyn here I'd come!

This life of ease, however was merely a lull. I finally caught up with the war outside of Aachen, along the German-Belgian border. When we got to the replacement depot, or "repple depple," as it was called, we were organized into replacement units – new meat to be chewed up at the front. I was in the front of a line of twelve rookies, a squad, one of three such lines which would be the component of a platoon. One of the officers said, "I need a squad leader, any volunteers?" There weren't any. "We'll take whoever has the most experience." He started going down the line, asking each man how long he'd been in. I said "eleven months," figuring that would be on the low end. As it turned out, this was one drawing I won. I was it. That was how I became a squad leader at nineteen. I was in charge of eleven men. I had always craved being in a position of leadership. Now, here it was, thrust upon me.

I looked around and counted. We were almost a hundred and fifty men, going in as replacements for a company of about two hundred and fifty men. I did the math—one hundred and fifty out of two hundred and fifty were wounded or dead and needing replacements. This was not a good place to be.

The policy of the military in WW II was to feed in replacements as the war wore on. Occasionally, a whole new division would show up—one that trained together. The men would know their officers and each other and have some cohesion. When we were lined up that night to enter the ranks of Company E, 110th Regiment, 28th Infantry Division, not one of the men in this particular gaggle had ever met the other. The 28th had been the Pennsylvania National Guard Division at the war's inception and had seen much action crossing France—it was the division marching through the Arc De Triomphe on the postage stamp what marked the victory in France—but it would probably be hard to find anyone from that original force now. When I was designated acting sergeant, the 11 men who were now dependent on me had no idea of who I was. Probably not a bad thing. "Jeez, not the Sonny Fox from Flatbush who couldn't hit two sewers?"

The Huertgen Forest sat along the German–Belgian border, about fifty square miles of dense woods, with tall fir trees that blocked the sun. It was a dark and eerie place where the thick lower branches of the fir trees were only two feet off the ground. The forest floor never got any sunlight. The Germans had timed the fuses on their shells to explode at tree–top level, thus dispersing the deadly shrapnel over a wide area. A substantial number of our casualties were from this shellfire.

We went up to the front in the middle of the night. We were in a column on the left side of a road making our uphill climb. On the opposite side of the road I saw soldiers being on foot and on stretchers. It was surreal; the replacements going up, the wounded streaming down with bandages on their heads. One wounded GI was shouting, "It's those God damned 88's, those God damned 88's." That was the German artillery.

As we were walking up to the first positions under fire, I felt a combination of fear and elation. Fear of what might happen—elation that I was okay. That first walk up there was the first time I'd ever been under fire. I found out that I could make it. I was scared shitless, but I could cope.

When my squad moved into its position in the Huertgen, we weren't even told where the enemy was. My first job was to take the frozen body of a dead American soldier out of the slit trench I was to occupy. I didn't stop to think about what I was doing. I just did it. After all, I had to settle the squad in. Being responsible for eleven other guys was very important to me.

It was raining and cold, a damp, penetrating cold that went through your bones. Nighttime was frequently below freezing and damp and fog was everywhere. I had one change of socks, which never dried so my feet wouldn't stay warm.

Overall, in the Huertgen Forest, the 28th Division suffered 6,184 combat casualties, plus 738 cases of trench foot (because our feet were never dry) and 620 cases of battle fatigue.

CHAPTER 6

Explosion and Surrender

Blessedly, after about three weeks in the Huertgen Forest, someone figured out that it might be time to give the 28th time to heal its wounds and regroup. The 4th infantry division replaced us during a night maneuver. This kind of move, replacing one division with another, is a very tricky procedure under enemy fire. The new unit coming in is shown its positions and should get a briefing regarding the "situation and the terrain." It is important that the enemy not know what is going on lest they see an opportunity to attack during the transition.

We were loaded into trucks without the foggiest notion of where we were heading. Away from the Huertgen Forest was good enough. Some hours later we ended up in a town in Luxembourg called Hosingen. We knew that the Aare River lay just to the east of the town, that the river was the border with Germany and that the ridge line on which the town was built was our MLR—Main Line of Resistance.

What we didn't know was that Hosingen lay 15 miles due east of Bastogne. We also didn't know where our minefields were because the unit evacuating Hosingen forgot to leave the map overlays behind. It was only when a German soldier, tired of his war, decided to walk down the road to our town one crisp November night and surrender, that we were able to get an inkling as to their dispersion. He drew an overlay for us of our minefields.

We were elated to be occupying a town with real houses. After spending all that time freezing in water-laden foxholes, it felt like we were being taken to a resort. We were assigned a house on the north end of town as our post. One of my squad insisted on running up curtains for our little house. In my naiveté, I had clearly anticipated the army's "don't ask-don't tell" policy. But my policy was "don't ask–don't tell–don't know." I knew nothing about homosexuality at that time.

Our time in Hosingen was spent, for the most part, in patrolling, rather than any sustained fighting. We would trek toward the river, and from a copse, fire mortar shells into the town on the opposite bank. Once when we had set up to do some firing, the mortar squad discovered it had left its sighting mechanism back in town. It seemed like hours hanging out in no-man's land, waiting for them to retrieve the sight.

See, no one actually WINS a war. The stupider side loses.

The most aggressive action we attempted almost ended in disaster. Some higher-up decided it was time to dislodge some of the German soldiers who had come back into the space between the river and our lines. My squad and another were to leave the town and take up a firing line on a hill across a valley from the Germans. As we pinned them down, another company would sweep in from the south and attack the flank of the German troops. I am sure some West Pointer learned that classic maneuver studying the Civil War. The problem was that we had taken the same route and occupied the same space on the hill for the previous two days. This would be the third day in a row that we would be using the same route and tactic. That made me somewhat dubious about this small piece of the war.

I was the lead man in our contingent of about thirty soldiers. As we approached our final position, I saw a German soldier whom I had clearly surprised, leap to his feet and scramble down the hill. Since we were not to start firing until a certain time, I dropped, rolled onto my back and pumped my rifle up and down, the appropriate sign that I had seen something.

The Lieutenant came scrambling up to me and I reported what I had seen. Clearly troubled and unsure, he nevertheless urged me on. My squad took its place and waited for the signal, at which time we would start firing. But the attack never came about. At the appointed time, we started firing across the river on the Germans. We heard firing in the distance that indicated that the company that was supposed to sweep in from the south had gotten mired in another firefight. Meanwhile we were getting some pretty accurate fire whizzing at us from the German side. They had, after the two days of preparations, figured out where our gunfire had been coming from and had no trouble locating us there on the third day.

After a reasonable amount of time, it was decided to call off this magnificent maneuver. As we started back the Germans started creeping up the hill. They had been below us the entire time, awaiting our arrival. Our daily rehearsal had given them time to prepare an ambush. We thought our combat was over for the day so it came as a shock when they opened fire on us with burp guns. The sound of burp guns is memorable. They were the simple hand held machine pistols the Germans had developed. They spat out a large number of rounds very quickly with a sound like a burp—hence the name we had given them.

I zigzagged and flopped. Zigggged and zagged and flopped—getting quite winded in the process. When I landed in an eight-inch deep beet furrow, it felt like a six-foot deep foxhole. That feeling lasted until a bullet tore through my sleeve. The spat of dirt that kicked up between my arm and my body indicated that the beet furrow was not a good place to hang out. Tired beyond fear, I simply stood up and ran toward the fallen trees behind which men who had made it were counter-firing.

I later discovered that the bullet that tore through my sleeve went through my thermal undershirt, too. The others marveled that so many had been firing at me and I had escaped unscathed. Even more remarkable, not one man was hit. Fortunately, burp guns were not very accurate.

When we got back to town, the Lieutenant, for the first and only time, uncorked a bottle of liquor and quietly passed out shots to each of us. As I recall, no one had a sense of elation. No one wanted to talk about it. We were all exhausted, and despite the liquor, very sober.

As we got into the second week of December, we noticed a rise in the clatter of equipment and tanks coming from the German positions across the river. After a couple of nights of this I reported it to the Captain. His orders instructed him to double our patrols. Since we were a mile or more away from the next position north of us, that meant loading into a jeep in the middle of the cold December night and, without lights, driving to a midway point between our company and the adjoining one. Not only was it freezing, but we understood the only way we would discover our lines being infiltrated was when they started shooting at us.

My other concern was the report that on occasion, the Germans had infiltrated and strung piano wire tautly across the road at about neck level. That meant if you were sitting in the front seat and ran into one of these you had a good chance of being neatly decapitated. When I had that position in the Jeep, I carefully fixed my bayonet on my MI rifle with the sharp edge facing front, and made sure my head was not above the blade of the bayonet.

Although nothing happened on our two weeks of increased patrols, the grinding noises that indicated big machines were being moved from the German positions was getting more ominous. What we were hearing was Field Marshall Von Rundstedt positioning his panzer divisions and all the manpower that could be found for one last gamble by the Reich—a push out of the Ardennes through our lines and on to Antwerp.

He had chosen his attack point wisely. First the cover of the Ardennes kept his concentrations from being spotted. The front along which he decided to attack was held by two divisions. On the South was the 28th, on the North the 106th, a division that had just arrived on the front. It had never been in battle and was totally unready for this level of assault. We were dispersed along a large front with huge gaps between our positions. Although we had been sending our warnings for two weeks about the increased level of activity, back at SHAEF HQ they apparently did not believe the Germans were capable of such an offensive maneuver.

On the morning of December 16, 1944, I was awakened at 5:20 AM by artillery screeching over the farmhouse. I ran to the foxhole a few yards from the building and jumped in to find my sentries.

"How long has this been going on?"

"About 20 minutes."

I started back to the house to get the rest of my squad out. As I got close to the door, I heard an incoming and dove under the butcher block alongside the entrance. The shell passed over and I started to extricate myself but could not get free. The battle was beginning and I was stuck under a butcher block! I started to giggle. All hell was breaking loose and I was going to end my life stuck under a goddam butcher block.

I finally broke loose and dashed into the house to find my mighty band of warriors cowering in the potato cellar. I shouted them out of there and into our prepared positions on both sides of the farmhouse. Unfortunately, that meant I was out of contact with those on the far side of the building. I was with two of my squad, the others were scattered about.

At 5:30 AM, the artillery barrage lifted and green signal lights arched into the sky. The attack was officially on. Since our position was in front of the town, about 500 yards closer to the German lines, I am not sure they knew we were there. At any rate, we were able to fire at their troops without any coordinated response from them. At one point, I heard some Germans walking down the road just on the other side of the hedge that separated us from that road. As they approached our position, I pulled the pin from a grenade. I rose up enough to catch a glimpse of three soldiers chatting as they walked, as though they were on a stroll down the Unter Den Linden. I tossed the grenade and watched long enough to register their startled reaction. Then, I slid back into the fox-hole to avoid the explosion.

It is amazing what I was able to see in those seconds. After one pulls the pin on a grenade and releases the lever, there is a pause of 4.5 seconds before it explodes. Perhaps, I had three seconds to scan the scene. I am sure I am remembering all of this as it happened. One of the men was wearing a Red Cross armband. I did not know that prior to tossing the grenade. If I had the time, would I have tossed the grenade far enough away so they would not have been harmed? The solder wearing the Red Cross armband had on dark rimmed glasses and he was young. They were all young, perhaps my age—19. At the moment of their death, they might have been talking to each other about their girlfriends or their schools. They seemed not to understand they were in the middle of a war and there was a battle going on. All of this I saw in those three seconds. All of this I remember 66 years later. What if I had decided to confront them with my rifle and they surrendered to me? I would have had to keep them in our emplacement, along with my two members of my squad, for several hours. Could I have gotten to know them as we awaited our uncertain outcome?

The vividness of that close encounter did change my feelings about the nature of war. More than the husks of burned out buildings, or graphic pictures of soldiers strewn about a battlefield, it was seeing these three young men, just feet from me, alive with energy and enjoying each other's company. Then, in a flash, they were no longer alive. I believe it is that instantaneous transformation, playing out as it did, that has kept those images alive today.

It was a long morning and it became afternoon. I had no way of contacting our HQ in town. I had no way of knowing how the rest of my squad members were doing in their emplacements on the other side of the farmhouse—facing the German lines.

We were very alone.

About three o'clock in the afternoon I heard the creaking roar of tanks coming up the road toward us from the direction of Hosingen. I had no idea whose tanks were making their way toward us. It was very tense until the turret came into view and I saw it was two of our Sherman tanks. The tankers told me they had been dispatched from reserves and had been "shooting Jerries" all the way in. That meant the Germans were behind our lines. I checked and was relieved that none of my men had suffered casualties. The tankers told me they had been assigned to re-establish contact with my position and they were now under my command. Irwin, the kid from Brooklyn, now had infantry and armor under his command!

After positioning my small army, I walked back to town and dropped in on Captain Friker to find out about our grand victory. He informed me that the Germans had reached our battalion and overrun it. That would be several miles behind us. Clearly, the battle had not gone as I had supposed. I was to return to my outpost and was to be reinforced by a ranger squad. (Ranger squads were much like today's black berets—an elite fighting unit.)

So now I had my squad, the ranger squad and two tanks. While I waited to be promoted to Field Marshal, I also had to figure out how to hold onto what was becoming an increasingly exposed position. Most of the fighting in the next twelve hours was sporadic and centered in the town. The next morning, December 17, we were taking some sniper fire, but most of the fighting was taking place in the town itself. I was standing near one of our tanks, directing some suppressing fire in front of us when two tanks appeared on the horizon on the ridge line leading into Hosingen.

"Ours or theirs?" I asked.

The tanker had his field glasses pinned to his eyes.

"Square fenders. Theirs."

As this dialogue was occurring, the turret of one of the German tanks tracked until the Panzer's 88 gun was aimed squarely at us, and the tank fired a round. It was right on. It hit the turret of the tank behind me but glanced off and exploded about 100 feet away. Had it hit the rounded surface squarely, you would have been spared this story. That shot was the end of the shortest tank battle in WWII. The Sherman tanks had 75 MM low trajectory cannon, the Tiger tanks had high trajectory 88 MM cannon. Our tanks were outgunned and they knew it. The American tank commander buttoned his turret, put the tank in gear, backed into the kitchen of the farmhouse and roared off. Our other tank, having heard from the first tank, also performed the time-honored maneuver known as, "Let's Get the Hell Out of Here."

One tank going at full speed makes a mighty noise. Two tanks raise the decibel level to a painful crescendo. As these two tanks roared off, I ran after them, yelling, "Come back. Come back," surely one of the most poignant and futile gestures of WWII. I suddenly felt VERY naked in that position.

I dispatched one of the men with a message to the captain saying that if I did not hear to the contrary, I was going to pull my squads back into the town to join the rest of the company. By three o'clock, not having heard anything, and not being sure my messenger had even gotten through, I started sending the soldiers on a run through a cemetery, at odd intervals back into Hosingen. Only one man got creased in the abdomen, the rest made it okay.

This time my audience with Capt. Friker was even more somber. Regimental was gone, about fifteen miles behind us, and divisional had signed off saying "Good luck." Although we had held our position, the Germans had kept going behind us. Now we were thirty-five miles behind German lines. We hadn't moved. They had. We had no hope of any reinforcements arriving and no air support. My squad was assigned to occupy and hold one of the few buildings in the center of town that we still controlled. All through the night our perimeter kept shrinking. It was a surreal night of burning buildings and tanks clanking and sporadic outbursts of gun fire. And I kept dropping off to sleep. I could not help it. The next morning the Captain decided that we had no alternative but to surrender, a decision that seemed very sensible to me at the time. We were down to a handful of houses we'd held on to as long as we could.

We surrendered to the Germans at 11:00 AM on December 18, 1944. We walked out of the few houses we had left in the town. We hadn't taken many casualties in our own unit and had destroyed our jeeps and our weapons. Out we came, with our hands raised high. My emotions were wildly mixed. Relief at being alive, fear of what was about to befall us, but also a keen curiosity about what this new experience would be like. I was curious to walk through the looking glass and see the German side of the war. I think my concerns were mitigated by being part of an organized surrender. I was still with my unit. I was still an American soldier. The scene just beyond our houses underscored the wisdom of the Captain's decision. The Germans had brought up tanks and artillery, and they were all aimed at the few houses we had been holding. They were about to level us.

That day we were walked from that field, back toward the original German lines—the Aare River, the border between Luxembourg and Germany. We had to go past the position we had held when the attack started. When we passed a number of German bodies, one of the guys in my squad piped up, in a fairly loud voice, "Jeez, we got a lot of 'em, didn't we?" as we were marching UNDER GUARD by the Germans! He may not have gotten a Purple Heart for those shins that I kicked, but I kicked him hard enough so that he should've. The Germans kept us marching through the afternoon. We found more and more of our division assembling. As it turns out, the Germans got their first big bag of American POWs in the opening days of what was to become known as The Battle of the Bulge. At seven thousand, five hundred men, it was the largest mass surrender in the entire war.

Like thousands of GI's, we were marched eastward by the Germans well into the night. That first night, we went into a church and sat up in the pews for about four or five hours, sleeping as best we could. The

Germans had given us no food. No water. The next day we were marched again. No food, no water. That night, we slept in a hayloft in a farmhouse where we found some onions and ate them ravenously. On the third day, the Germans marched us again. It was icy cold. We must have covered a good fifty miles with no food and no water. Eventually, we got to a dark railhead in Gerolstein, Germany. We were in a huge circular building—had it been used for engine repair in the past? We settled down on the concrete floor and slept as best we could until morning.

The next morning the Germans gave me and another GI a pair of shovels and told us to shovel the manure out of the boxcar we were going to occupy. It was much smaller than American boxcars, one of the 'forty-and-eights' I had started my journey on from Omaha Beach. When we finished shoveling the shit as best we could, they gave us our ration—one can of head cheese for two men—and locked us into the box-car.

There were about seventy-five of us. We were so tightly packed there was not enough room for everyone to sit, much less lie down. The sound of those iron bolts locking with a thud went sent a chill through my already chilled body. I would have been even more chilled if I'd known how long we'd be locked in there. We were sealed in there with no waste facilities and no windows, just a little grill with holes in about four places that let light and air in. In mid-December there wasn't a lot of light to let in and it was damn cold. I was exhausted, freezing, hungry and thirsty. We all were. But when the train started to move, I was so tired that I fell asleep standing up. If you had to piss, you had to get to the sliding door and try to piss out the crack. Of course, you wouldn't always make it, so over a period of time a yellow rime built up. After a few days, dysentery set in. We could only use our helmets. We would hang them on the side, so that was sloshing around. We had no food, just the one can of head cheese. That was it, from the time we got into that boxcar until we reached our destination seven days later.

We left the station and went a ways and stopped. For the next few days, we alternated some progress with long waits. I suppose their rail system was being decimated by our planes and moving their troops and supplies took precedent. Our boxcars full of human freight were low priority. On Christmas Eve, we were on a railroad siding, standing still, when we heard bombers flying overhead. The British were bombing the rail yard. You could hear the bombs whispering down—Shhhhh. Whish-hhh. Shhhhhh. When you can't run, you can't hide. In combat you can move, dig in, seek cover or shoot back. To be sitting there, listening to the bombs coming down, with no alternative but to wait and hope each one missed—seemed to make the word 'hopeless' totally inadequate. A lot of praying went on in that train. Very loud praying. I think one of the voices might have been mine. Later, we found out that eight GIs in the back of the train were killed when shrapnel came through. That was Christmas Eve, 1944.

Merry Christmas.

After a few days in the boxcar, one of the men said, "There's gotta be a way we can all sit down at once. Let's try something. You'll see, it'll all work out." American optimism. There we were, seventy-five men in a car meant for forty. But this guy had an idea and he wasn't going to let it go by. "Okay, everyone get organized by size place," he yelled. And in the gloom of a December afternoon, we shuffled around as the guy gave us orders. It wasn't as if we had a lot else to do. "The little guys move down the center, the bigger guys move to the back." So we all moved around that car until we were in some sort of size place. This took hours, HOURS. When it was all over, about half a dozen guys were still left standing. Another scientific experiment gone awry.

We all sank back into our semi-stupor of huddling ourselves against the relentless cold, the growing hunger and the sense of helplessness. With no food or water, cigarettes became very precious. There were vivid moments, like when you saw the amber light of the ash glowing in the dark as a guy puffed on it. Sometimes, you'd see the glow move in the dark as one guy handed a cigarette to his buddy behind him. Sometimes, the glow would go out.

"Where's the cigarette?" the buddy asked.

"You've got it," the first guy answered.

"No, I don't." And he didn't. Another hand, apparently, had reached out, taken the cigarette and snuffed it out.

It took us seven days to reach Bad Orb, Germany, fifty miles north of Frankfurt auf Main. Seven days and seven nights, locked in that boxcar. The time seemed endless. One of the GIs had a pocket size copy of the New Testament. I borrowed it one day just to have something to read. I have no memory of what portion I read, or of any religious significance I took from it. I was just giving my brain something to divert it.

In thinking of how we survived the ordeal, I can only guess that my body went into a kind of hibernation. Certainly my metabolism must have shut down to barely awake. About the only activity would have been making my way to the crack in the sliding door of the boxcar to piss. Did we talk with each other? Aside from thinking of food and what would happen to us when we got to prison camp, I have no recollection of how the interminable hours were passed. The train would stay in one place for hours—or days—and then lurch forward. Would this be the final leg? Then it would stop. I remember the gloom of the short winter days with the light sifting in through the four narrow openings near the top of the car. I think I never stretched out full length during the seven days. I sat with my back against the cold side of the boxcar, my feet stretched out before me. And so the hours—the days and nights passed. In hibernation. I came as close as I've ever come to really losing it, being locked in there.

After several week in Stalag 9B—the now, presumably Juden-Frei POW camp—all the non-coms, Sgts. Corporals and PFCs, were sent north to another prison camp, 9A, in Westphalia, near a town called Zeigenhain. I was still in a state of resignation and helplessness. We all were. The days were heavy on your hands and it was cold and you were hungry. You had no control over whom or what you were.

Did our families know we were alive?

How much longer would it be before our troops were able to liberate us?

How would each of us react to our new status—especially since the Germans had already shown they were ready to dump the Geneva Conventions on POWs by separating the Jewish GIs?

How long could we last on the restricted amount of food and the absence of adequate medical attention?

Maybe that small part I had built up inside of me that no one was going to get at and hurt was going to help keep me upright through this new challenge.

And then there is the "Odd Couple" part of the story. To understand this part, let me start by describing the sleeping arrangements in the Stalag. The main furnishings were three tiered, wooden bunks, enough to hold 240 POWs in each building. The 'mattresses' consisted of three or four slats across the width of the narrow wooden frame, topped by straw. That was it. That was our bed. We were each given one thin, worn blanket and assigned a bunk. It was cold at night in the winter in the barracks. It quickly became evident that the only way to survive was for us to double-up so that by sleeping with a buddy you would gain body heat and an extra blanket. As far as I know, we all did that.

How I ended up with a GI from Tulsa, Oklahoma I don't recall. I do know that the skinny Jewish kid from Brooklyn and the churched guy from Tulsa qualified as THE odd couple of our barracks. We had some really interesting discussions about religion. For instance, he wanted to know if Jews really used the blood of Christian children in making their ceremonial foods. The only Jews he had ever brushed up against back home were merchants in stores. We slept together every night until liberation, this person from the far side of the moon and I. We shared our meager rations and our stories and tales of our families. When he was one of the ones chosen by the Germans to go out one night and work on filling bomb holes in the rail lies created by our bombers, I felt compelled to volunteer to go with him. After we returned home we traded

Christmas cards for a couple of years. I cannot remember his name—though I believe his last name was, of all things, Irwin. If I believed in a personal God, I could make a case that the reason I ended up in Stalag 9A was to personally undertake the sudden and accidental reeducation of the kid from Tulsa.

And then there were our constant companions, the German guards. Our days started with roll call. We would line up along the length of the barracks in a double line and our designated spokesperson, termed the 'confidence man', would report, in German, on our numbers. He would stipulate how many were standing there, how many were ill and, each day there was the phrase I still remember, "und eine mann sheissen." Loosely translated as "one of our number is in the outhouse coping with dysentery."

For the most part, except for meal times, the guards stayed outside the barracks. As long as we did not disturb them, they left us alone. One day, an older German guard who probably was a soldier in WWI and was now drafted into service as a prison guard, came into our barracks. One of our guys was lying ill in his bunk and this older German shuffled over to his side. He removed a clump of newspaper from his great coat and carefully unwrapped it. Inside was a small piece of meat. He quietly handed it to the GI, patted him, turned and exited. I happened to be in a place to witness this quiet act of kindness. Such a strange and unsettling exception to how I had categorized the entire German population. I wonder if that person had lived in Sodom or Gomorrah, if God would have found that one act sufficient to spare their destruction. Clearly it was not enough to spare German cities. Months later, when we were being trucked to an airport for evacuation after liberation, we passed through one of those cities. The wrecked blocks of buildings were vivid testimony to the tragedy that Hitler and his madmen had brought on to their own people.

Back home, my family was reading of the Battle of the Bulge (a name for this engagement that we did not know of until we returned home) and wondering about my fate. It was sometime in January when they were informed that I was MIA—missing in action. They had to live with this uncertain status-not knowing if I was alive or dead. We were allowed to write special form postcards from the Stalag on a few occasions. In 1945, mail service from Germany to the United States was, shall we say, circuitous, involving the International Red Cross. It was not until an early March day, about 6 AM, that my parents received a call from their mailman who had been sorting through the mail for his daily route and spotted the first card from me. He knew of my status and was so excited he called my parents with the news. It may seem odd to know of the celebration at 2515 Ave. Y that day upon hearing that their son was a prisoner in Nazi Germany.

There was one "older man" (he must have been twenty-eight) in my barracks at who somehow decided to take me on as his mission. He became my mentor. Why did he choose me? I honestly do not know. After the war I found he was an economist who wound up at the Federal Reserve. The most astonishing thing is, a few years later, we discovered that his mother lived in the same building my parents had moved into on Riverside Drive.

One day, he said, "I want you to do two things. I want you to shave and I want you to wash out your pair of socks." It seemed like such a silly thing to ask. Who the hell cared? It wasn't as if the U.S.O. was coming to the stalag to entertain us. Every day in camp was the same. We were all in the same unshaven, neglected state. But I respected this man and decided to do it.

You have to understand—we had one razor and one razor blade for two hundred and forty men. We had an outhouse with nothing but cold water. Forget shaving cream. To shave meant that I had to stand there, in the freezing January weather, in the cold outhouse, shaving with a dull razor. But I had committed myself to doing it, so I stood there on a cold January day in the outhouse and shaved. It took about 20 minutes, and every time I cut a follicle, it brought tears to my eyes. By the time I finished shaving, my hands were frozen, my fingers about to fall off. But I did it. Then I took off my socks, washed them as best as I could, brought them in and put them on the one pot-bellied stove we had in the barracks. It was a difficult thing to do and more easily left undone. But I had decided I was not going to wallow. I had taken back control of my life. Yes, I was still a prisoner, but in some very important place inside of me the barbed wire had come down. I had learned that even under the most hopeless of circumstances, one does not have to be helpless.

I learned another valuable lesson through this experience—man cannot exist without a social structure. Until I entered military service, the social structure I grew up with was the civilian one. When I was inducted into the Army I entered a social structure that was totally military based. Rank dictated who we obeyed and to whom we deferred. When I became a sergeant, I automatically assumed power over eleven other soldiers. They were not to question my competence or my abilities. I had three stripes and that was it. And when we entered the Stalag, we were supposed to continue to treat our community as American soldiers. However, especially since we were all non-coms, that structure went out the window. For a while there was no recognizable social order within the camp. Gradually, a new structure valid for this peculiar situation emerged. Language facility helped. The ability to give a haircut was valuable. No one ordered us to create this new hierarchy. No one designed it or designated its components. It evolved to meet the needs of this time and this place. The day we were liberated the stalag structure disappeared and the military organization was once more in place—at least until our discharge.

For the most part, we were almost as bored as we were hungry. In response to this, I helped to organize speakers into a Chautauqua circuit. We were in five barracks, about 240 in each building. The other four impresarios and I conducted an inventory of prisoners who could speak on a topic. Any topic. We turned up a Ranger from Yellowstone National Park and the editor of the Bisbee (AZ) Bee. We organized a speaker's tour from barrack to barrack. We would announce the schedule in the barracks and pick a location among the bunk beds for each discourse. The lectures attracted any number from a few to as many as a hundred. The speakers who drew the largest crowds were—the army COOKS! As the pains of malnutrition spread, the experience of listening to recipes presented by these heretofore reviled members of the establishment turned out to be irresistible. Recipes began to sound like poetry.

Sausage.

Lobster.

Chocolate.

The very words took on a lascivious flavor. All this purposefulness helped take my mind of the crushing boredom, and the ever present hunger pangs

Our daily ration consisted of a cup of weak tea in the morning, a cup of soup of very mysterious origins at noon, and a loaf of bread at night. The bread started out being shared by five men, then seven and eventually was reduced to being shared by ten prisoners. We developed a routine to insure fairness in the selection of the pieces. Each evening became a kind of vespers ceremony. We organized ourselves into communities of ten and each night a different member of this group would slice the bread. He would cut the slices as equally as possible, and then lay each slice face down to hide any air holes which might lessen the quantity of bread one would be getting. The next step was to draw from a deck of cards. This would dictate the order in which we selected our slice. Obviously the preferred position was first, so if any slice looked larger than the others, one could lay claim to it. The ceremony of the bread took longer than the actual consuming of the slice. It was not as though we had a lot of other things on our agenda. It was a weight loss diet that really works. When I was finally liberated I weighed in at 105. I am 6 feet 3 inches tall.

Then I added Newscaster to my POW resume. The French prisoners had somehow managed to rig a radio. They had been prisoners for over four years—since the fall of France in 1940, so they had time to figure that out. They would listen to the communiqués from the BBC and then, each day, they would recite them to one of our men, who understood French, at the point where our compound fences touched. He, in turn, would translate the communiqués from both fronts for the five of us who would then be responsible for presenting them each night in our barracks.

At six o'clock at night, we would put someone at the door so that if a German guard was coming in I could switch to a lecture on something innocuous. Then I would, by memory, describe what was happening on the Western and the Eastern fronts. Toward the end, when the Russians were closing in on Berlin, they stopped to regroup at the Oder River. For two weeks there was no further movement on the Eastern front. Every night, when I got to the Eastern front, it was the same news. Finally, one night, someone shouted,

"That's what you said last night, and the night before that..."

"If you don't like the news," I phumphed, "get someone else to do it!"

A physiological fact about starvation is that it reduces the functions of the male glands and enhances those that are more female-like. Thus our facial growth grew more soft and silky. Our voices went up in pitch. That night the shouted exchange was rather squeaky and petulant.

One of the bitter ironies in WWII struck Stalag 9 about two weeks before liberation. A high point of our days was watching the contrails of the B-17s as they made their way Eastward over Germany on their daily bombing runs. Sometimes there would be hundreds of them and the deep, pulsating noise of their four engines was the affirmation that the war was moving into its noisy final stages. As the front moved closer to us, our fighter planes were buzzing around, strafing German columns, freight trains and pretty much anything that was moving. We crowded the entrance to the barracks to watch as much of that show as we could. Though we restrained ourselves from cheering so as not to piss of our captors, there is no doubt that the sight of this armada of American power was a tremendous boost to our morale. One morning we watched as a P-47 banked and started diving directly toward the stalag. My guess is that a German guard in one of the guard towers had fired his machine gun at the planes and the pilot decided to take him out. Unfortunately, when we saw the smoke break out on the leading edge of this wing, we all knew that eight, fifty- caliber machine guns were firing thousands of rounds straight at us. I immediately hit the floor and found that at least three of my buddies were already ahead of me.

We were lucky. We were digging slugs out of the wooden bunks for days. The French were not so fortunate. Eight were killed that morning by "friendly fire." As we watched the bodies being borne past our compound, the sadness was accentuated by the realization that after five years as POWs, they had been killed by their ally as liberation was at hand.

The German Commanders started getting very nervous. As the war came closer, orders came down to them to move all prisoners towards Kassel, which was further into Germany. There were two reasons why that wasn't a good idea. We were in such terrible shape it was thought that many of the men would not survive the trek, and the Allies had control of the air and were strafing everything. We weren't sure that the Americans would identify our column of men as POWs. The Germans were determined to move us out of there. We were determined to stay put. We spent the night organizing. One third of the men were assigned to not get out of their bunks the next morning. They were supposed to say they were "too sick." The next third of the men were assigned to start dropping into the mud when we were outside and ordered to move. They were to say, "I can't move. I am too weak" If we were forced to move out, the last third of the men, of which I was one, was assigned to start jumping the guards (ten men to one guard) when it got dark. The next morning, the guards came into our barracks.

"Raus, Raus! Schnell!" On cue, one third of the men moaned in their bunks. The guards couldn't get them out of bed. The Germans gathered the remaining two thirds of the POWs outside in the pouring rain. When they started moving us out, guys started dropping into the mud, as planned. I stifled a laugh. I couldn't help it—it looked so fake. The Germans were pissed. They started waving guns around and firing shots into the air to prove they were pissed. Meanwhile, the French POW'S were moving out. The Russians were moving out. The British were moving out. The Germans didn't understand the unreasonable Americans. One hour later, we still didn't know if they were going to start shooting us, or what. One third of our men were in their bunks, hundreds more were lying in the mud. The rest of us were facing those gun-waving Germans. The American Captain tried to reason with them.

"The war is over. The American Army will be here in a few hours. Anyone who gets hurt here, you will answer for it."

The German commander pleaded, "Give me just 240 of your men to move to save face." The Captain said no.

The Germans were getting itchy. They wanted to get away before the American Army arrived. Finally the standoff ended. We were allowed to return to the barracks. The Germans took off. All except for one little schmucky German guy who had keys to all the cell blocks. He kept walking up and down the street in his great coat, holding the large wooden locks with the keys attached to each compound piled one on top of the other. Of course they were all empty now, save ours. By early afternoon, March 30, 1945, even he'd disappeared.

Now the defeated German Army was streaming past the camp. We understood why we were told to stay low and out of sight. There's nothing more dangerous than a defeated army; discipline breaks down, you don't know what they might do. About three o'clock in the afternoon, we got word that SS troops had come into the camp. We remained still, hoping they would assume the camp was empty. It was spooky. We didn't know where they were or if they were staying. It turned out that they went into the compound where the Germans had lived, to look for food. Apparently, they took what they could and they left. A half-hour later,

American tanks of Patton's sixth armored division started streaming down the hill toward and around the camp. It was the sight we had been praying for. Especially since, during long days in the Stalag, we had sung our own version of "The Battle Hymn of the Republic":

We're a bunch of Yankee soldiers living deep in Germany
We eat black bread, a little soup and a beverage they call tea
And we have got to stay right here 'till Patton sets us free
And we go rolling home—
Come and get us, Georgie Patton
Come and get us, Georgie Patton
Come and get us, Georgie Patton
And we go rolling home.

Patton had finally come.

We climbed up onto the roof and screamed and yelled and cheered. I looked at the GIs coming into the camp and said, "Boy, are they fat." Of course, they weren't. We were all pretty skinny by then. Our camp was liberated on March 30, 1945, on Passover, the Jewish holiday that celebrates freedom from slavery. If you want to celebrate the festival of freedom, that's not a bad way to do it.

Dad, older sister Shirley, and me.
Check out the two poses—
Shirley, feet together—hair
carefully combed. Sonny, legs
splayed, cap on backward and
sucking his thumb; a perfect
insight into our two personalities.

Parents Abe and
Gertrude Fox in a serene
moment. Serenity was
not always the hallmark
of their 59-year marriage.

Sisters Shirley, center,
Phoebe, right and a rare
appearance of 11-year-old Irwin
with his hair combed.

The Living Arts

The New York Times

Americans captured at
the Battle of the Bulge
being marched to boxcars
for transport to
Bad Orb, Germany.

Photographs from the National Archives

Maj. Fulton Vowell, an American war crimes investigator, at a Berga cemetery where Jews were buried in unmarked graves.

Where G.I.'s Were Consumed By the Holocaust's Terror

A Filmmaker Helps Thaw Memories of Wartime Guilt

By ROGER COHEN

BERGA, Germany — Four plain wooden crosses stand in the cemetery above this quiet town in eastern Germany. One of them is inscribed "Unknown Allied Soldier." He is unlikely to be an American, because the G.I.'s who died here were exhumed after World War II and taken home. But the mystery of this soldier's identity is only one of many hanging over Berga and its former Nazi camp.

On a cold, late March day, with rain falling on the graves, a thin, soft-spoken American stands

But when the other soldiers embarked, he was immobilized with a foot infection. He remained in Indiana while his fellow infantrymen were plunged, within weeks, into the Battle of the Bulge; two regiments were lost. Thousands of American soldiers were captured, and several hundred who were Jewish or who "looked" Jewish ended up in Berga. Up to now their fate has received relatively little attention, partly because the surviving soldiers long tended to repress the trauma.

"I could have been among the captured or the killed," Mr. Guggenheim mused. "I never wished I had come to Europe. Anyone in the infantry who wishes for war has something wrong with them. But I've thought a lot: why in the hell am I here and they not?"

About 60 years after it all happened, Charles Guggenheim made a stunning documentary re-creating the unique separation of Jewish POWs at Stalag 9B. I finally learned about the terrible fate of those who were sent to the slave labor camp at Berga.

After getting the information that I was alive and a POW, my mother sent letters on a form provided by the international Red Cross. Unfortunately neither the letters nor the food packages ever made it to the camp.

Here is a German still from the documentary showing the just captured American troops being escorted by the German guards on the way to the railhead for the start of the seven day boxcar trip to Bad Orb.

Back at NYU and obviously enjoying my status as a BMOC and the extracurricular activities.

The lead item in the Winchell column that set of a frenzy of delicious prospects in the Fox 'Tribe' but, apparently, a dose of dismay on Park Avenue.

Johnson & Johnson heiress Fifi Johnson and Sonny Fox (of the textile tribe) are closer than a band-aid and a blister...Leis Rocky

Here is the way a letter from the front looked upon arrival home. Known as "V-Mail," it was a way of reducing letters to film to make it easier to transport the huge volume of mail in both directions.

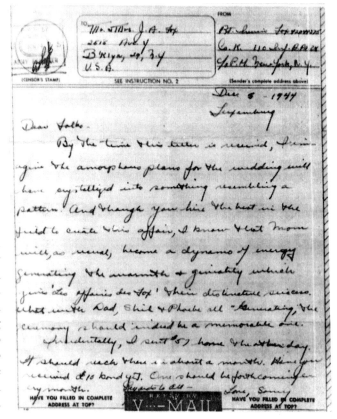

CHAPTER 7

Repatriation and Home Again

Stalag 9A was one of the first prison camps liberated by the Allies, and no one was quite prepared with an evacuation plan. The result was that although we were no longer prisoners, we were still in the prison camp, and, as it turned out, would be for another week. The diet improved somewhat, though more by quantity than quality. When the American soldiers came through asking for volunteers to guard the increasingly large number of German prisoners pouring into the open areas inside the prison gates, I eagerly responded. One might assume that I was anxious to torment my tormentors. I remember being motivated by the thought of getting better rations. We were moved to the quarters previously occupied by the guards who had been guarding us. I took up my position in the guard tower, with the very machine guns that had been trained on us now trained on the thousands of Germans milling about below. Since we were quite depleted from our starvation rations of the past several months, we did not make very good guards. I, for one, was constantly falling asleep on my post.

The irony of switching from prisoner to prison guard in 24 hours was not lost on me. I was allowed to use a German POW as an orderly, to clean my room and make my bed. It was also my responsibility to give the prisoner his lunch. I tried to short ration him, but I found I could not. The young German who was that day's orderly did not seem like an enemy. He was now the bewildered and helpless one. But the Americans who were occupying the area, men from the 80th division, were not so ready to forgive. One of the soldiers expressed his outrage at the condition he found us in by selecting about twenty Germans from the compound. He would run them up and down the company streets shouting, "Raus! Raus!" until they were exhausted. He would return them to the prison compound, pick out another twenty and start the ritual all over again.

Finally the day came when the Army moved us out of Stalag 9A and we were truly starting our journey home. We were flown out in C46's. As we flew over the cities and towns of Germany, we could see the vast destruction inflicted by the allied air force and artillery. I viewed it almost objectively. I have no memory of the thrill of revenge. I suppose that I was emotionally numb—or thinking only of getting home. We were taken to Camp Lucky Strike, one of several tent cities near Le Havre that the Army had constructed and decided to name after cigarettes. We were among the first POWs to arrive and were met by well-meaning Red Cross ladies who plied us with greasy donuts and coffee. Needless to say, we wolfed them down with little regard for what this diet was going to do to systems that had become accustomed to thin soup and ersatz bread. One unfortunate put away 18 donuts and promptly died. In the next days, we were switched to eggnog and other more appropriate food.

It was in Lucky Strike that I heard of the death of FDR. Although I was born while Calvin Coolidge was president, and lived through the disaster of Herbert Hoover, my first awareness of matters political started with FDR. In all those years of growing up, going to school and fighting a war, he was the only President I had known. The emotional impact of his death was muted, though, by my need to know that I was going to get food again and anxiety about when we would be leaving. When we left on a troop ship I immediately volunteered for KP. Not because I felt that I should, but. I would be closer to food. My anxiety about where the next meal was coming from would last for a while.

Looking back, the battles and the prison camps were a voyage of self-discovery. Going through that at nineteen ended up being the seminal and shaping experience of my life. I was tested in many ways and I found that I could deal with all of it. I don't recommend that particular path to enlightenment but it certainly changes you.

If you survive.

Fourteen years later, in 1979, I found myself in Brussels producing a TV special for HBO starring Tony Randall. It was a piece of fluff called The International Festival of Magic, which was being held in Belgium. I realized that I was not too far from the town of Hosingen, Luxembourg, where I had been captured. For some reason I felt a need to go back, perhaps for closure. When the taping was finished, I rented a car and drove east. I arrived in Bastogne and visited the museum commemorating the battle of the bulge and those who had died in that huge struggle. On the drive from there to Luxembourg, I dwelled on how I would be received. When they discovered my story, they would probably want to buy me a beer…maybe even insist I stay overnight.

As I drove through the Luxembourg countryside, I recognized some of the places I had been such as Clervaux, a charming town, built in a pass, with part of the city clinging to a hill. It had been regimental headquarters and we were taken there one winter's day for the only shower and change of clothes I had in all the time at the front. Finally I approached the sign announcing I had reached Hosingen. I was somewhat disoriented at first. The town had grown and it started further out than it had in 1945. Eventually I found my way to the center of town and walked into the police station. The commandant spoke French, so I resorted to my high school French to tell him why I was there. La guerre. Les Boches. Un prisonier. He seemed quite unimpressed with my tale, but did direct me to the road leading to the farmhouse we held when the battle started.

Driving down that road, between the town and the farmhouse, a flood of sense memories came back. There was no one around at the farmhouse. I parked the car and wandered to the spot I had been on when the tanks were spotted coming up on the other side of town. It was exactly as I had remembered. I looked at the farmhouse. I could see the new bricks that had been used to patch the gaping hole made by one of the tanks. I always felt a bit outraged that this American tank had damaged some man's house after it had withstood five years of war. The farmer emerged at about that time. I addressed him in my limited French. I explained that we had lived in that house during la guerre and that I wanted to apologize for the damage done the house. He explained that he had bought the farm some years after the war, and had no idea of its history—nor did he seem very interested in it.

No beer. No invitation. My dreams of being carried off on shoulders and hailed as a hero evaporated in the slanting autumn sun in Luxembourg. I left Hosingen, stayed at a hotel in Clervaux overnight, and returned to Belgium. Although I had not been acknowledged in some wonderful way, I had achieved my objective. I have never thought about returning since that trip.

HOME AGAIN

I came home on a sixty-day leave. The evening I returned to my parent's house on Ave. Y, I found the whole neighborhood turned out to cheer my arrival. A banner was strung up across the road welcoming me home. While I sat in the kitchen eating my first home cooked meal, about twenty or thirty people were crowded into doorways and sitting on appliances. Before coming back, some of us had speculated on how we would be received. Had we let people down because we had surrendered? Would people be polite but reserved? Looking around the house that night, I had my answer.

After my experiences I couldn't sit still. Mostly, where I wanted to go was bars. My mother became my buddy and we'd start hitting the bars when they opened—around eleven o'clock in the morning. Other than at bars I spent most of those sixty days at the dentist's office. The result of our POW diet was that my gums had receded so badly that decay had set in. The Army wanted to take out all of my teeth, but my father wouldn't let them. He sent me to a dentist who was a pioneer in root canal. He saved a lot of my teeth. Mind you, this was before the days of high-speed drills. It was only a little better than prison camp.

Following home leave, all POW's were given two weeks of R&R-rest and rehabilitation. Hard to tell whether we were supposed to recover from the prison camps or from our home leave. In any event, the next place I went was a bit of all right. The army had taken over the toniest place in Lake Placid—The Lake Placid Club. It was the place where old money went. They had just three beds in each room. And maid service!

July 1, 1945

Dearest Folks –

This ain't the Army, Mr. Jones! It's all the things I imagined and more. Two fellows and I have a beautiful room with cross ventilation, private bathroom with tiled shower and bathtub, fresh towels and soap for each man. The grounds are exquisite and, best of all, there are free milk and donuts at all times…

On Saturday night, the army would invite the young ladies of the old money crowd to come to their old haunt and dance with the GI's. That's how I met Fifi Johnson, of the adorable face. I discovered that Fifi was the daughter of the Robert Wood Johnson—of the Band-Aid Johnsons. More of that later.

By August, it was time to be shipped back to my final post, old Fort Benning. This time, I was not going to be ordered about by some scrawny red-neck in basic training. I joined the School Troop detachment, so called because they put on combat demonstrations for the candidates at OCS who were in the process of becoming officers. That was the fun part of my Army career and it was reflected by the change in my army specialization number. I went out a "746" (classification, rifleman) and came back an "288" (classification, playwright.) I was amazed that the army had a classification number for "playwright." I may have been the only soldier ever to have had both those classifications. I wrote radio scripts, had my own jeep and even got a half hour a week on the radio. I could hear the radio great, Norman Corwin, in my head as I wrote those wonderfully, overripe scripts at Fort Benning. Being a playwright in the army sure beat being in a foxhole.

I had an office. I could go to the motor pool at anytime and check out a jeep to zap off to Columbus whenever I felt it useful. There was a drama group on base. I got to play the lead in one of their productions. I found a synagogue in the classy part of Columbus (yes there was a classy part) and my friend Lester Tanner, whom I had met at Lake Placid, and I met two lovely Jewish lasses. They wore gloves and were reasonably proper—but, hell, they were girls and we could pretend we weren't in the army for a while when we were with them.

A dividend was meeting their parents. One of the mothers still had her Jewish/European accent. There was something fascinating about the mix of the southern drawl with the minor key accents of Galicia. There was something appalling about the mix of this accent with the same racist sentiments about the blacks that others used. To hear it from Jews, just after our people had suffered such a huge disaster resulting from the senseless discrimination of the Nazis (and the Poles and the Hungarians and the French) was, at the very least, perplexing. You would think that, as a sorely beset minority, we would be the most sensitive. Indeed it proved to be so as the civil rights movement developed.

Private John Hammond Jr. was in my barracks. He was an astonishing anomaly in that setting. He was a descendant from a wealthy family, with connections to the Vanderbilts—a graduate of Yale with cousins high in the ranks of the military and the State department—and at least ten years older than me. Here he was, a private in Fort Benning. Let me reproduce at this point a small piece of the Wikipedia entry on John, just so you understand this phenomenon.

John Henry Hammond II (December 15, 1910 – July 10, 1987) was a record producer, musician and music critic from the 1930s to the early 1980s. In his service as a talent scout, Hammond became one of the most influential figures in 20th century popular music. Hammond was instrumental in sparking or furthering numerous musical careers, including those of Benny Goodman, Charlie Christian, Billie Holiday, Count Basie, Teddy Wilson, Big Joe Turner, Pete Seeger, Babatunde Olatunji, Aretha Franklin, George Benson, Bob Dylan, Freddie Green, Leonard Cohen, Bruce Springsteen, Arthur Russell, Asha Puthli and Stevie Ray Vaughan. He is also largely responsible for the revival of delta blues artist Robert Johnson's music.

When I came upon John, he had already been instrumental in helping Benny Goodman bring in a black pianist—Teddy Wilson—to his trio, one of the first moves toward breaking the color barrier in the big band era. He had discovered Billie Holliday. He had produced many albums and was one of the major forces in the jazz world. So what was he doing here—as a private? What he was doing was trying to integrate the U.S. Army. John had been promoted and busted a few times for his disregard of the stupid segregation of the military. He refused to call on his family connections to get him out of his position, where his talents were obviously wasted. For whatever reason, John Hammond adopted me as his friend. I had some wonderful conversations with him and took an informal course on the history of jazz as shared by one who was shaping it.

After our discharge, I lost contact with John Hammond, Jr., though I read about him from time to time. Then, about twenty years later, John and his new wife moved to Weston, Connecticut, the very town where I was living with my family. I got to spend more time visiting in his home and enjoying his tales, his energy and his commitment to using music to enable racial integration. By then, though, the world of music had changed. It changed in 1964 when four Yorkshire lads appeared on the Ed Sullivan show. John's kind of music was no longer the big seller and John's role in the music industry had attenuated.

I was in Fort Benning when the War finally ended.

August 15, 1945

Dearest Folks –

Well, the death watch is finally over. When the news finally came, it took about an hour for it to get around. When it did, Columbus and Fort Benning took a back-seat to no one in the way of celebrating. The bus into town took everyone on free, cars were loaded and motorcycles and pogo sticks came into play.

Columbus' main street was littered with ticker tape and crowded with cars. When I first saw the sight I gaped in amazement. Every car was weighed down with laughing, screaming people. Civilians picked up soldiers and soldiers picked up civilians. The horns and cowbells, sirens and firecrackers lent to the color of the spectacle.

I wasn't the same skinny kid from Flatbush any more. My opinions were colored by what I'd seen.

At the same time I began thinking of our country—what lay ahead for it now that the war was over and we had emerged triumphant. What about the dissonances in our own society? How would we handle those?

November 6, 1945

Dearest Folks—

It matters not which town, city or hamlet you visit in the South. You leave with the same impression. The South is a sick land!

It is sick physically and it is sick mentally. Its land is eroded and worn; its people ill and pale – and their minds filled with hatreds and bigotry.

They are living in a non-existent world. They are living in an age that is past and they don't know it yet.

Sooner or later, those people they suppress – those religions they "tolerate" – those liberties which are theirs alone – will overcome the narrowness and half truths of the "White Supremacy." The Atomic Bomb has brought the reckoning that much closer.

The British will learn their lesson in India. The French and Dutch will learn it in Indonesia. It's an evolutionary process which will triumph or destroy.

I was supposed to be discharged in early November, but the Army, in its stately fashion, moved slowly. By the end of November, 1945, I was merely going through the motions of being a GI and still taking care of the radio program. Finally, in December, 1945, the day came that I was waiting for.

DAY OF LIBERATION

Dearest, Darling People...

Oh, the power of the prayer! Oh, the joy of being freed from an involuntary servitude. Sing of pin stripes and red socks... of table-cloths and silverware... of skyscrapers and subways... of wine, women and song...

So, start looking at clothes, people. And start working on that New Year's Eve.

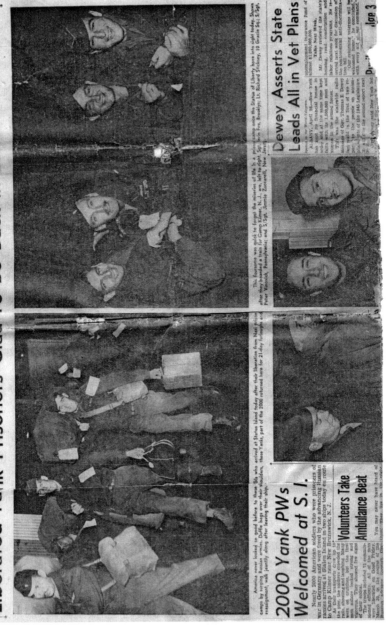

Liberated Yank Prisoners Glad To Be Back in Land of the Free

America never looked so good before to these GIs who arrived at Staten Island today after their liberation from Nazi prison camps by surging Russian armies. Duffle bags over their shoulders, these Yank, part of the 2000 returned here for 21-days furlough and reassignment, walk jauntily along after leaving their ships.

This foursome was quick to forget the miseries of life in a prison camp once the Statue of Liberty hove into sight today. Soon after they boarded a train for Camp Kilmer, N.J., are, left to right: Sgt. John Fox, Brooklyn; Lt. Richard Dickson, 10 Gould St., Brooklyn; Peter Valenick, Pennsylvania; and S/Sgt. Jimmie Zaccarelli, New.

2000 Yank PWs Welcomed at S. I.

Volunteers Take Ambulance Beat

Dewey Asserts State Leads All in Vet Plans

age 3

As some of the first returnees, we were the subject of some curiosity. One of my sister's friends decided, after seeing this newspaper photo, she wanted to date me. Turns out she thought I was the dashing one with the moustache!

Here I am on home leave in 1945, following my liberation. I was rapidly replenishing my body with home cooked meals—I had weighed in at 105 pounds by the time the cavalry arrived.

With Grandma Goldberg outside our home on Ave Y in Brooklyn.

Performing one of my sterling radio dramas that proved I deserved my ASN 288 designation of "Playwright."

CHAPTER 8

Candid Microphone

I went home and back to NYU. My original class had graduated in 1945, and I wanted to finish as soon as possible. The professors were wary of the returning GIs. We had been tested and we knew they couldn't intimidate us. Plus, we had a lot of time to make up for and we wanted to get on with our deferred lives. We were motivated.

I became an A student, the comptroller of the Washington Square College undergraduate budget and a devotee of the jazz clubs around the village. I worked at a radio station, WINS, from 4-8 AM, keeping the program logs. I made a buck an hour. After finishing my stint, I would start my day at NYU. This meant leaving about 3:30 in the morning for the cab ride down. I loved New York at that hour; the lonely figures scurrying along to some unknown destination. The garbage trucks removing the tied bundles of waste products from the stores and offices that line mid-town Manhattan, the smell of the marble floors in the building that housed the station on 44th St as the cleaning women went about their early morning chores. When Skye Masterson sings about "My time of day is the night time of day" in Guys and Dolls, I am with him on that stage.

I graduated from NYU in 1947 with a degree in television and radio production. Three weeks later I went back to Alan Funt to ask for a job. He had just sold the radio show, "Candid Microphone," to the ABC radio network. Alan took me on. As I always say, I got my first job in radio because I was smart and talented...and because my mother knew his mother.

When we started were just four of us—Alan, Phil Pollard, Al Slep, and me. We were the ones who produced "Candid Microphone" for the sixty-five weeks it stayed on the air, inventing it as we went along. We were on once a week for a half-hour at 8 PM. When we first started we were using wire recording, which came out of WW II as a German invention. Editing wire was a hellish thing to do. To edit the recordings you had to use scissors to cut the wire, then hold on to both ends for dear life, because if you let go of either end, the wire would go BOINGGG and you'd end up with about a hundred knots you'd have to take out. So you'd hold on for dear life, and then pull it through to where you wanted to make the second cut, cut that and hold on tight. Then you'd take the two ends and tie as tight a knot as you could. Finally, you'd take the lighted end of a cigarette and weld the wire together. At the beginning, that was how we had to edit the first few shows. It was nuts.

We were working eighty hours a week inventing the ideas, writing the skits, going out and taping them, editing the stuff. We did everything. I was having a ball and getting paid for it—thirty-five bucks a week at first, then I worked my way up to sixty-five bucks a week. It was my first job in radio and I thought it was terrific, even though Alan was a difficult person to work for. I learned a lot from him, including the meaning of the word "chutzpah." I watched it in action. Alan never took no for an answer; never assumed that something was not doable just because somebody said so. He was equally brilliant and temperamental, would throw pencils at people and scream a lot. He was a madman but we had some funny times. Some very funny times.

Alan had a two-room office suite at 52 Vanderbilt Avenue, which he shared with an accountant. Their desks butted against each other and the chairs faced one another. Throughout all our shenanigans, that accountant was sitting at his desk, working on numbers. It was insane. There was a second office, where we kept the tape recorder.

One of our shenanigans involved chaining our secretary to the desk and calling a locksmith, without telling him why he was coming up. Only the locksmith was a half-hour late, so by the time he got there the poor girl's foot was getting red, which made it look even more convincing. Alan greeted the guy in the office. The microphone was hidden in the box of Kleenex and, as usual, the accountant was working busily at his desk. The locksmith was a crusty old guy from the Lower East Side . . . the kind of guy who's seen everything.

"Ver's the lock?" he asked.

Alan pointed to the secretary chained to the desk, "Right there."

The locksmith looked at the secretary chained to the desk, then back at Alan.

"You chained this voman to the desk?"

Alan said nonchalantly. "I do it every day, only this time the lock jammed."

"Vat kind of thing is this?" the locksmith asked. "Vy you lock her up?"

"Ahh, she's a clock watcher. She's always leaving too early. The only way I can make sure she stays until she's supposed to leave is by locking her to the desk."

Certain he was in the loony bin, the locksmith got right to work.

"Don't vorry, Miss," the locksmith assured the secretary. "I'll get out of here."

At the adjoining desk, the accountant didn't even glance over as he continued to scribble his numbers. Alan asked the locksmith, "What, you've never seen anything like this?"

The locksmith shrugged his shoulders, "Out vest maybe."

I was laughing so hard by now that my head was in the filing cabinet. The locksmith quickly unlocked the woman and left, as fast as his legs would carry him. Alan told me to get downstairs on the double. "He's on his way to the police to report us."

I raced downstairs and ran out to Vanderbilt Avenue. Just in time to stop the locksmith who was, indeed, on his way to the police.

Another time, we put Phil Pollard in a steamer trunk, trussed it up with rope and called a moving guy. When the mover came, Alan pointed to the trunk and gave his own address as the delivery point.

"Take this and leave it there. And don't answer any questions. Just leave it outside the door and leave. Just get it done! How much will it be?"

"Twelve dollars."

When he and his assistant started to move the trunk, they heard banging from inside. The moving guy jumped.

"What's that noise?"

"What noise?"

The mover and his assistant picked up the trunk again. Bang, bang, bang. From inside the trunk.

"What's that noise?"

"Nothing. I don't hear any noise." Alan insisted. "Here's twenty dollars. Keep the change. Now move it out of here."

What was more likely to arouse suspicion than telling the guy to keep the eight bucks change? Finally, at the very end of this whole thing, they started to move it one last time and Phil started moaning, mournfully.

"Uhhhh….. Uhhhhhh…"

Pause. Beat.

"Get another mover. Keep your twenty dollars!"

And he's out the door. Again, I had to run downstairs and stop him from going to the police. And the whole time, the accountant was sitting there, doing his accounts.

While I was working on "Candid Microphone," I started dating Fifi Johnson again, the heiress I had met in Lake Placid. Although I enjoyed her company, I was always aware of the disparity of our backgrounds. Once, I went to her Park Avenue digs to pick her up. The rooms were vast and the furnishings screamed good taste and much money. Her father stood in the middle of one of the rooms. Tall. Spare. The Ur-establishment. I told Fifi how uncomfortable all this made me feel. In response, she sweetly refused to sit anywhere in a club where the minimum or cover would kick in. She insisted the bar was just fine, thank you. While this was going on, Al Slep, one of my cohorts on the show, who supplied Walter Winchell with items from time to time, slipped him one. One day, I opened the *Daily News* and leading Winchell's column was this little gem:

"Johnson and Johnson heiress Fifi Johnson and Sonny Fox (of the textile tribe) are closer than a band aid and a blister." "Sonny Fox of the TEXTILE TRIBE??" First I laughed myself silly. Pretty soon the band aid was removed. Our relationship, as Winchell would have written had "gone pffft."

After 65 weeks, "Candid Microphone" went off the air. Later, Alan would do some of the same stunts on television. Almost all the good stuff we'd done on radio, he did on television. My theory is that it was funnier on radio because it was not so literal. You could make up your own pictures as you listened to the dialogue. Anyway, I was out of a job.

Then I got a call from Arch Oboler, who was the other big guy in radio, besides Norman Corwin. He had just come back from Africa with a bunch of audio-tapes he'd recorded there. He'd heard about my work on "Candid Microphone," called and asked if I would help him edit the tapes. Next thing I knew, I was on the 20th Century and the Chief bound for Los Angeles.

It took four nights and five days. In '48 L.A. was a small, unsophisticated place. There were only a couple of places where you could go and eat. I was not overwhelmed. Plus, I was staying at Arch's ranch house up in the hills above Malibu. I lived there for about two and half months, feeling like I'd gone to the nether regions of the world. Arch had never been in the war because he was '4-F', unfit for service, so he compensated by buying military vehicles, like the Amphibious Jeep known as "The Duck." It was a big, wide ungainly thing and the only vehicle he'd let me drive. When I drove this amphibious vehicle down Sunset I felt like I was in a float in a parade!

After two months, it was clear that nothing more was going to happen with the tapes so I said goodbye to Mr. Oboler and came back to my town. The first thing I did when I got home was to hit the Stage Delicatessen for one of its mighty pastrami sandwiches, washed down with a cold bottle of Dr. Brown's Cel-Ray tonic.

CHAPTER 9

I Become the
Voice of America

In 1950 I applied for a job as a correspondent with the Voice of America. It was a civil service job so I had to go through a full field investigation by the FBI and be cleared by the State Department. But first I had to ask my mother about petitions. She was head of various organizations and, politically, an emotional left-winger. Whereas other people signed petitions, my mother would run around looking for petitions. So I sat her down.

"Ma, can you remember all the organizations you joined, because the FBI is going to be asking a lot of questions?" Of course, she couldn't remember them all. Fortunately enough, neither could the FBI, because they cleared me. My Civil Service label was 'temporary indefinite'. Nice. Really makes you feel secure. But the grade was good and there was fair money—especially since I was still living at home.

The VOA was headquartered in Washington, DC, but most of its news operation was in New York at 250 W. 57th Street. Here was truly the Tower of Babble. So many different language desks, all concentrated on piercing the iron curtain and getting the American story into the homes of those in Europe and Asia where the information flow was severely regulated. The Russians spent an enormous effort toward jamming our signals. The contest was never ending. Switch frequencies—find and jam. Start a new higher powered transmitter—increase the power of the jamming generators. One of the paragraphs in my job description instructed that I had to be able "to cover any subject no matter how obscure or abstruse." After I looked up abstruse, I was ready for my new career.

I had a wonderful time learning my craft as a correspondent. I interviewed important persons, like King Faisal of Iraq, who was later assassinated, Eleanor Roosevelt and Madame Vijaya Lakshmi Pandit of India. Just being able to say her name marked me as a smooth reporter. The thing I enjoyed most was striking out and covering the United States as a roving special events reporter. My job was to make us explicable to people around the world. So I got a chance to go to places I would never have gone—Fargo, North Dakota, Butte, Montana, Walla Walla, Washington. It was the first time I really saw my country. I ended up being 3300 feet under Butte, Montana, in a copper mine. I met the owner of a radio station in Walla Walla who left to go fishing for two weeks at the start of the salmon season. He had all the salmon cleaned and tinned and gave it to his employees. I spent about three weeks in Carroll County, in backwoods Georgia, with a dark-skinned farmer from India. In the 1950s, people in that part of Georgia were probably racist and I had my concerns about how this sweet natured farmer who had been brought over here to experience this part of America by the New York Herald Tribune would fare. I was a long way from Flatbush. I'm not sure how much the rest of the world learned about this country, but I learned an enormous amount about the variety of lifestyles and outlooks that it takes to make up America. Even when the country looks like everyone in those blue states or those red states are oddballs and really stupid, I try to keep in mind the innate decency of most of the populace.

One of the most difficult problems we had trying to explain America to the world in the 1950s was the acute disparity between how wealthy we were, and how poor and damaged the rest of the world was as it emerged from the cauldron of World War II. Europe and Russia had been ravaged. Japan's cities had been bombed to smithereens—and two of its cities nuked. Trade had halted and progress stopped for five years in most of the world. The United States had suffered many combat casualties, but our mainland had remained untouched. This huge gulf made it difficult for others to feel any identity with us. This was brought into clear focus for me when I spent the weeks showing my Indian friend our universities and the farms with their tractors and combines. He found all of that wonderful, but totally useless to him. It was not until we happened on a black sharecropper with a horse drawn wooden plow that had steel sheathing that we made contact. The young Indian farmers eyes lit up as he realized that he could improve the efficiency of his two-and-a-half acre farm by putting similar metal sheathing on his Ox drawn plow.

One night, this dark-skinned farmer from India and I knocked on the door of a poor white farmer's house. He was a sharecropper. We had interrupted their dinner around a trestle table, benches and a single naked light bulb. They invited us in to share their dinner with no apologies and with the greatest dignity. They were warm and welcoming. From this experience I learned that a person can have a blind spot about the color of people's skin but that doesn't make one evil. I also learned that this is an incredibly vast country with great beauty and great strengths. When I was a Vice President at NBC, I had to remind people that the part of the country we were flying over was what it was really about. It wasn't just about New York and L.A.

Perhaps the most effective program ever produced by VOA was designed to get me a date. At least I could personally measure the efficacy of that broadcast.

Four of us owned a sloop that we kept at the Throg's Neck Yacht Club. It was the seediest yacht club this side of the Mississippi but it was cheap. One morning, we were having breakfast at a diner just before taking her out. One of our foursome, Dick Hall, showed us pictures from a windjammer cruise he'd taken in Maine that summer. He had been away for a couple of weeks and had met this tall, lovely, curvaceous blond lady named Gloria. He showed us color photos, and we all ooed and aahed.

It was Halloween Eve, 1950, at a restaurant named 17 Barrow Street when I first met Gloria. The personification of that photograph looked even more brilliantly beautiful. She was the shiksa dream of every Jewish boy growing up in Brooklyn. I was smitten with her but she was dating my friend. She was also, at that time, the Executive Secretary of the New York State Association of Young Republican Clubs, working for an interesting guy named Cliff White. Gloria's job took her to Albany, so my buddy stopped seeing her. I kept corresponding with her. I would write her Ogden Nash type poems and she would respond. We kept this going for about six months. Then, that faded away.

I was still at the Voice of America when I heard that she and Cliff were back in town. This was 1952, two years after I had first met her. I was still not all that secure about women; especially such a goddess. It wouldn't have occurred to me to call her up and say, "Hey, I hear you're back in town. Want to have dinner?" That was too direct. I had to be much more elliptical. So I went to my boss at the Voice of America.

"I've got a great idea for a series—young people in politics. There's a guy I know named Cliff White, President of the N.Y. State Association of Young Republican Clubs. We can talk to him about it. Oh, yeah, and we get the Democratic Clubs, too." My boss thought that was interesting and gave me a go. I called up Cliff and said I wanted to do this series, "And I want you to be in it. Do you want to have lunch with me and we'll talk about it?"

"Sure."

"By the way, why don't you bring Gloria along?"

"I already thought of that."

So Cliff and Gloria came to lunch. On the way back from lunch, I said to Cliff, "Do you mind if I ask her out?" I asked him permission to ask her out. It was like asking her father. He said it was fine so I finally caught up with her. "How would you like to have dinner one evening?"

She agreed. That was how Gloria and I started. But I had to use the Voice of America to get my first date. By the way, I did the interview with Cliff and it was broadcast. All over the world, people are still waiting for the second episode of "Youth in Politics."

By the summer of 1952, Gloria and I were going steady. Then I was asked to cover the Korean War for the Voice of America.

CHAPTER 10

Another War

My job in Korea was to cover a part of the war that most Americans never knew about. The War was a UN action. Sixteen countries sent troops there. It wasn't just America and the Koreans. I don't know why the Ethiopians decided to send troops but they did. Colombia, Greece and Turkey, the Thais and the Commonwealth, the French and the Benelux countries all sent battalions or brigades.. The Italians had an 'Ospidale' unit in Youngdongpo and the Swedes contributed a hospital ship. There was a kaleidoscope of people from around the world in Korea. I was to cover everybody but the Americans, who were very well covered. One of the techniques was to go up to the front and do what we called "hometowners." I'd hook up my tape recorder to the battery of the jeep, have the guys line up and talk to people back home. They'd say "Hi" in their language, and things like, "I'm Kamal Attaturk and I'm from Ankara. Hi, Mom, I'm fine. Say hello to everybody." Since those countries didn't have correspondents, I became their bridge to home. They were all so eager to have me there that they gladly fed me the best they had to offer. I found it extraordinary that each unit had the same uniforms, they all drew down the same rations, but each country was able to maintain its own identity and cuisine at the front. In time I found myself deciding whom to cover by what I wanted to eat that day. If I wanted curry, I'd cover the Thais. If I wanted ouzo, I'd go to the Greeks. If I wanted hot hors d'oeuvres and red wine, I could go to the French, because even if there were a battle raging, they'd have hot hors-d'oeuvres and red wine.

Most of the heavy fighting was over by the time I arrived in September of 1952. The Chinese and North Koreans kept pushing, The South Koreans, Americans and other allies kept pushing back, but the line stayed pretty much where it had been when the North Koreans began their incursion in 1950. When I was generating stories, I knew there would be a built-in delay between the time I sent the tapes back to New York, and the time the appropriate language desks would be using them. I decided to get some Christmas features done in November so they would be timely when broadcast. One day I visited the Belgian front. I explained I wanted some of their soldiers to sing the French version of Silent Night, right there on the battlefield. I did express my regrets that the front was so quiet.

"Why do you say that?"

"Oh, I had this concept of hearing the words for Silent Night against the counterpoint of booming artillery."

They considered that for a moment, conferred, and said, "Wait here." Then, suddenly the hill was alive with men running back and forth, unspooling wires as they ran. After about ten minutes, the soldier retuned and announced they were ready. They had rigged up explosives at various places and connected the charges to a central point. Anytime I wanted to hear an artillery burst, I just was to cue them. And so it went, the soldiers singing sweetly and then, on my cue, the sound of incoming artillery.

Silent Night-BOOM.

Holy Night-BOOM.

I received kudos from the New York desks for this wonderful piece. Call it heightened reality.

After I'd been there for a while, I realized that Greek Independence Day was coming up on April 30. That gave me an idea. By that time I had made friends with a lot of people up at the front. So I called Col. George Koumanakis, who was the commander of the Greek Battalion. I told him that I understood that Greek Independence Day was coming up.

"Yes," he said. "Please come up to the front and be with us. We're going to have bazouki music and Ouzo. It'll be a great celebration."

"I'd love to," I answered. "But there's one thing I'd like you to do. I want you to invite the Turkish general staff to come as your guests."

"Do you understand what Greek Independence Day celebrates?!" he sputtered.

"Yes, your independence from Turkey and Turkish rule, I understand that. But, George, we are all now brothers fighting under the same UN banner. It's time to put that aside.

"Okay," he said, finally. "For you, I'll do this."

I hung up with him and called up my friend, Altimur Killic, third lieutenant in the Turkish Brigade.

"Al," I said, "Greek Independence Day is coming up. I want the Turkish General Staff to be there."

"Are you kidding? Do you understand what you are asking?"

I repeated my 'gipper' speech. "C'mon, Al, we are all brothers under the UN banner. You've got to do it."

"All right, all right. For you, I'll do that."

"Great."

About two days before Greek Independence Day I get a call from Altimur. He tells me I've embarrassed him.

"I talked the General Staff into going but we've never received an invitation."

So I call up the front. When I say "call up the front," you have to imagine me sitting in the correspondents' billet in Seoul, putting a call through I-Corps which went into Division then into Battalion. In those days there was no direct dial. But eventually, I got Colonel Koumanakis on the phone at the Greek front. I tell him what I heard. He didn't think the Turks were going to come so he didn't invite them.

"They're coming!" I said. "Get them an invitation!"

He promised to send the Turks an invitation.

Now comes the day. I drive up to the front. Fortunately this sector is quiet and they've got everything spread out. A feast. And here come the jeeps carrying the Turkish General Staff. We start drinking ouzo and eating moussaka. Pretty soon, the music starts and so does dancing. And now it is Greek arm around Turk; Turk arm around Greek. I'm broadcasting this momentous occasion and I'm thinking, "The skinny kid from Brooklyn has done it! Hundreds of years of internecine warfare are over. I have made this moment happen. I've done it!" Six months later, on the island of Cyprus, they were killing and raping each other again. But, for one shining moment on the Korean front, there was Camelot.

By February, 1953, I was half way through my six-month posting and began thinking of my return home. I realized that instead of just retracing my route from New York, I would like to meander across the rest of the world—Asia, the Near East and Europe. I also realized if I did that, Gloria might not be hanging around when I landed. I called Gloria June Benson in New York and suggested that if she came to Japan, we could get married there and then take the long way home through Asia and Europe for our honeymoon. She said she would think about it and call me in a couple of days. Mind you, she did not have a ring. We were not officially engaged. I had met her parents just once. But Gloria called and announced she was coming. We planned to get married in April.

Meanwhile, truce talks, which had broken down, resumed in Korea at Panmunjom in March 1953. The result was that in April, one day after Gloria arrived, Operation Little Switch—where we exchanged sick and wounded POWs with North Korea—began. And I had to cover it. But I had found time before she arrived to go the PX in Tokyo and pick out an unset diamond. (Yes, they sold even those at the PX!). I had it set at

Mikimoto and, when Gloria arrived in Tokyo, I gave her the ring and we were engaged. We then went to our house. Actually, when I say "our," it was shared with Bob Alden of the *New York Times*, Jim Greenfield of *Life* magazine and Mary and Ted Aligretti. Ted, who was and ad agency maven, was there to help the first TV network, NHK, get on the air. We all shared an 11 room Japanese house. That night, Ted and Mary and Gloria and I polished off four bottles of champagne and a great deal of sake. The next morning, I left Gloria and went to Panmunjom for a week to report on the exchange of sick and wounded POWs from both sides. Later, Panmunjom was to be the strange setting for the armistice negotiations and, ultimately, signing. It was the first time you could actually see the enemy face to face. We came from our sector, the North Koreans came from theirs. They all met inside a building and screamed and yelled at each other. One could stand outside while negotiations were going on and watch artillery strikes in the nearby combat zones. During these final rounds of peace talks, ground activity had largely come to a halt, but artillery and mortar fire continued until the cease-fire was signed.

During that week, while I was away from Gloria, I stayed on the "peace train." This was, in fact, a hospital train that had been converted for the correspondents to use. It had rudimentary desk space for the portable typewriters and bunk beds for our use. For CBS and NBC radio broadcasts, they had rigged up a closet, which was more or less soundproof. The army provided a phone line to Tokyo, from where the networks transmitted the broadcasts to New York. There was half an hour between the CBS use and the NBC feed. I arranged with my friends, George Herman of CBS and John Rich of NBC, to use that time to chat with my abandoned fiancé back in the strange world into which she just been plunged. So for almost 30 minutes nightly, the broadcast I hoped would not be heard was an intimate love chat originating from the broadcast booth at Munsan-Ni. At some point there would be a timid knock informing me that NBC would be on the air in a few minutes, could they please get in. Then I went back to Tokyo and got married. Twice.

Gloria and I got married on May 1, 1953. And May 3, 1953.

The only legal and official marriage you could undertake in Japan in '53 was in a Japanese location. First you had to go the American Embassy and get all the paperwork, then take that to a Japanese ward office. This turned out to be a concrete pillbox-like place, where people came to pay traffic fines and electric bills. We walked up to a counter and gave the papers to a clerk. Then we gave them thirty yen, which was nine cents in those days, and after everybody stamped it, they shoved the paperwork back at us, and we left. As we came out of this plain little concrete installation, I turned to Gloria. "Well, we're married." I remember the stricken look on her face. It was not the way she had dreamed of it. But we had provided for that.

Two days later, we got married in the Tokyo Army Chapel. We had hoped to get a rabbi and a minister but finding a rabbi in Tokyo in 1953 was not easy. We finally had to go with a Methodist chaplain, but I negotiated the ceremony. For example, I explained, I would not kneel and we excised or modified some of the passages. Gloria was fine about that. Some of the people who attended were the Bureau Chief of Time/Life and the Senior Editor of *Time* magazine. Pulitzer Prize winning photographer, Max Desfor, a Pulitzer Prize A.P. photographer, took our wedding photos. The Voice of America, unofficially, audio taped the ceremony.

Our reception at the Tokyo Club had about 75 guests. A three-piece band. A three-tier cake. Hot and cold hors d'oeuvres. It cost $125. Then Gloria and I went on our honeymoon to Kyoto. While we were having a snack on one side of the vast cafeteria at the Tokyo terminal, I noticed a Japanese gentleman at a table way across the other side, with a pair of field glasses aimed squarely at my bride. In 1953, beautiful blonde women were still a comparative rarity in Tokyo. In Japanese culture, the nape of a woman's neck was perceived to be very provocative. When we were on the subways of Tokyo, Gloria in her sundress would be closely observed and commented on by teenagers who found the exposed section of her neck very, shall we say, diverting.

We had been in Kyoto for about four days when, I got a call from Tokyo, saying, "You'd better get back. They just fired you." While we were playing blissful newlyweds, the Voice of America had decided to have a RIF—a reduction in force. They were closing down the operation in Korea—my wedding present from the State Department. So I went back and started giving away all my stuff —my jeep, the furnishings in the billets in Seoul—all the things that previous correspondents had cajoled and conned out of the Army to make life a little more comfortable. My largesse became known up and down the peninsula. What I did not know was that when my friend, Bob Alden, heard about the closing of the VOA bureau, he filed a piece for the *New York Times*. Another friend, Bob Pierpoint, filed a similar report with the CBS morning news, and Walter Cronkite included it on his radio news broadcast.

I got another message which sent me back to our Tokyo embassy— for a ten PM call coming through from my boss at VOA in New York. "A terrible mistake has been made," he said. "We're not going to close the Korean post. As a matter of fact, we'd like you to be our Chief Correspondent for the Far East for the next two years."

It was tempting, but I turned it down. A life of flitting around South Asia was not what I envisioned as a newlywed. I agreed to stay on only until they found another correspondent. Before we ended the conversation there was a pause. Then, "You have a lot of friends there, don't you?" Indeed I did. So I awaited my replacement—for six more months.

During that time, Gloria and I set up housekeeping in a couple of different apartments, and I kept doing my work. A large number of stories had to do with the UN effort at reconstruction which was going on during the fighting, as territory was retaken and secured. I remember producing a documentary from a bombed out textile factory. Numerous Koreans were sitting on the floor of this roofless space, laboriously hammering the cogs of wheels back into a semblance of straightness. Somehow, that factory was going to come back to life.

Later that day, I was at the residence of Ellis Briggs, our Ambassador. He asked me, as he made us a martini, "Do you think they will make it back?" I thought of all the schools I had seen, in open settings when there were no usable buildings, with the children studying from what books were left. Even at the height of the war, where possible, schooling went on. I recognized, in the personality of the Koreans, a strength that often brought them into conflict with Americans. Unlike the Japanese, they did not bother to hide their emotions. This sometimes led to fist-fights between Americans and Koreans. They were not interested in being polite or to defer. I thought of the scene I had seen that very day at the textile plant.

"Oh, yes, Mr. Ambassador. I think they will make it." I now own a Korean made sedan and drive it with a special frisson of satisfaction.

I stayed in Korea for another six months awaiting my replacement, but I was eager to come home and start my new life with my wife. So I resigned from the VOA in September 1953, cashed in my return trip ticket, and Gloria and I set out on a four month trek: Hong Kong, Bangkok, Rangoon, Delhi, Istanbul, Athens, Italy, France and home. At this point, I two and a half years of news coverage on the Voice of America under my belt. As a correspondent, I'd had to write as well as report. I thought I was headed for a career in news. When we got home, in early 1954, Ted Church, the head of CBS-TV News, met with me and agreed that he would recommend me for hire. The next day he got fired. I don't think it was directly linked to our meeting.

There I was, back in the U.S., twenty-eight years old and married. We had knocked around Asia for four months, and my savings were now just about drained.

I needed a job.

In my travels around the country for the VOA, I had the chance to meet people such as the recently immigrated European family that had won a homestead in a newly irrigated area. At this time they were living in a basement of their home—the only part that had been built.

As a correspondent covering the Korean War. This was Panmunjom, the site of the negotiations that led to the armistice. There has never been a peace treaty.

Here is the wedding party after the Army Chapel service on May 3, 1953. On Gloria's right, Jimmy Greenfield, who in addition to being a Time Life correspondent served as our best man. Next to last on the right, is Bob Alden, New York Times reporter, who played the part of Gloria's Dad and gave her away.

Our parents sent out hundreds of invitations to the wedding with the assurance that no one was going to fly 30 hours on propeller driven planes to attend. It saved a lot of anguish about cutting down the list of invitees—but our take of wedding gifts was severely attenuated.

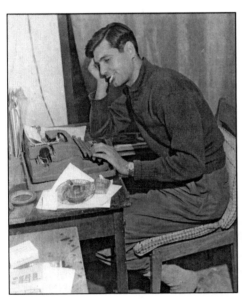

When I was covering stories in Korea, this was my home—a room in the correspondents billet in Seoul. Out back was a small concrete building that was our correspondents' club—drinks 25 cents a pop.

The war in Korea was a United Nations undertaking with combat troops from sixteen countries. Here are some of the armbands I collected along the way.

CHAPTER 11

You're the Finder. Find It

In 1954, the following bulletin was circulating around television stations:

"Man Wanted For Job In Television. Must have keen intelligence, curiosity, imagination, taste and the ability to communicate. Must be a good teller of tales. He ought to be able to carry a tune and play some sort of musical instrument. He may be a teacher, a coach, an aviator, a forest ranger, almost anything. He should have been an athlete, experience which has given him insight into children's likes. A man's man, he should have an adventurous bent, a generally relaxed sort of person who has a sense of humor about himself. A man who can talk to a boy, man-to-man."

At least I wouldn't have to know "abstruse."

The new show would be called "The Finder." Determined to have no children on the show as props, the show's creator, Dick Hartzell, realized that "The Finder" would stand or fall with his choice of master of ceremonies. But was the right man ever born? According to the "Man Wanted" circular it didn't seem likely.

As soon as the circular hit New York, two friends of mine called and told me they had read about this new kids' show on a new educational television station in St. Louis, looking for a producer/performer. They thought I might give it a shot.

At this point, my experience was in radio. I had never done television and didn't particularly want to be a performer, certainly not a personality entertaining kids, but I needed a job, so I wrote to the station in St. Louis. They called and said, "Fly out here and we'll give you an audition." I told them I didn't have enough money to fly out there. They said they'd split the ticket with me and I booked a flight.

Now, how to audition?

This was 1954, when everybody was a folksinger, so I went to a friend who played the guitar and said, "Make me a folksinger." He taught me three chords and how to sing "Froggy went a'Courtin'." That was part of my presentation. Another friend had written a song about "Henry-the-Hummingbird," the only bird that could fly backwards. I got a friend to make a Hummingbird puppet. This was plain pipe rack time with not a lot of bucks to spare. Henry the Hummingbird was made out of a rubber Spalding ball (25 cents), a piece of wood, a spring and a couple of feathers. It was cute. I could make the wings go up and down. I wrote some dialogue for Henry, a smart bird with an attitude, had my wife pre-tape it, put it all together and flew out to St. Louis to audition for the show.

Only I'd never been in front of a camera before. When that 35mm lens came in close, right up to my face for a close-up, all I wanted to do was run. But I stayed. Did "Henry." Sang "Froggy" and all that stuff. When the audition was over, Dick Hartzell took me to lunch.

"A lot of people have auditioned for this job," he said. "Pretty much, they've all been smoother and glibber than you. But I think you're at the beginning of whatever you're going to become. So if you want the job, it's yours."

That was how I became "The Finder." Five 45-minute shows a week—I was to host and produce—my salary would be $125 a week. I flew back to New York, where I bought a second-hand Ford, our first car. Gloria and I drove across to St. Louis and sublet a fifth floor walkup, our first real apartment.

The 45-minute show was to air at 4 PM, Monday through Friday. The premise was that I found interesting things and brought them back to the studio for the kids. I'd find whatever I could afford, grab anyone who was coming through town.

It was the first time I'd ever performed and the production budget was zilch. I had two assistants, one of whom was an unpaid volunteer. We broadcast from the girls' gymnasium on the campus of Washington University in St. Louis where our office was downstairs in a kitchen— with the stoves still there. We had no money and no ratings but we had fun, inventing things as we went along.

Before the station even went on the air I decided to see if 'chutzpah' would work in St. Louis.

This was 1954, the second year of the Corvette, the glamour sports car in America. The final assembly plant was in St. Louis. One day I called up the district manager for Corvette. I told him I was starring in a kids show called "The Finder."

"This is what we're offering you," I said. "If you give me a Corvette, free, for one year, we'll use it as the signature vehicle on the show. Every day, it'll be on the air at KETC. We'll film it for the opening of the show."

You have to remember I was pushing an educational station which wasn't on the air yet. We would probably have a viewership slightly higher than the test pattern and we were programming for 6–12 year olds. If my asking was the definition of chutzpah, his answer might serve as the definition of "putz"—he said, "Yes." So for a year, I got to drive this wonderful white Corvette convertible, with "The Finder" written on the side in red letters. My other car was a second hand Ford.

As an article written at that time said, "His job requires him to travel to the office in a low-slung white sports car, but his work is as demanding as any in town. The job: searching for constructive and interesting things for kids to learn from, five days a week."

One day, I was driving the Corvette to a personal appearance at a public school in an unfamiliar neighborhood. I drove around and around but I couldn't find the school. Some kids were standing around and I pulled over to ask them where the school was? One of the kids looked at me, looked at the car, stepped back and said:

"You're the Finder. Find it!"

The Ford Foundation was operating a center at Ann Arbor for the distribution of programming to the new Educational TV stations. They asked us to make a pilot for them. After they screened it the word came back, "we like the show. Tell Mr. Fox he doesn't have to sing." "The Finder" became the first children's TV program seen on many of the new stations. My career as a folk singer, however, was over.

It took three months for the show to kick in. After a while, it managed to get its own personality. Dick Hartzell and I became great friends and Gloria and I were enjoying St. Louis.

The other members of this new, educational station were a wonderfully varied bunch. Ranlet Lincoln looked like his name. He was tall and somewhat gaunt. He had a mellow voice, a deep laugh and a keen intellect. His wife was also tall and slender. They were the quintessential WASPS. I told Ran that when the next pogrom came, I would stand next to him and depend on "innocence by association" to protect me. Many years later he became the Dean of Continuing Education at the University of Chicago and had an early morning show on Channel 7 discussing heavy issues.

Mayo Simon, on the other hand, looked, and acted, as though he should have been a Rabbi with deeply philosophical examinations of perplexing moral issues. He was in charge of features. Later he became a TV and feature film writer.

The ingathering of this odd collection of young folks, pretty much all of us in our twenties, provided Gloria and me with a nexus of friends who were terrific company. Some had just started families, others, like us, would begin that journey while in St. Louis. When we invited a bunch of our cohorts to our apartment for a Thanksgiving dinner, we had to instruct them to bring chairs.

It was on a Thursday, several months after the show began, when I started to realize that our kids' show actually might have viewers. On Thursdays, our big date was to go shopping at Bettendorf's, the biggest supermarket in St. Louis, and then eat at the counter. That Thursday, I was going down the canned fruit and vegetables aisle when I heard a little girl's voice pipe up:

"Look, Mommy, it's him."

"Yes, darling," I heard the mother's voice answer in a patient tone, "they eat, too."

That was the first time I began to have an inkling that there would be any recognition. There really were people out there...

By the way, it was at Bettendorf's that I took a major step toward accepting the fact that I was now an adult. I know, with all of my experiences in the war and now as a married man, I should have made that transition by now, but there was still a part of me, I guess, that still had to leave Brooklyn.

That night, at the supermarket, I was walking down the candy aisle and passed the Hershey milk chocolate bars—with almonds. They were sitting in boxes of 24 bars. At that time, a bar of Hershey's with almonds still represented a luxury to me.

"Wouldn't it be nice," I thought, "if I could, someday, just buy a whole carton of those bars?"

I started to push my cart on, and then stopped.

"Wait a minute. I am married and living in my own apartment. I earn the money and I can bloody well use it as I see fit."

I reached up and put the carton in the cart and walked on, head held high. Dammit, I was a grow-up!

After several months I had acquired a few acolytes who used to come to the studio when we broadcast. They were eleven and twelve years old and they'd hang around, pulling cable and such. They became my first real fans. When the time came for me to leave, they picketed the station with signs: "Sonny stays, or else." There was even a picture of a knife dripping blood. There weren't a lot of them but they were a vocal group.

Recently, after 55 years, I received an e-mail from one of those kids. Here's a shocker—he's retired. The thrill was to be remembered by him and to discover how significant being a part of that experience had been for a 12 year old.

That was when it was fun to be on television. We were young. We were inventing television. It was a low-risk place to cut your teeth. No one could tell you what you couldn't do because nobody knew what you could do. If you flopped one day, you were on again, doing something else, the next day. It didn't cost you your job so we pushed as much as we could push. We were inventive. We had to be inventive because we had no money.

Overall, it was a nice laboratory, a splendid place to get your feet wet in television.

Zero Hour for Channel Nine

By Peter Wyden

After 18 Months of Preparation, Non-Commercial Educational TV Station Goes on Air Tomorrow— Irwin (The Finder) Fox to Star in Program Beamed to Children

Although I had not yet done my first television show, I already had my first feature. Reporter Peter Wyden went on to write some important books and father Ron Wyden, the current Senator from Oregon.

HIS job requires him to travel to the office in a low-slung white sports car, but his work is as demanding as any in town.

The job: Searching for constructive things, people and places that will fascinate today's hard-to-fascinate children and telling the youngsters what he finds.

His qualifications: He talks amusingly enough to keep his pretty wife in stitches and is equally at home among Senators and jet pilots. Measuring an athletic six feet and three inches, he is a born mimic and story teller, his voice changing effortlessly from character to character. He sings, plays guitar and sails his own sloop. For a living, he has hidden radio microphones in butcher shops and celebrated Christmas as a war correspondent with Ethiopian troops in Korea.

Just back from a trip around the world, he is brimful of anecdotes about exotic countries. And among his closer friends is a puppet called "Henry the Humming Bird," which suffers from hay fever and takes a critical view of human behavior.

This culture-conscious answer to Superman is 29-year-old Brooklyn-born Irwin ("Sonny") Fox and you'll be meeting him shortly as "The Finder" on the program of the same name over KETC, the educational television station on Channel 9.

Here is the set for "The Finder," and the guitar which I was going to use to become a famous folks singer—until the Ford Foundation wrote, "Tell Mr. Fox he doesn't have to sing."

With my wife, Gloria, in the fabulous Corvette I promoted. My license plate should have read, "My other car is a second-hand Ford."

When Phil Davis appeared on "The Finder," I became a character in a Mandrake strip! I adjudge that one small step toward immortality.

CHAPTER 12

Let's Take a Trip

It started with a phone call.

"Hi, my name is Ted Sack. I am a producer at CBS-TV and we're starting a new program for children this spring on CBS. We're looking for a host. Would you be interested?"

So how did a hot shot CBS producer even know there was an educational station in St Louis, much less a show called "The Finder" that had been little noticed in St. Louis? It turns out that *Newsweek* magazine was preparing a story on this new phenomenon called Educational Television. To illustrate the kinds of shows being provided they selected some shows being distributed by the Ford Foundation. Since "The Finder" was probably the first children's show in that mix, they did a sidebar on it. The writer of that article was subsequently visiting Irv Gitlin, Vice President, CBS-TV Public affairs on an entirely different story. As she was packing to leave, she asked, "So Irv, what else is going on?" He apparently mentioned his plans for a new kid's series for the following spring and that he was looking for a host.

"Oh, you might want took into this guy in St. Louis," she remarked, and left.

"Would you be interested?"

The shortest span of time measurable to man is the space between that question and my answer. That weekend, CBS arranged tickets and Gloria and I flew to New York. On Saturday morning, I went to 485 Madison, CBS headquarters. I went up to the office of Irv Gitlin, CBS VP for Public Affairs, the man who was behind the show. After a short chat, he told me he had a copy of a piece I had done on "The Finder." We watched it together.

It was a feature I'd done on the flight Lindbergh had made across the ocean in 1928. There was a Lindbergh Museum in St. Louis, so I'd been able to get a lot of artifacts and film clips for the piece. When the lights came up, Irv turned to me and said, "Is that representative of the work you've been doing?"

"Actually, that may be the best thing I ever did out there," I replied, in my most disingenuous manner.

"I think it's pretty good," he said. "Okay, the show starts on April 20th. It's sustaining (no sponsors), so I can only offer you three-and-a-quarter."

Three-and-a-quarter what? Month? Year? I was too shy to ask him. Then he told me I had to move back to New York by February.

"I don't have enough money to move."

Irv said he'd have CBS move us there. We shook hands on it and that was it. No callbacks or auditions. No pilots. No sponsor. That was TV in 1955. I floated on air all the way back to the hotel, where I told Gloria,

"I've got a weekly show on CBS and I think it's three-hundred-twenty-five dollars a week. Do you realize if we never earn a buck more than that, we're set for life?" That was a lot of money in 1955. We went back to St. Louis and I told the head of KETC that I was leaving to go to CBS.

"Are you sure you're making the right decision?" he asked.

Yeah, I was sure. Soon after that we said good-bye to Dick Hartzell and St. Louis and moved back to New York. It was April 1955, eleven months after I'd left to start "The Finder." Six months after going on air. That left KETC looking for my replacement.

The *New Yorker* had fun with that. First they reprinted the ad that KETC was running:

FINDERS KEEPERS

The Finder, man to find people, places and things to stir the imagination of young people. Daily TV program KETC, St. Louis. Experience helpful. Talent essential. Must have own sense of humor. Present Finder leaving soon for CBS and network show after only six months.

– Help-wanted column, the Times.

And then they added this poem:

Gone is the Finder
"Why did he wander?"
The children all thunder.
Of none were they fonder,
To no friend more tender,
Than that six months' wonder.
What spell was he under
So far to meander
From kin and from kinder?
Could it be, in all candor,
He did but surrender
To promise of plunder,
To visions of splendor–
Of spenders far grander,
Of venders still kinder–
At CBS, yonder?

April 1955, I went on the air as the host of CBS-TV's new series, "Let's Take a Trip." Each week I took the same two kids to a different location. Ginger was nine and a half, Pud was ten. We did live remotes every week, which was challenging and expensive. In 1955, we used the same cameras, tripod dollies and other equipment we used in the studios. No lightweight, hand held cameras. We connected those cameras with thick, heavy coaxial cables to a mobile control unit. We traveled all over: to the Truman library in Independence, Missouri, an aircraft carrier, Chinatown, a bread factory, a rope factory, a shoe factory, to spring training with the Dodgers.

It was especially meaningful to me to be at Ebbets Field in Brooklyn, where I had seen my first professional ball game at 12 years of age. Now I was back, hanging out with PeeWee Reese, Roy Campanella, Duke Snyder and the rest of the "Boys of Summer." And then there was the "Old Perfesser"—Casey Stengel who when Pud and Ginger said goodbye to him at the end of the show, turned to Pud and said,

"Pud you keep on practicing. You could become a good ballplayer. And Ginger, ahh, you could become a good secretary."

Ginger never forgot that statement, though I recognized him as a man who had been born in the 19th century and was speaking 19th century ideas.

When "Let's Take a Trip" premiered, my parent's apartment on Riverside Drive was crowded with family watching their "Sonny Boy" make his network debut. Meanwhile, "Sonny Boy" was at Floyd Bennett Field in Brooklyn, explaining the new phenomenon—helicopters. The show climaxed with the rescue of a Coast Guardsman from the chilly waters of the Atlantic. When the program ended, my mother's mother, "GG" (for Grandma Goldberg) came into the kitchen. "So Gert, that was very nice, but from this he could make a living?"

To her generation, making a living meant working ten hours a day, six days a week cutting cloth for pants, like Grandpa did. The idea that a grown man could frolic for half an hour, once a week, with a couple of kids, did not sound like a serious way to make a living. But "Let's Take a Trip" turned out to be more than a living. It was an absolute joy.

The first reviews were glowing. The *New York Times*: "*A good children's show in television is hard to come by. It is a happy assignment, therefore, to report on a refreshing and welcome departure from the usual children's fare. Judging by this week's premiere of Let's Take A Trip, it can be unhesitatingly recommended.*"

And from *Cue* magazine: "*The weekly tours of Pud Flanagan, Ginger MacManus and Sonny Fox to interesting spots in and around New York are the best thing that's ever happened to young viewers with lazy fathers. Each Sunday the two moppets become the envied representatives of millions of small-fry who'd like to visit a fire station, ride a tugboat or inspect a dairy farm. The show's popularity stems largely from travel-guide Sonny Fox and his policy of making the two youngsters do things rather than take a spectator's tour.*"

"Let's Take a Trip" came on every Sunday, right after Camera Three, a highly intellectual program; not exactly the best lead-in for a show designed for nine to twelve-year-olds. The result was that we never had a large audience, but we probably had an involved audience. We had a wonderful relationship, Ginger, Pud and I. I loved doing the show and was having a terrific time, getting that $325 a week. Gloria and I had one child, Christopher, who had been conceived in St. Louis and was born a few months after I started Trip. Now Gloria was carrying our second offspring. I was happy as a bug-in-a-rug, but I didn't know if this was all going to disappear in ten minutes. We were still living in a hotel, when we found an apartment in the North end of Manhattan.

"They want an eighteen-month lease," I said to Irv Gitlin. "Should I sign it?" He said yes, the show is a winner. Hoping he was correct, I signed the lease. He turned out to be right. The show was on every Sunday for the next three years, even though it never had a sponsor, William Paley, CBS' owner, and Frank Stanton, President of CBS, kept it on because they loved it and because they thought intelligent programming for young people was part of their responsibility, like the news division.

They were not asking news or public affairs to be profit centers. CBS also produced the Leonard Bernstein hosted "Young People's Concerts." The accountants had not yet moved into the executive suites and the grown-ups were still in charge.

Each week we presented "Let's Take a Trip" live – with Murphy's Law working full-time. Live remotes in a different location every week was tough. Some of the top people working in sports today cut their teeth on our show. Of course, there were also the perils of the live remote.

We did a show in Manhattan's Chinatown, to show Chinese New Year's customs and the New Year's Day Parade. But when we got down there, we found out there was no New Year's parade in Chinatown. Instead of a parade, each 'tong' (neighborhood association) went around with dragons, noisemakers and fishing poles. People held out red envelopes on their fishing poles with money inside, for good luck, and the 'tongs' snagged them. It was very authentic but it wasn't a parade. And we'd promised our audience a real live Chinese New Year's parade. So CBS start organizing all the different 'tongs' into one large group for us to shoot. They went all over Chinatown, rounding up other people, including the Chinese high school marching band. CBS decorated the streets and did whatever it took to persuade them to march down the street in a New Year's parade. By Sunday it looked like a parade was organized to happen.

Before air time a crowd of onlookers had gathered. After all, we were the only show in town! Our floor managers had urged the police to keep everyone off the streets since our entrance had us walking up the street to start the show. One-minute before air, Pud, Ginger and I were in our positions in the middle of the street. (I did not have the microphone, my usual ID. I was to pick that up after our walk.) The police, having been given their charge to keep everyone off, proceeded to order me and the kids off the street. With perhaps fifteen seconds to go, I finally convinced New York's Finest to let us cross the street and start the program. The show was divided into two parts. In the first part I would be upstairs with Pud and Ginger and Mr. Lee, who was going to tell us about the food and the customs. In the second part we would all come downstairs to watch the parade. It had taken a lot of persuasion to create this fake parade, line it up and kick it off at the moment we wanted them to kick off.

We went through our dress rehearsal and, on cue, the parade started and the tongs marched and the Chinese High School band in its fancy uniforms made a splendid showing. Looking good. Except many of the groups thought that was the show and they began to take off on their own, spreading out all over Chinatown to grab the cash filled envelopes before the other tongs got there first. So CBS emissaries went galloping up and down Mott and Pell and the surrounding streets, corralling our dissipating parade and getting them reorganized for the actual show.

Now we were on the air, but when our floor manager shouted "standby," the leaders thought it was time to start the "parade." So the "parade" began to march. While the kids and I were still upstairs, learning how to say 'hello' in Chinese, the "parade" was underway with no cameras to cover it. By the time the kids and I got downstairs, much of the "parade" had passed. Finally, the Chinese High School marching band, the last of the "parade," did pass by. The cameras focused on their retreating backs as though this was a REALLY interesting aspect of Chinese New Year! We're live on CBS. Now what? I found a dragon costume lying on the street and picked it up.

"Mr. Lee, get in the back!"

Mr. Lee got in the back, I got in the front. We started dancing in our dragon costume. The director and cameramen had no idea I was in there, but they were so grateful to have anything to photograph, they immediately started shooting the dragon from every conceivable angle. I kept checking my watch. "Keep dancing, Mr. Lee," I said, as the cameras rolled, "keep dancing." When I figured we had gotten close enough to the end of the half hour, I threw off the costume. I thought I could hear the gasps of surprise from the truck.

It became known as the year of the Fox

On another Sunday, "Let's Take a Trip" decided to salute the U.S. Coast Guard. The Coast Guard was the one part of the armed forces that was never celebrated. When they were notified that they were going to be featured on CBS, every Admiral in every base was at his set, surrounded by family and friends, happily watching their service finally being honored. We were originating from a pier on Staten Island in the middle of nowhere.

Now, when you do live television, you have an 'A' and 'B' game plan, depending on whether the show is running short or long. At one point in the show, they said Plan 'B' (which meant the show was running short.) So instead of getting on the boat with the kids and sailing off into the harbor with the end credits rolling, I was to stay on the pier and fill while they sailed off. The kids get on the ship. The Captain is all excited and smiling, knowing he's on television. "Full speed ahead!" Only, in his excitement, they forgot to take up the gangplank.

CRRRUNCH.

The gangplank dropped into the Upper New York Bay, split into kindling. All over America, Admirals were sinking under their desks. Anyhow, the ship sailed and I'm at the end of a deserted pier on Staten Island, having been given the signal to stretch. Usually, when the floor manager—the person on site in touch with the director or AD back in the bus—gives the 'stretch sign', it means they need anywhere from ten to thirty seconds extra. You don't start a whole series of new things; you just let a little air into what you're going to say anyway. Knowing that, I took some pauses and used a few extra words. I was just about at the end of a thirty-second fill when I saw the floor manager holding up three fingers. That meant I had three MINUTES left. A long three minutes. They had screwed up the timing. There I am, on the CBS network, live and I'm at the end of a deserted pier. On Staten Island. Alone.

I talked about next week's show. I talked about doing your homework, talked about anything I could think about. But I was all alone, so

I talked about anything that popped into my head, figuring I'm making a fool of myself on the whole CBS network, live, for the longest three minutes of my life. Finally when I figured I had filled about two and a half of the three minutes I said goodbye and left them to run a very slow crawl with the credits.

Ah—live TV.

Two of the most interesting programs were the ones with George Balanchine of the New York City Ballet and the famous sculptor, Jacques Lipschitz. Lipschitz had his studio in the Hudson Valley, north of New York. The first of our two half-hours were set in that studio, where he showed us how a sculptor goes about shaping marble and wood and other materials into huge—or small—pieces that seem to be both inanimate and alive. We did the second half-hour in the place where the clay statue is cast in bronze through the 'lost wax' process.

Jacques had married either late or a second time, I do not recall which, but the result was a young child of about eleven for whom he could have been the grandfather. He told me that since he was unlike the fathers of her classmates, and his 'job' was not like the other daddy's jobs, his daughter felt a strangeness in him. To try to break through, he had invited her classmates to take a field trip to the studio so he could show them his work and talk of being a sculptor. While there, he served them donuts and hot chocolate. Subsequently the teacher had the children write thank you notes to him. They all thanked him for the refreshments. Not one mentioned the sculptures. Jacques Lipschitz told me this poignant story to contrast it with what happened when our show decided to devote two half hours to him. "Now," he concluded, "Now she is impressed and excited about my work and impressed with her father."

I will spare you the details of the Lost Wax process and other portions of the two half hours, mostly because I have forgotten them. What I have not forgotten is Lipschitz' statement, "It takes as much work to make a bad sculpture as a good one."

I have remembered that as I have looked at shows that failed, a book that did not work, or a script or a screenplay that doesn't quite make it. The fact is that a person actually got the book written, or a team of people got the show on the stage or the film produced, and those creators should be respected for the work and commitment that went into the effort.

The press stories on our show continued to be good. A couple of them described Pud and Ginger as "the two luckiest kids in America." Here they were, one week with the Dodgers at Ebbets Field, another with a Seminole tribe in Florida, and getting paid for this. Except that at Ginger's private school in New York, the Grace Church Elementary School, Ginger's classmates were putting her through the kind of hellish experience kids can specialize in. They resented her success and made their jealousy quite clear. One boy even pushed her down a flight of steps. It culminated in a petition, created and signed by her classmates, asking the school to expel her. When Ginger asked her best friend why she had signed, she was told that if she hadn't, she would have been ostracized. Ginger, at least during the week, did not feel like the "luckiest kid in America." She was not expelled, but to this day she remains hurt by the entire experience.

Two years after the start of "Let's Take a Trip," an evolving situation finally had to be dealt with; Ginger and Pud were growing up—especially Ginger. The pre-pubescent charmer with her pigtail and spunk was beginning the inevitable transformation into the body of a teenager. The consensus was that the essence of the show would start to change if we kept going with teens instead of younger kids. The problem was not as apparent with Pud, who still looked as he did when we started. I suspected his mother made him smoke cigars or whatever to stunt his growth. In any event, it was decided since they started together, it would be better to bring on two new performers in the nine to ten year-old age range. Pud's mother registered her dismay that "just because Ginger is growing boobs" that was no reason to dump Pud.

It was then, in April 1957, I came up with the suggestion, "Let's have an open call." The idea of opening the selection process to any kid sounded like a great way to draw attention to the show and it appealed to my wimpy-past history—let's give everyone an even shot. Of course I had never been at an open call—nor attended one.

On that day in April, it seemed like every boy and every girl in the New York metropolitan area answering to the age description showed up. The line stretched out the door and around the block. Hour after hour, the director, Tim Kiley, the producer, Steve Fleischman and I greeted every child. After a while they all began to blur. It felt like every boy had freckles and was pounding a baseball mitt and every girl had a pigtail and was hugging a doll.

I later found out that in that line was a ten year old young actress named Patty Duke. She was escorted by her omnipresent agent. As hour followed hour, Patty became sicker and sicker, but her agent would not let her leave. According to Patty, she got within ten places of us and finally had to leave.

We did finally discover my next two charges, Jane and Jimmy. Though I felt that neither had the singularity of Pug and Ginger, both were fine and we worked together for almost a year. Many decades later, Jimmy Walsh, now a successful Wall Street Executive, invited me to lunch, along with his teen-age daughter. Midway through lunch, he turned to me and asked,

"Was I good?"

After all those intervening years, this successful accomplished man still needed the assurance that, as I told him, he was, indeed, "good."

During the first year of "Trip," Goodson-Toddman, the most successful game show producers in TV, came to my agent, wanting to discuss the prospect of hosting a game show. I went to Irv Gitlin at CBS and said, "I don't really want to do game shows. Can you give me some reason not to?"

"Like what?"

I asked if CBS could put aside a fund for me to develop kids' show. I presented some ideas and Irv said he'd get back to me. A short time later he reported, "I've arranged for twenty-five thousand dollars in development money." I was thrilled. That was a lot of money in those days. I called my agent and told him I didn't want to do the Goodson-Toddman show, told him about Irv's offer to develop children's TV programs. When Mark Goodson found out that Irv Gitlin was making it possible for me not to do the show, for which Goodson-Toddman was partnered with CBS, the shit hit the fan. I got a call from Irv Gitlin to come in and talk to him. Irv had to withdraw the offer.

That was how game shows started coming into my life. I was more curious as to how the experience would work out than I was anxious to actually host these shows. I was quick at grasping the rules and pretty soon I became the game-show try-out host in New York. I didn't take it seriously. I thought it was just for fun and focused on my real job—"Let's Take a Trip." Then a new kind of game show came along and my career was going to take one more highly centrifugal turn.

Ginger, Pud, and an energized (note the raised fist) Sonny cutting an album for CBS records. They took away my guitar, but I got to sing anyway!

With Jacques Cousteau aboard his famous boat the Calypso. In the 1950s, these weekly remote excursions were truly unique.

Joan and Jimmy with President Harry Truman at the Presidential Library in Independence, Missouri in 1957.

With Joan and Jimmy and an ad-libbing seal.

June 17, 1956 Ebbets Field, Brooklyn. Ginger McManus on the mound pitching to catcher Roy Campanella. We spent two days hobnobbing with Duke Snider, PeeWee Reese, and the boys of summer.

With Joan and Jimmy on an aircraft carrier, clearly moored, but, nevertheless, impressive.

Around the Dials

World Scout Jamboree a Stirring Program

By BOB WILLIAMS

TELEVISION yesterday did more to advance the cause of international brotherhood and understanding than a thousand speeches.

Sonny Fox

For one hour over the CBS network (Channel 10 here), viewers visited the 8th World Boy Scout Jamboree, just getting under way at Niagara - on - the - Lake, Ontario, Canada. It was arranged with the co-operation of the Canadian Broadcasting System, as a special Let's Take a Trip program, interrupting for one week the show's summer vacation.

THE BILLBOARD
MAY 7, 1955

TV Borrows Education Field Trip Practices

Let's Take a Trip (TV)
Host, Sonny Fox. Cast, Ginger MacManus and Pud Flanagan. Script, Bob Fenwick and Bob Allison. Producer, Ted Sack. Supervisor, Irving Titlin, CBS director of public affairs.
(CBS-TV, 3:30-4 p.m., EDT, April 24.)

Like so many good things, "Let's Take a Trip" is so simple in concept it is only amazing it was not done before. It seems that the field trip has become standard practice in all levels of education from kindergarten to college. So why not do it on TV?

This week, its second, "Let's Take a Trip" originated from the studios of United Productions of America. There, friendly emsee Sonny Fox and his two young friends, Ginger, 9, and Pud, 10, were shown every step in the production of an animated sponsored film, "Second-Sight Sam," for the Health Information Foundation. The kids were allowed to try their hands at a couple of the chores and to carry the transparencies from one worker to the next. CBS cameras got good shots of every step on the process.

As guided tours go it was as interesting as they come, for both young and old. Gene Plotnik

---

Herald Tribune MONDAY, MAY 9, 1955

By JOHN CROSBY

Good Kid's Show

"Let's Take a Trip" is what we used to call the Chicago school of television. And what is Chicago television? Well, "Zoo Parade" and "Ding Dong School," for example, which are among the last remaining examples of it on the networks.

I once asked Jules Herbuveaux, of WNBQ in Chicago, how "Zoo Parade" came into being. "Well," he said, "every father ought to take his kids to the zoo—but about 80 per cent of them don't. So we take the kids to the zoo."

* * *

You'll find this is not only a fine, wholesome, educational show for your children but one that they'll thoroughly enjoy—if they're anything like mine. My only problem—and I expect you'll encounter it, too—is that my son and daughter want Pud's and Ginger's jobs.

Copyright, 1955, N. Y. Herald Tribune Inc.

"Let's Take a Trip" hits the Trifecta! Here are three of many positive reviews.

CHAPTER 13

Challenge and Corruption

In 1956, while I was hosting "Let's Take a Trip" I got a call from EPI, the producers of the immensely successful "64 Thousand Dollar Question," which aired on Tuesday nights at ten o'clock, hosted by Hal March. It was the big show of the year on CBS. In fact, it had become a phenomenon. The competition among the three networks, CBS, NBC and ABC, was intense—especially in prime time—8 to 11 PM. In those three hours, many millions of dollars rode each night on the ratings each program produced. The sponsors and their ad agencies, scrutinized the Arbitron and Neilsen data every morning, when the "overnight" were available.

CBS realized that on "The 64 Thousand Dollar Question" the contestants were becoming celebrities on their way to the top prize and then they went off and got exploited by others. There was Gino Prato, the humble shoemaker, whose expertise in opera made him a big winner, The Marine Captain who was an expert in cooking, Joyce Brothers, the psychologist who was a whiz on boxing. CBS decided why not bring them back to face a challenger? We can call it The $64,000 Challenge. Instead of one isolation booth, we'll have two isolation booths. Everybody wanted to host the show. The commitment of CBS to launching a sister version of Question was viewed as a sure-fire, prime time winner in the coming year's schedule and every host, would-be host, actor or wannabe was calling his agent to push to host this important new entry.

When I was called in to do an audio run-through for Joe Cates, the producer/director, I knew I was just one of dozens trying out. A couple of days later, Joe called me up to his office and said, "Let's listen to this together." We listened to me hosting The 64,000 Challenge run through on audio. When it was over, Joe asked, "What do you think?"

"I wouldn't hire me if I were you," I said.

"I agree," he replied. "I don't think you're ready to do this yet."

We were both right. At this point I had less than two years of experience as a performer. I'd done my first show in a converted girls' gymnasium in St. Louis for seven months, My next show—"Let's Take a Trip"—was a low key kid's show done on location, with never a studio audience and no sponsor. I was too green to host the spin-off of the phenomenal $64,000 Question.

I went back to doing "Let's Take a Trip" every week on CBS, figuring I'd never hear from them again. "Let's Take a Trip" was slated to do five shows from the West Coast. Gloria and our five-month-old son, Christopher, were going to join me out there. I was surprised when I got a callback to do the pilot for "The $64,000 Challenge." Actually it turned out there were two pilots being done, one with me and one with a popular radio host, Ted Brown. Now I was caught up in the prospects of the prestige of a primetime network show—and the big bucks that came with it. It was just ten days before the program was going on the air and they still didn't have a host?! I stayed in New York and did the pilot, sending Gloria and Christopher out to the Coast, planning to take the red-eye out to L.A. and join them. After the taping, a whole bunch of very important people went to dinner, including Mr. Charles Revson (Mr. Revlon). At one point he turned to me.

"If you do this show, we're going to have to change your name."

"Why?"

"Because no one's going to believe that a person named 'Sonny' is giving away $64,000."

"Mr. Revson," I said, "with what you're going to pay me, you can call me anything you want."

Such a smart ass. The host's salary was going to start at fifteen hundred a week—an absolute fortune. When I took the redeye out to L.A. to do Let's Take a Trip on Sunday, I knew Ted Brown would be doing a similar pilot on Sunday night. I wondered if that was the last I'd hear from them. Monday morning, the phone rang in my hotel room in L.A. When I picked up a voice said,

"Bill Fox, please."

"I'm sorry, you have the wrong room."

"Don't hang up. This is your agent and that's your new name. You have the job!"

I was the host of The $64,000 Challenge? I couldn't believe it. And I couldn't believe 'Bill' Fox was my new name. I thought that they were going to ask me. I had a name all picked out—Steve Fox. SF. I wouldn't even have had to change the towels in the bathroom. But nobody had asked me, and the money was too good to turn down. So I accepted the offer and flew back to New York with my wife and child on Wednesday. "The $64,000 Challenge" would premiere on the coming Sunday. It would also be my debut as 'Bill' Fox, host of the show. Of course, Sunday was the same day I was on, every week, as 'Sonny' Fox on "Let's Take a Trip." The *New York Times* had fun with that. Val Adams wrote, "CBS today announced that Bill (Sonny) (Irwin) Fox is to be the host...."

On Sunday night, April 8, 1956, amidst hype, hoopla and opening night telegrams from William Paley and Frank Stanton, "The $64,000 Challenge" made its debut. The announcer said, "Here's your host, Bill Fox!" Contestants on "The $64,000 Challenge" were viewers who claimed they could match knowledge with the big winners from The $64,000 Question. The challengers were exhaustively tested before they challenged a specific winner in the category that had earned the champion his/her title. While one was answering, sound was cut off from his/her competitor's booth. Prizes were graduated in amounts of $1000, $2000, $4000 and so on, up to $64,000. The questions got more and more complex the higher the stakes, with as many as twelve parts. I blew one of those questions on the first show I hosted.

The champ was Policeman Redmond O'Hanlon and his expertise was Shakespeare. The challenger was another Shakespeare expert, a New York fireman named Martin Van Outryve. We were on one of the multi-part questions – "Name the fathers of several women in Shakespeare plays and the corresponding play." The challenger had answered all parts of the question correctly. Now it was the champ's turn. When Policeman O'Hanlon named Polonius as the father of Desdemona in Othello, instead of Brabantio, I accepted his answer. Partly because I was nervous. Partly because, before the show, I had been told by the producers to "expect a tie." Expecting a tie, I heard what I thought I was going to hear when he gave a wrong answer. I was also nervous and obviously wasn't listening hard enough. Opening night jitters. I was so busy trying to do a good imitation of Hal March that I didn't even know I'd accepted a wrong answer until the show was over. Within 20 minutes after the show went off the air, CBS received 12,000 calls of protest. It was such a to-do that they had to call the fireman and policeman back the following Sunday to start over again.

Then, in the middle of the week following the debut show, I get a call from EPI, the production company. "We have a problem about your name."

"What?

"There's a Bill Fox already on the AFTRA rolls."

The union rule is, after you've established a professional reputation using a name, even if it's not your real name, nobody else can use it. "CBS, three sponsors, two ad agencies and nobody checked the AFTRA rolls?"

"No. What's your real name?"

"Irwin."

There was a pause that went on a beat too long. "I've got a great idea. Let's change my name each week and then people who don't even like the show will tune in just to hear what they're calling the schmuck this week."

The guy said he'd call back. The second week of The $64,000 Challenge the host intoned: "Now, here's your host: Sonny Fox." Bill was gone, never to be heard from again. I have this fantasy that somewhere, out in backwoods Iowa, Mom and Pop are sitting on the porch, a-rockin' and a-whittlin'. "Whatever happened to that Bill Fox?" she asks. "He seemed like such a nice young man."

Ah, the short life of Bill Fox.

From then on, for the next five months, I did both shows on Sunday. I would get up at four or five o'clock in the morning and go off to that day's location for Let's Take A Trip. I would do the show, then come back about one o'clock in the afternoon and try to get an hour or two nap. Then, at six o'clock that night, I would take the subway down to Studio 42 on 52nd Street, where we shot Challenge, around the corner from the studio that was the home of the The Ed Sullivan Show. It was exhausting. By the end of the first month I was pretty good at imitating Hal March. But I wasn't doing Sonny Fox. Or even Bill Fox, for that matter. Then they started to pressure me. David Levy, of Young and Rubicam, called me up to his office overlooking 42nd Street.

"I'm going to pile up $64,000 on my desk," he said. "So you understand the importance of what it means when you say "$64,000 dollars."

Next, they started giving me line readings about the cigarette commercials. Pretty soon there were dozens of voices pounding away at me. On top of that they would say, "If a guy loses, kiss him off, get rid of him." But if a guy got to the $16,000 level, then lost, I could see the defeat in his eyes. His whole life was in shambles. I wanted to reach over and give him a hug, say it's okay. But they would tell me, "Get rid of him!" I always found that hard to do.

The questions for "Challenge" were kept in a vault at Chase Manhattan Bank. A Vice-President of the bank would bring a copy of them on stage and, as the announcer emphasized, they had just been removed from the bank's vault. That was the truth, but not the whole truth, since I had just reviewed a copy of the questions in my dressing room so I could review the questions and get the pronunciation correct. It was all done with tremendous pomp and circumstance. Having had so little experience as a performer it was really something to walk into that theatre with a house band, two sponsors, three ad agencies. I usually developed a headache before I went down to the studio every Sunday night. I did get renewed after the first thirteen weeks but the pressure kept mounting. I was not smart enough, nor mature enough as a performer, to be able to resist the twisting that went on.

And then, the killer.

That night, the contestants were Billy Pearson, the jockey, versus Vincent Price, the actor. The subject was art. They were both art collectors, very knowledgeable. They had both answered all the questions correctly until we were up to the $64,000 level. The $64,000 question was one of those twelve-parters they loved to create. Vincent had already answered all twelve parts of the question correctly. Billy had answered some and skipped a few. Now it was time to finish. I had the questions and answers on two sides of a large card. With the sound turned off in Price's booth, I said, "Let me review the questions you have left." When I turned the card over my eye fell on a word. I said "Van Gogh" before I realized that "Van Gogh" was the answer, not the question! Seconds later I realized what I'd done, but it was too late. Billy pretended not to have heard me. I pretended I wasn't there. There was no air left in the studio because everybody had had a deep intake of breath. Somehow I finished doing the show.

Once it was over, there was a gigantic reaction. Headlines screamed in the papers. Editorials. They ended up calling it a draw and Pearson and Price split the $64,000. As for me, it was just a matter of time. I did the show for another few weeks but it was awful. I would stumble on people who were whispering until I came up, and they stopped whispering. Then my agent called and said, "Sunday was your last show."

You have to understand the incredible impact of those quiz shows on the audience. I would walk down the street on a summer Tuesday night in Manhattan, in our neighborhood, when Hal March's show was on. This was before air-conditioning so all the windows were open. Out of every window came the sound of The $64,000 Question. Everybody was watching. They were all watching Challenge, too, on Sunday nights, when I was hosting. What was so embarrassing was I wasn't getting fired from a show that was a failure. I was getting fired from a show that was a howling success. Part of me wanted to shrink away from the world, because it was a very public execution. And part of me was relieved. The perception of the people in charge was that I wasn't cutting the mustard and they were right. I wasn't. Not on their terms. I never took the show as seriously as they would have liked me to take it. Civilization was not depending on it. At any rate, it was an interesting time. Ralph Story, a lovely man from L.A. who was very relaxed and low-keyed, and much more seasoned than I as a performer, took over and the show continued to be one of the most-watch prime time programs.

In reflecting on that bleak period of my professional career, I learned a valuable lesson—there is a difference between failing—and failure. I had failed as host of a prime time game show. I had taken on a challenge I instinctively knew I was not ready for—even tried to avoid. A door opened and I walked through it—even as I had done in St. Louis and on my first show on CBS. This time I failed. The important lesson was to accept that as part of risk taking and move on. I was building my family. I now had enough money to buy my first home in Connecticut. I was still hosting Let's Take a Trip on CBS every Sunday. There would be other doors. There would be other triumphs and other disappointments.

I had failed in a very noted way.

I was not a failure.

Two and a half years after I was fired from "Challenge," it was revealed that first, "Twenty One," another highly rated quiz show, and then others, including "Challenge" and "Question," were rigged. Answers had been given to contestants, and, at least on "Twenty One," instructions were given on which answers to skip over, when to mop ones brow, and so on so as to heighten the tension. It quickly became a national scandal.

At that point, I was just pleased not to be involved. I was never questioned nor called before the Senate investigation committee. I was as appalled as anyone. I had always assumed that the producers, having exhaustively examined the knowledge of the contestant understood that person's strengths—and weaknesses. If the producers wanted to keep a contestant on for another week, they would construct a legitimately difficult question that played into that person's strength. If they wanted to dump the contestant, they constructed a question that was not at the center of the contestant's knowledge base. Here is an example of how that worked—and did not work. The candidate for becoming a contestant is an expert on 18th century English poetry. The tests prove he does have an encyclopedic knowledge in that area. He is given the category of English Literature and starts his climb. After three weeks, it is determined he is not registering with the audience and should be dumped. That decision could have come from the producers, Mr. Revson or the network. In any event, the contestant found the next week that the question was about Beowulf. English Literature, but far from his expertise. He failed.

When Dr. Joyce Brothers came on $64,000 Question she was the perfect example of how these shows were cast. Here was this paradox of a blonde, winsome psychiatrist who was an expert on boxing. She was doing fine through the $16,000 level, answering the most complicated questions thrown at her. Alas, Joyce did not wear makeup, and Charles Revson, owner of Revlon and the principal sponsor of the program, decided she was sending the wrong message to America's women and should be dumped. So, at $32,000 the question was about referees of boxing matches. Still legitimate in regards to the subject, but clearly a curve ball. The trouble was Joyce answered it correctly and went on to win the top amount.

In the months after I left, the pressure from the sponsors, and likely the networks, began to make the producers bolder and more arrogant in pre-arranging the outcomes. Even a child in a spelling contest, Patty Duke, at that time 12 years old, was taught how to cheat convincingly. To compound the venality, when she was subsequently called before the Senate Committee, she was coached by the production company on how to lie to the Senate. She was 15 at the time. All this I found out much later, from Patty. I am totally convinced that when I hosted "Challenge," in its initial months, any control was through construction of the questions, not the giving of the answers.

Except by me. I was apparently inventing "Jeopardy," Merv got rich. I got fired.

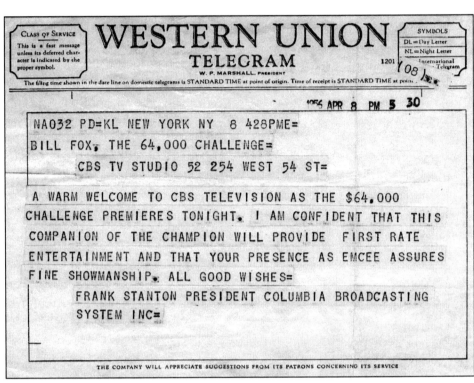

The heady stuff of opening night on "The $64,000 Challenge," such as this telegram from the President of CBS. The "champion" he refers to in his message is "The $64,000 Question," which in its one year on the air was the most watched show on TV.

Sonny MEETS THE CHALLENGE

by Sid Bakal

AS A RELATIVE newcomer to big-time television, Sonny Fox, who hosts the new "$64,000 Challenge," hasn't been around long enough to develop stock phrases and dull cliches about himself in answer to questions. As a result, he emerges as a frank and refreshing personality.

Fox, a stringy, easy going six-footer, discussed his now-famous fluff, committed on the very first CBS program over lunch the other day. That was the occasion when he passed as correct, a wrong answer in the Shakespeare category. It erupted into storm signals for a week.

Was he worried about his job at that time?

"Well, to tell you the truth, I wasn't," said Fox with a disarming smile. "You see, this is the first commercial show I've had in nine years of television and I hadn't started to live up to my new income. Besides, when I heard about it the next day from the producers, the agencies and the sponsors, they also reassured me at the same time that everything was okay, and that they realized it was a natural error due to nervousness on my first show.

"But I'll tell you how nice people can be," he continued. "Before I came to New York for 'Let's Take A Trip,' I did a children's educational program in St. Louis called "The Finder." After the first '$64,000 Challenge' show, one of the St. Louis papers called the producers, and said they were con-

(Continued next page)

13

All the early reactions were, like this piece, mostly favorable.

The moment that really blew it. Jockey Billy Pearson and Actor Vincent Price were at the final $64,000 level—and I asked an answer! Van Gogh may have cut off his ear, but by mentioning his name, I ended my prime time career.

'Don't fire Sonny,' scream his fans

By JOHN LESTER

When fans of Sonny Fox heard he would be replaced on The $64,000 Challenge if he didn't stop the "fluffing," they swamped the program and CBS-TV with wires, letters and phone calls. The tenor of their protests was that they didn't mind the "fluffs," liked Fox and "would you please let him alone?" Now the producers, who've been auditioning replacements for the past several weeks, don't know what to do.

Virginia Graham subs for the vacationing Bess Meyerson on CBS-TV's Big Payoff, daily at 3. P.M., beginning Monday . . . Which reminds that Payoff may switch to NBC-TV which once carried it as an hour-long Sunday series.

Lloyd Nolan repeated his TV version of The Caine Mutiny Court-Martial on the BBC-TV the other night and was a bloomin' smash.

Lester

and all incorporate another "policy": the use of many "new faces" in supporting roles . . . Jerry Colonna in England for a six-week tour of the British Isles.

Note to confrere Burton Rascoe: Glad you rapped the You Are There version of the O. K. Corral gun-fight last Sunday. It was loaded with inaccuracies, as you pointed out. The researchers treated Wyatt Earp almost as badly as they did Joan of Arc some time ago. Any idea what's going on in that series?

"Born Yesterday" set as an NBC spectacular with Paul Douglas playing "Harry Brock," the rich junk-man. Both Mary Martin and Judy Holliday have been mentioned for the dumb blonde role of "Billie Dawn" . . . The Vic Damone show will stay on CBS-TV.

Trendex Top 10
(Week Ending May 7)

New "$64,000 Challenge" hit the No. 4 spot on the Top 10 Trendex list its first time out, joining sister-show "$64,000 Question," which retained its No. 1 slot in the May outings. Top 10 evening programs for the week ended May 7 are:

$64,000 Question, CBS	39.4
Ed Sullivan Show, CBS	38.1
I Love Lucy, CBS	37.8
$64,000 Challenge, CBS	31.9
Hitchcock Presents, CBS	29.4
December Bride, CBS	27.9
Hit Parade, NBC	26.2
Trust Your Wife?, CBS	26.2
This Is Your Life, NBC	25.9
Red Skelton, CBS	25.8

This John Lester piece reflects how widespread the issue became. The chatter went on for some weeks before the axe finally fell.

I sent my replacement, Ralph Story, a note welcoming him to the show and wishing him well. This was his sweet response. Ralph carried the show for two more years until the scandal swept Challenge and every other big money quiz show off the air.

Dear Sonny –

As you must know, the mail which comes in to the program collects over at CBS, then is dumped over at EPI a month later. Yesterday I got some telegrams from old friends who evidently hoped to congratulate me on the first show, and amongst the wires was yours.

I wanted you to know that it was very much appreciated and very nice of you. The little black cloud seems to have dispersed, temporarily at least. And the admirable way you conducted yourself under the difficult circumstances of the change-over revealed a very fine person, indeed, one greatly admired both at EPI and elsewhere. This, of course, made things much easier for me and I wanted to add my thanks with this note.

Being fresh and green to both New York and Television I have no way to repay your kindness .. except to say thanks and hope that we meet someday soon.

Very sincerely,

Ralph Story

Mr. Sonny Fox
900 West 190th Street
New York, New York

Dear Sonny:

Now that the "sturm und drange" is over, I want to express to you my personal feelings about everything that has happened.

I wish everything had remained the same, but unfortunately in the pressures of our business, changes often occur. You have been most considerate in this very trying period. And I want you to know that I sincerely appreciate all of your courtesies.

When you get a breath, why don't we have lunch?

Sincerely,

Steve

Steve Carlin was CEO for EPI, the producers of the Challenge. After my firing, I received this letter from Steve. While I did not dispute their judgment that I was inadequate, I was disappointed that no one from EPI had the guts to speak to me directly. I was not inclined to accept his offer of lunch.

CHAPTER 14

Game Shows

When my hosting stint on "The $64,000 Challenge" came to an end I continued doing "Let's Take A Trip" and walked away with a sense of pleasure after every show. I would have happily put game shows behind me, but Goodson-Toddman was very kind. I became the fill-in host for their shows, "To Tell the Truth," "The Price Is Right" and "Beat the Clock." One week, I was the substitute host on shows on all three networks.

When one takes over a show as a substitute host, as I did when Bill Cullen when on vacation from "The Price Is Right," you try not to screw up the guy's show. Just do it and give it back to him in the form in which he left it. But live TV had its unpredictabilities, so it sometimes turned bizarre. I was in the middle of hosting "The Price Is Right," live, at the Hudson Theatre on 44th Street in N.Y., on one such occasion.

"Okay, Panel, if you'll look at the curtains, June will be coming through with the next item up for bids."

All eyes went to the curtain, where, at that moment, June was supposed to be coming through in a mink coat. Instead, what I saw was the curtain starting to billow, as June tried to find the opening but couldn't locate it. Then, more frantic searching, but no June. Just more billowing. The audience is getting restless and my eyes are widening as the billows get much deeper. Still no June. The audience starts to laugh. I'm trying to pretend nothing's happening. Finally, one of the panelists, in a burst of chivalry, leaps out of his chair and throws open the curtains, revealing a stage hand, totally frozen, like a deer caught in the headlights of an oncoming car. Then June staggers through in her mink coat. She's laughing so hard that rivulets of mascara are streaming down her cheeks. The audience is falling out of its chairs. I'm standing there thinking, "This is not happening. I'm going to wake up." Finally, I came to my senses.

"Everybody stop!" I said. "June, go back." Shut the curtains. Now panel, please look at the curtains for the next item up for bid."

June came through the curtains again, still laughing. Still mascara stained. The audience applause saluted her successful entry. Somehow we fumbled to the end of the show.

"The Movie Game" was a syndicated daily show, produced in Hollywood, which I hosted in 1970 for the first six months of its life. The format had to do with questions regarding movie lore. We used stills, costumes and props—but not movie clips. Too expensive. The schedule was to shoot five shows a day for two days—take a week hiatus and then shoot the same schedule again. It was produced on the old Republic studio lot—a place replete with the ghosts of a lot of movie history. My assistant host—or co-host, or whatever, was Army Archerd, the *Variety* columnist. Bob Stivers, the producer/director, knew that by signing Army, he was plugging into a lot of Hollywood stars who would ordinarily not be available to a daytime syndicated game show. Indeed that is the way it turned out. The problem was that throughout most of the show, Army had nothing to do. He interviewed one of the stars at the end of the program. Army's wife, who was always on the set, was clearly miffed that I was the host, not Army. The producers seemed to be walking on eggshells where this key Hollywood player was concerned. Once I was criticized for not introducing Army with enough awe in my voice. I never read *Variety* so my appreciation of the importance of the personage was clearly not up to their standards. First I did not speak "$64,000" with enough reverence. Now it was the words, "Army Archerd."

I did get the chance to work with the "Duke," John Wayne. Imagine, this icon of the movies actually sat there through five tapings of a week's shows. I had an air-conditioned trailer for myself sitting in an adjoining studio. In between tapings I was asked if Mr. Wayne could sit in my retreat. He arrived with a friend and proceeded to play a mean game of Klabyash in the middle section, while I hunkered down on the sofa in the rear area and read the *Time* magazine cover story on him that had just come out. It was rather special, reading a paragraph, and glancing up to see his considerable presence ten feet away. There would be a bit about dragging his first wife around by her hair and my look would be a disapproving scowl. Then I would read of some accomplishment—and I would give him my benign look. Of course Wayne was so into his card game he was never aware of my editorial glances.

On the thirteenth week of the series, Bob Hope had been corralled by Army to be on the program. As the fifth taping of the day wound down, and I was starting my closing remarks, Hope sauntered up to me and observed that since this was the end of the first cycle, it would be appropriate to celebrate. With this remark he removed a pie from behind his back and pushed it into my astonished face. At that moment, all the cameramen who had been likewise armed started hurling pies back and forth. The show ended with a throwback to the time of the Keystone Kops, which for all I knew, might have been filmed in this very studio. I was back in my trailer, wiping the stuff from my suit, when there was a knock on the door. Standing there was the icon of American comedy. Hope said, "Your friends put me up to that. Are you all right?"

"Mr. Hope," I replied, "if I have to get a pie in the face, better it should be from you than anyone else."

We smiled, shook hands and he left. What a nice person to care about me enough to make that gesture.

One day, around this time, I realized I hated doing games shows. And

I didn't like myself as a game show host. I really wanted to get back to what I had started out doing all those years ago—I wanted to produce. My epiphany, as a performer, came one afternoon when I was guest hosting "Beat The Clock," a mindless stunt game that I actually enjoyed because of its lack of pretension. The host, Bud Collyer, always ended the show by saying "and God Bless you."

One afternoon, as I was ending that show's taping, I heard a voice saying, "and God bless you." I stood there, stunned. I don't say God bless you. Bud says that. I finally understood. I was playing at being a game show host. When I did "The Finder," that was me. When I did "Let's Take a Trip" that was me. What I did on camera was an extension of me and I was the best me there is. But this was me trying to be the game show host, doing the things I thought a game show host was supposed to do. I finally got it. I can give it to you fast or slow, loud or soft, but it has to be me. When I can be an extension of who I am off camera on camera, it works. My epiphany helped me understand my discomfort with game shows—or at least why I didn't take them seriously.

Perhaps Oscar Wilde expressed be best when he wrote, "Be yourself—everyone else is taken."

CHAPTER 15

The Wonderama Years

It started in 1959. One day my agent, Harold Cohen, called and said there was a weekly four-hour children's program on WNEW-TV Channel 5 in New York, called "Wonderama." The station was interested in me hosting because they wanted to upgrade the quality of the show.

At this point, I had done three years of CBS' "Let's Take a Trip," so going to a local station and doing a cartoon show for kids seemed like a step down. One gets a little snobbish about such things. But sustaining my mortgage and supporting my family, which by now had grown to four kids, necessitated my taking some sort of job. So I signed on. I was determined to make this a special program, full of all the important things kids should know about.

I worked very hard on the first three shows, which were all about rocketry. This was 1959. When President Kennedy was elected he'd said, "We shall go to the moon this decade." Space exploration was really in its infancy. I got some old footage of rockets and got some old pioneers together. I did a very earnest job. The first three weeks were marked by tremendous effort on my part to single-handedly upgrade the level of children's television in this country. At the end of the third week, I was called in by the station manager.

"We didn't hire you to drive away children," he said. "The ratings have plummeted. From now on, you will only do three minutes of live material and then a cartoon."

I could have walked out and said the appropriate thing to vent my anger, but I swallowed it. I needed the job so my offended pride took a backseat. I went back to doing this expurgated version of the show. In between tapings, to keep my young audience from becoming restless, I started playing with the kids and talking with them. After a few weeks, the production executive said, "Why don't you do some of that on the air?" Gradually, I started bringing the kids in the live audience into the picture. Pretty soon the ratings started climbing. The reviews got better and better. It took me a while to understand—this was what it really could be about. We did "Simon Says," and we played "Stump Sonny," in which kids would ask me questions that could only be answered with an answer from the encyclopedia. We did joke-telling contests and spelling bees. We brought on Joe Papp's Shakespeare actors, Roberta Peters' opera people, Leonid Hambro from the New York Philharmonic. I did a show with the nation's outstanding athletes, who pointed up the importance of keeping physically fit. I did a show on Israeli life, taped in Israel, giving youngsters insight into that land's rich heritage. One week, all the children in the studio were blind. We talked of their ambitions, examined Braille, and in other ways tried to break down the "otherness" of living with a handicap.

To interest children in news events, I started to include a children's news segment with young reporters (11 or 12 years old) on the show. We were able to get press credentials for our crew of free-lance "legmen"; including a report by an eleven-year-old correspondent on the Special Security Council debate at which the United States and the Soviet Union exchanged charges of espionage following the U-2 incident. We conducted a mock presidential primary on "Wonderama," just before JFK defeated Humphrey. Three boys, representing each of the contending candidates made campaign speeches, distributed pamphlets, posters and buttons. The mock election was held by the studio audience. We were able to present these features along with "Bugs Bunny" and "Simon Says."

I did develop a small coterie of guest performers who made repeated appearances on the show. Perhaps the most memorable was a skinny, bearded young Canadian who was a magician/escape artist/math genius named The Amazing Randi—actually James Randi. Randi had the gift of not only doing truly amazing things, but was comfortable with the kids. I still do some of the shtick I learned from him to amuse younger folks, but his escape feats were the kind that I am not interested in replicating. One time we parked a derrick outside the studio on 67th street. We rigged Randi in a binding he designed around his ankles, strapped him into a straitjacket and hoisted him, by his feet, 40 feet above the street. This was a stunt concocted by Randi. When I asked him how long it would take him to escape and come down, he answered with, a twinkle in his eye, "How long would you like." Yet as he was ascending, his head pointed straight down, I suddenly wondered what in the world was I doing. What if the harness gave way and he plunged to his ghastly death. Live. On "Wonderama." Actually, as I learned later, I wasn't too far from that prospect. After Randi successfully descended to our applause, he told me he had come down earlier than he had planned because. "I heard a couple of rivets pop from my ankle harness and thought maybe I ought to cut this short."

Perhaps the toughest audience Randi played to was not even on the show. I approached him about doing a show for my son Chris' fifth birthday at our home in Weston, Connecticut. I proposed he stay for the weekend and join us on Saturday night for an especially interesting set of guests for dinner. He accepted and on Saturday afternoon, standing on the raised ledge in front of the fireplace, Randi proceeded to work his magic that would baffle and amaze Chris and his four friends. Randi's first act was to show them a dollar that mysteriously appeared from one of their ears and have them sign the bill. The bill then mysteriously disappeared. Then Randi took an unpeeled banana, peeled it, broke it in half and presto, there was the dollar bill—with their signatures! I had watched close up and was in wondrous rapture at how he did this under such close scrutiny—and I still don't know how he did. The kids, however, were singularly unimpressed. When that routine was finished I heard them ask, "Mr. Fox, can we go out and play now?"

I learned a valuable lesson. To kids of that age, there is no such thing as magic—or, perhaps to put it better, the whole world is magic. They applaud for Tinker Bell and they believe in witches and ogres. Why shouldn't a dollar bill find its way into an unpeeled banana? If the fairy godmother can turn a pumpkin and mice into a royal carriage, what's the big deal about a banana?

All Randi knew was he was bombing, so for this audience of five five-year-olds, he redoubled his efforts. He worked that room until his veins were popping and rivulets of sweat were coursing down his face. The kids were scratching odd parts of their bodies and moving restlessly until the time would come when they could run outside and play. Randi recovered from this experience and today, with his established foundation, is dedicated to challenging all evidences of the supernatural. Perhaps this is his revenge against the fairy godmothers and witches and ogres and all that magic stuff. He did win a MacArthur Genius award. I guess he grew up okay.

After a while, I wanted to see if we could do a show for four hours without a single cartoon. We did and we never lost a single ratings point. Another time, I decided I would try to explain some elements of the theory of relativity. I suppose this could properly be termed "hubris." I used pictures and diagrams to show that the heart is not only a muscle but a clock and that at ninety percent of the speed of light a yardstick would shrink from thirty-six inches to eighteen inches because the rest would become energy. I planned to use music and poems and charts. Then the Sunday came. Interspersed between "Bugs Bunny" and other cartoons, there I was, talking about the "theory of absolute rest." It was probably a disaster. It certainly was in the studio. The cameramen stood there, their jaws hung slack, their eyes glazed over, and a little dribble coming out the side of their mouths. I thought I could hear young kids all over the metropolitan area saying to their older sibling, "Marty, what's he talking about?" And the answer, "Bugs Bunny will be on in a couple of minutes." Later, when I checked the ratings, I found we hadn't lost a single ratings point. At least it was an attempt; if the kids didn't actually get it, maybe they grew a little by reaching for it.

It was satisfying to me that on "Wonderama," I was able to bring some sensibility into the show, along with the fun and games. A year after JFK was assassinated, we arranged for a couple of schools to have students draw pictures of what they remembered about the assassination and the events following that tragedy. It was clear from the sketches we received that the trauma of that event had deeply affected the children. We traveled to Kennedy's burial site in Arlington Cemetery. There we taped interviews with young children who had come to pay their respects. We made a twenty-minute special out of it, though when I taped the narration it took a while for me to get through it without breaking down. That was the wonderful thing about "Wonderama"—we could balance the silly with the substantial.

Producing a four-hour mini-telethon every Sunday required us to develop some segments that could be included every week. One of the earliest and most successful took advantage of the fact that every kid loved jokes or riddles—and every child was up for a game. For the joke-telling contests we'd pick four kids and they'd tell me a joke up to the punch-line. If I knew the joke, they sat down. If I didn't know the joke they got a prize. As for the jokes—there were jokes that were funny. And jokes that were funny because the kids telling them were so adorable. Like the one from the quintessential eight year-old kid—red hair, freckles, a space between his teeth and a lisp—you can't get more eight-years than that.

"You've got a joke for me?"

"Yeth," he lisped. "How many featherth (feathers) on a bird?"

"I don't know how many feathers are on a bird."

"How many striptth (stripes) on a bee?"

"I don't know."

"What time did Thinderella's fairy godmother tell Thinderella to come home from the ball?"

"Midnight."

"How come you know so much about the fairieth and nothing about the birdth and the beeth?"

A pretty good joke.

Another time, my assistant came to me and said a kid was going to tell me a joke and there was no way I'd know the punch-line.

"Why not?"

"Because he's going to tell it to you in Greek."

Hmmm. I asked if the mother was there. I was told she was upstairs. We always stashed the parents away because once we got rid of the parents the kids were mine. So I went up before the show began. "Is the mother of the young man who's going to tell me the Greek joke here?"

She raised her hand.

"Would you be able to write the answer down for me phonetically?" Sold the kid out like that. Wrote it down for me. When we have a joke segment and the little Greek kid comes up to me, I have the phonetic answer cribbed in my hand. I put my arm around him and said, "So you've got a joke for me?"

"Yeah."

"You're sure I'm not going to know the answer?

"Yeah, I'm sure."

"Okay, tell me the joke."

So the kid tells me the joke. "Kalo, kostunyaka koumonyika dub dub dub..."

I looked at him and said, "That old one?" Now I read from my cribbed notes in my hand. "Tamara tzikidos, moussakalonous blah blah blah."

The kid says nothing, just starts to walk away.

"Wait a minute. Aren't you amazed that I got that joke?"

"No. You know all of them."

After a few years, every kid in the New York Metropolitan Area wanted to be on "Wonderama." *McCalls* magazine wrote that "a ticket to 'Wonderama' is the hottest, hardest to-get ticket in town." They weren't wrong. It was tough to get tickets because we only had about seventy-five kids in the audience, once a week. That wasn't a lot of kids. There were waiting lists a mile long. I once got a telegram from a mother that said, "Before my child gets married, can we please get a ticket?" I sent back a letter with two tickets and a note—"In case by now your child is married." You got tickets in one of three ways: you could be on the waiting list; you could know someone in the sales department; or you could know my mother. Every Monday, I'd come to my desk and find a letter from my mother: "Dear Sonny, the following children must get tickets."

One day, I said to my mother, "Ma, how do all these people know you're my mother?"

"I don't know," she answered, then added in a classic phrase, "it just comes up in conversation."

In the course of "Wonderama," we tied in with the N.Y. Football Giants. I was a committed fan of the team and by arranging, for example, a contest to be water boy for a day, I got to spend time on the sidelines during game time, attending practices, and becoming friendly with their beleaguered coach, Allie Sherman. The three years Sherman was coach were losing years for my beloved team, and they were difficult years for Allie. He was a graduate of the University of Alabama and spoke with a soft southern accent. He was slight of build and on the field looked even smaller surrounded by the behemoths of the team. One evening when we were dining together he told me a story that made me aware of the unique power of TV in general and "Wonderama" in particular. His daughter was a loyal fan of the program. During the run-up to the drawing that would select the Water Boy/Girl to be part of the team for one game, we awarded two tickets each half hour—holding out the ultimate prize until late in the morning. Allie found out about this when his daughter came screaming to him with the joyous news that her friend had won two tickets and had invited his daughter to go with her to see The Giants!! This was a young lady who could go to any game and sit in the owner's box. The fact that the tickets came from "Wonderama" made them special!

After establishing our sway over the audience, we began receiving invitations to bring the show to different countries—to tape all or part of "Wonderama" on location there. Israel was followed by Denmark, then Finland and, finally, Portugal. In each case, a kid's local TV show had gained enough standing to warrant generous offers of underwriting expenses with very modest requirements regarding the quid pro quo. This not only led to four-hour programs themed to those countries, but to an extraordinary personal opportunity to deepen my understanding of an important aspect of civil society.

I learned that while we would be taping in Portugal, they would be celebrating the 50th anniversary of the "Miracle of Fatima." Clearly, since I am Jewish, I had only a vague awareness of the significance of this, but an immense curiosity. I did know that Fatima was, as Lourdes in France, a place pilgrims journeyed to pray for healing or to give thanks. The story of Fatima, a rural location in Portugal, was that in 1913 three shepherd children were playing in the field when The Virgin Mary appeared to them. Over time the Catholic Church accepted this as a true miracle, and a large wooden statue of the Virgin Mary was created and housed in a wooden shrine. Later a large tabernacle was built with a main hall and, similar to the Vatican, had curved arms spreading out on each side as though to embrace those who entered. Outside the Church a huge, paved space, perhaps a quarter of a mile long stretched toward a stainless steel cross.

When we first arrived, a week before the event, this vast space was totally empty. We toured around, made our arrangement to return for the ceremonies a week later, and departed. We continued to tape our other features until two day before the start of the celebration. As we traveled back toward Fatima, we began passing pilgrims on their journey: They came on buses, on foot, and in Mercedes Benz cars. Some had taken vows of silence during their journey. Some had vowed only to eat bread and drink water during their sojourn. Some drove for a few hours. Some walked for a week.

Some were coming to give thanks for the healthy birth of a child or the recovery from a husband's serious illness, sitting up, propped up or lying flat. Some would be present in wheel chairs or on gurneys.

In the hours leading up to the ceremony starting at noon, I watched old women make that long journey on the pavement, the quarter mile journey, from the cross to the church—even climbing the steps and moving down the aisle to the altar—on their knees. The path became littered with bloody bandages that had come off those knees on the way.

When the ceremony finally began, under the hot sun, there were 750,000 pilgrims in that huge space. Chairs had been set up in countless rows. Red Cross personnel and doctors and nurses were on hand. In the front were six or seven rows of the sick and the lame.

At noon the prayers began, interspersed with hymns and Ave Marias. The hours passed. I began to hear the whistle I soon recognized as emergency calls to help someone in the crowd. It could be heat exhaustion or dehydration or illness. Throughout the 24 hours those whistles were a constant counterpoint to the ritual.

At 11 PM, the statue of the Virgin Mary was removed from its shrine and started on an hour's journey throughout the entire space. The spotlights from the TV crews covering the event followed the Statue as it progressed and the pilgrims sang Ave Marias until it was placed back in the shrine.

The ceremony continued through the night, but we decided to get a few hours of sleep at our nearby hotel.

The next morning, we returned to the proceedings. They were still underway with about three more hours to go. Finally, at 11 AM, the statue of the Virgin was removed for her final tour of the assemblage.

This time 750,000 people were waving white handkerchiefs to bid her farewell.

The reason I have dwelled on this experience at length, is to underscore the lesson I absorbed; that for many people, a faith in some supernatural force that can intercede in a desperate life is the emotional safety net that enables them to deal with forces beyond their control. The evidence of this need, so dramatically seen on the road to Fatima, in the littered bloody bandages, in the voices raised in supplication and in the ranks of the seriously ill and crippled—in all these faces—that need was, for me, poignantly and powerfully underscored.

I am not a religious person. I accept—I revel—in the history and culture and values I derive from my Jewish Heritage. But even in prison camp or battle, I did not turn to the God of my fathers. I envy those who have that abiding faith. If one truly accepts and believes, whatever the religion, one has an emotional resource I don't have.

We did include an edited version of Fatima in our presentation on Wonderama.

One day in November 1964, the phone rang and it was a person from the office of the Senator Elect, Robert Kennedy. I was told that while in DC as Attorney General, each Christmas season he would visit the poorer neighborhoods in the DC area and distribute games and toys. He wanted to initiate the same effort in New York and would I accompany him. While being thrilled at this approach, I responded with my usual chutzpah, "Okay, here's the deal. If the Senator would come on 'Wonderama,' and chat with the kids, I would spend the two or three days with him they asked for." An hour later the call came back saying he would indeed come on "Wonderama." Thus began a four year association with this remarkable man.

The visits to the barrios and ghettos of New York came before the studio visit, so I was mostly in the position of watching RFK. I was wary regarding him since I remembered his time on the House Un-American Affairs Committee. I had heard stories of his arrogance as Attorney General. I do remember that when he got out of his limo he was not wearing an overcoat, even though the weather was December cold. Seeing this, I took my coat off. I did not want to look any less... I don't know, fit? Daring? By the third stop I realized I was not running for office and that being warm beat improving my image! I would arrive ahead of him to warm up the crowd and get them in a holiday mood. Working a big crowd in the cold outdoors setting was something I had almost no experience with, but I quickly developed some tactics that were adequate to the occasion. When the Senator arrived, he would speak for a reasonably short period and then plunge into the crowd shaking hands, acknowledging kids and seeming to genuinely care about them. Considering the tragedy that had just struck President Kennedy, I thought it perhaps foolhardy, but quite wonderful. Even more so as I began to realize that deep down, Senator Robert Kennedy was a shy man.

We taped the first segment with the Senator on a day other than our regular tape day. We assembled about twenty kids, who arrived with excited parents in tow. At first the parents were seated in the studio. While we awaited the arrival of our special guest, I asked the boys and girls to share with me the questions they were planning to ask the Senator. One was about the national debt, another about Vietnam. They were referring to loose-leaf note books with questions undoubtedly reflecting suggestions by their parents. I quickly decided that we had to magically convert these little Walter Cronkites back into kids before the Senator arrived. The first thing we did was to remove the parents to a different locale in the building where they could see—but not be seen. Then I asked the kids if any of them wanted to know if he helped the kids with their homework? Did he ever spank them? Were they allowed to watch TV? Pretty soon these miniature mavens were morphing back into kids again.

When the Senator arrived I was struck again by his slender frame and his diffident manner. He seemed not to need to be dominating or bombastic. When we started the taping two things struck me immediately; he never took his eyes off the kids—not even to address me, and he was one of the few adults I know who knew how to talk not to—but with—kids. He was asking them about their likes and how they felt about things. The conversation went on for about twenty-five minutes and it was clear that the Senator enjoyed the experience. This started a tradition. Every year I would join him on his visits to the more depressed areas of town, and every December he would drop in to chat with another group of kids on "Wonderama." I think he was at his most human chatting with these young people. At this time he already had nine of his own and I believe he truly enjoyed our visits. As I got to know him our relationship extended beyond his studio visits. I would be in DC and let him know I was there. He would suggest dropping by the Justice Department at a certain hour. He would then drive me to the airport to drop me off on his way home to McLean, Virginia. He invited me to come home to dine with the family, but I too was anxious to get home to my kids and he certainly understood.

As the years went by, and I got to know him better, I could feel his sense of frustration at being one of 100 in the Senate, and a junior Senator at that. He had been at the center of things when brother Jack was President. Now he was on the periphery. I remember returning from taping in Bolivia and telling him about attending a gathering in La Paz at which our military attaché was recounting—boasting would be a better word—that he had just concluded a deal to get some America warplanes for Bolivia. This impoverished country, with its indigenous population, still living as it had in the 19th century; this land of a very wealthy few and almost no middle class, the last thing they needed were fighter planes. Who even wanted to attack Bolivia? When I had finished expostulating, The Senator quietly and almost sadly said, "I know. I try to change things but it is hard." It was clear he missed the power that came when he was Attorney General and his brother was the President.

One day I got a call from his wife, Ethel, to come to their N.Y. apartment at the UN Plaza to discuss a project. When I arrived, she announced that every year they would hold an all day reception for the families of the consular and embassy Officials stationed in DC at their estate in McLean. Virginia. As a highlight of the day, they would put on a show for the kids and, according to Ethel, this year her kids had voted that I be invited to be in that show. Of course I was flattered—flattered enough not to inquire how her kids in Virginia knew about me since my show was not seen there. I accepted, and some weeks later, when I was in the apartment, Ethel turned to me and asked, "So who do you have for the show?"

"What do you mean?"

"Well you are producing it, whom have you invited?"

"Ahhh…I see. Well I am working on it." I had about ten days and, of course, no budget. I grabbed Randi and he agreed to perform. I had a family with three young kids who did spectacular acrobatics on the trampoline. I arranged for a flat bed truck that we could use as a stage and, voila, we had the semblance of a show. It worked well enough. Later, the Senator returned from his labors at the Capitol and we ended up in his bedroom with a couple of martinis he had made, standing on a balcony overlooking the swarms of kids and their parents trampling through the estate. "Isn't this great," he remarked. And he meant it.

As "Wonderama" increased in popularity, I was increasingly wary of the effect on my four children. All their friends watched the program and the fact that they were my child could be a distorting factor in their lives. I decided as they grew old enough to appear in the audience, that they would each be permitted to come on the show once a year, around their birthday, and could invite one friend. Still, evidence of the infiltration of my status into their lives inevitably popped up. One Sunday, when Chris, our oldest, was about nine, he asked me "How come you are on television but you are here?"

I explained that we taped the show on Thursday and likened this to a photograph of me—that is, simply a picture. "The taped program is also a picture," I explained, "from Thursday." A couple of weeks later, Chris had an overnight guest and, after watching an early part of the multi-hour program, they adjourned for breakfast. I happened to be within earshot when I heard Chris' friend ask, "Chris, how come your Dad is on TV and he is here?"

I listened eagerly to hear the playback of my explanation. "I dunno," Chris replied. "I have two dads, one on TV and one here." So much for shaping that young mind!

Another incident showing how my standing as a kids host affected my kids' lives happened when I went to pick up 9-year-old Chris at a friend's house. Dana, my son of about 5, joined me. When I got there about six other kids tumbled out of the house and held out pieces of paper for autographs. I signed each one and, as I thought I was finished, there was Dana, holding out a piece of paper, asking for my signature. Clearly, having seen all the other kids eager to get my signature, Dana had decided it must be important, so there he was. I asked him for whom this was and he answered, "me." When I finished signing the note, Dana turned to the other kids and yelled, triumphantly, "I got it! I got it!"

One day, when Chris was in the audience, he was allowed to stand in the control room during a break. He turned to me and said, "When you die, will I inherit the program?"

The continuing fallout that came from being an icon to other kids required making adjustments. If I was taking my children to a concert or theater, I learned to wait until just before the lights went down to avoid have many young people come to me and ask for autographs. I did not want my time with my children to turn into personal appearances. Restaurants presented different problems. Having a quiet meal with the family would often result in interruptions from fans. I learned to suggest that if they would wait until desert time, I would be glad to autograph. My wife, Gloria, always was annoyed by these interruptions. I would remind her that when the interruptions stopped coming, we would probably stop being able to go out to restaurants.

"Wonderama" seemed like a simple show, just me and the kids for four hours every Sunday. Sometimes, people would ask what my secret was. I told them that there was no "secret." Working with kids starts with respect. I believe that kids are a unique part of our society. They're not little adults. They are very interesting people. I spoke with an eight year old while taping a pilot for Fox with kids called, "So Waddayasay." She told me straightforwardly about her trips to heaven every afternoon where she played with her deceased grandmother and other members of her family who were dead. She was matter-of-fact, charming and totally normal. I did not make fun of her. I did not disbelieve her. She was perfectly ready to chat about this extraordinary world of deceased doppelgangers in her eight-year-old fashion.

A unique bonus of developing this intimate quality of connections with my audience allowed me, over the years, to see inside their lives in unexpected ways. Each show day, when the children arrived, the parents were ushered into a screening room away from the studio. Once the parents left, it was me and the kids. For the five hours it took to tape the show, Often I would invite three or four of them to sit on the sofa and we would just chat—about boy hating clubs and dreams and likes and dislikes. On one occasion, I was listening to some young (9-11) girls describing the kind of man they would like to marry someday. Clearly, their description such a husband would be modeled on their experience at home, so when one young lady said, "I don't want a man who lies around on the sofa all day with the newspapers over his face." I immediately understood that scene.

The most startling answer, however, from another was:

"I want a man who won't hit me in the face."

Before I could react to that, she continued, "like my father hits my mother."

For some of my young friends, it was as though the parents had been shipped to the far side of the moon. Thank goodness for video tape. We never edited the show—except when we had to. This was one of those times.

Perhaps the most interesting source of glimpses into the complicated lives and feelings of my young charges came in 1965. We invited our audience to send in their letters explaining why he or she wanted to attend the inauguration of Lyndon Johnson. The smart money would have predicted that this prize would leave the kids cold. They were used to competing for toys and games. A presidential inauguration?

The letters, all handwritten, came flooding in; some were on paper torn from a school notebook, some neatly in ink, some scrawled in pencil. I could tell from the addresses that they had emanated from the all parts of the area—upscale, downscale, black, white.

While we pored through them, I began to realize that I was getting an unexpected insight into the angst and the ambitions of childhood, as well as their dreams and frustrations. I saved some of these letters and now, 57 years later, I can share some of these with you.

Tom Adelman of 520 E.90th Street wrote that he wanted to win,

...because my sister is smarter. My parents think I was born a failure. I would like to win and make them proud. If I were to win...I must let my twelve year old sister come,. I have $66 saved up and will pay her expenses but she must have an invitation too.

Solmerina Aponte in the Bronx wrote,

My teachers always ask me if I have anything interesting to say. I never do. Maybe this time I will be able to say something interesting for the first time.

Teri Sue Hall of Yonkers, N.Y. was one of the secure, purposeful ones,

I am going to be the first woman president of the United States of America. I feel a woman, if a good statesman, should not have to struggle

against male prejudice. I for one have already memorized the oath of office and I expect to make use of it.

Osher Sebrow, from the Bronx, incorporated a compressed story of his life in his entry,

The reason I would like to go to the presidential inauguration is because my mother pushes me on in science by taking me to labs in the hope of my becoming scientist while my father pushes me on in music in hopes I will become a violinist by bringing me records of violin concertos. . . . both parents say if that if you are exposed to things there is hope you may become that. So I thought that if I am exposed to the inauguration I may become president and make everyone happy including myself.

Areatha Pollard of Brooklyn was a Jr. High young lady, clearly frustrated in her social life and looking at winning this to finally get kissed. She wants to go...

. . . Because nothing exciting has taken place in my 12 years of life like being asked out, or being kissed by a boy or being around when gang fights are taking place, others have but not me.

Leif Rubenstein, 11 1/2 from Flushing, showed that compassion is still alive.

If I win the two people I would take along are my grandparents. To many this may sound silly, but to me it means a lot. They both lead a bitter life, never enjoy themselves, and are always unhappy. If I win I wouldn't care if I have to walk to Washington, It's just the feeling you get of helping two dear people you love to start a better life for themselves.

A cover note was added to this letter which read,

If I don't win, I am saying my congratulations to the lucky boy or girl who does.

Finally, for those of you who wonder about our younger generation—although these "kids" are the ones now doing the wondering—take heart.

Our Dear Sonny Fox,

We are a family of five boys. We are all well above average but our kid brother Stanley who is 12 yrs. of age is mentally retarded but our mom said we should be grateful because he is a borderline case and is a good looking kid, we all love him and would like to do something special for him. Stanley is very interested in our government. Last inauguration for our late President Kennedy, Stanley had gotten a tape recorder for Christmas and taped all his speeches and has them all memorized. His favorite is "ask not what your country can do for you but what can do for your country." We think if Stanley were picked he would be the happiest boy in our town of Wurtsboro and we would be happy just knowing we took the time to write and you cared enough to read this letter. We are Aaron and John, twins age 15, Jimmy age 16 and Eric age 17. We all took part in writing you this letter. Our town knows we are writing you and they are all praying for our brother, so with all these prayers, how can we not win.

I performed on "Wonderama" every Sunday for four hours over a period of eight and a half years. During that time I was, of course, aware of the special relationship we had built up with our audiences. But until I unearthed and reread the letters quoted above, I don't think I quite understood how unique this was in children's programming. Many programs have treated their young audiences with respect. Many have been educational and inspiring. I don't know another childrens show, however, that *listened* as carefully to its audience—that had a continual feedback loop that was at the very heart of our success. Being a local TV show helped. We were able to marshal the kids to clean up Central Park and hold carnivals for Muscular Dystrophy.

Isaac Bashevis Singer wrote this about kids,

"They still believe in God, The Family, Angels, Devils, Witches, Goblins, Logic, Clarity, Punctuation, And Other such Obsolete Stuff"

There is a gothic quality about children. They still hear those voices in the darkness that we have forgotten to listen to as we grow up. Henry James alluded to that in his novella "Turn of the Screw." I enjoyed probing their minds, taking that dangerous journey and seeing where it would take me. Having four hours every Sunday was a wonderful luxury because if you ask a child a question, the child will likely answer and stop after a brief time. Most of us will rush in to fill the silence. I found if you say nothing and keep looking and waiting, that's when the gold comes. You've got to let the silences hang in the air. There are very few silences hanging in the air in children's television these days. They try to compress everything, suck out the air from between words. On "Wonderama" I had a chance to explore what came out of those silences. I loved probing children's minds, loved seeing where it would take me. And I discovered that once you had their loyalty and commitment, you could take children anywhere.

I remember the 7-1/2-year-old girl with the big brown eyes standing alongside me at the desk which was my home base. She was telling me about her true love—

"He's 7 and 3/4."

"Oh, it's nice to have an older man in your life. And is he nice?"

"No, he does fresh things like putting his fingers through the bread." Said in a way that make you think how, in later years, she would lovingly mould him into a more gentlemanly individual. Then she related to me how her sister had lost two of the four tickets they had gotten for the program and therefore could not invite this special person to the show with her. All this time, she is relating only to me—and me to her. The cameras and lights and other children had melted away. This was an intimate conversation between me and brown-eyes. There was absolutely no one else around for this most intimate of moments. Total trust between us.

"Would you like to bring him back something from the show?"

"Yes."

"How about some Hebrew National Salami?"

"He's not Hebrew."

That conversation is the essence of what made Wonderama unique. An umbilical cord of trust that built a relationship that, after all these years, is still there.

I recently read Amy Shua's writings on raising her children in a way that accorded her the appellation, "Tiger Mom," meant in a not so complimentary manner. I started finding glints of what made "Wonderama" so connected to my young audience. Tactics on child rearing aside, her point is that achievement should precede self-esteem, not the other way around. When I was accused of being "cruel" to a joke teller if I knew the tag line, I denied that child a prize. Yes I did, because the children understood the rules of engagement. They lined up to try to prove that in this particular case, they could outwit me. Fair enough, if indeed they did. However, he or she understood it had to be fairly won. I was not going to pretend I did not know the answer or, out of some attempt to gain their affection, give away a prize not earned.

When I played Simon Says on "Wonderama"—and I did every week—the rule was that if they started to move without being instructed to do so by Simon, they were out. For the kids playing, that was cool. When we would first start, there might be as many as 75 contestants. I would catch a motion peripherally without being able to identify the exact individual who moved when they should not have. All I had to do was point in that approximate direction and usually not one, but two or three would seat themselves. They individually—all right, occasionally with reminders from their fellow players who had not moved that, "you moved"—sat down. They understood they were out. So, when a player won, he or she had a right to feel proud and to accept the gifts as deserved. If the child derived an elevated sense of self esteem from this, it was well-earned.

Except when the child who won did cheat and was not caught—then values like conscience and honesty came into play. Lee Aronsohn, co-creator of the very successful TV series, "Two and a Half Men," remembers it this way:

"I was 12 years old—the age at which a boy's major interests have just started their long migration from toys and cartoons to cool clothes and girls. Through a client of my father's, my two younger sisters and I received an invitation to appear on "Wonderama."

Did I want to go?

It was a tough call. Sure, I watched "Wonderama" every Sunday morning—everybody watched "Wonderama." But... it was a kid's show, and I was almost not a kid anymore. What would my neighborhood friends think? More importantly, what would the girls in my 7th grade class think?

In the end, however, greed and exhibitionism won out over any possible peer repercussions. I could win prizes! And I was gonna be on TV!

(As it turned out, pretty much everyone thought it was cool that I went on the show—my first exposure to the eternal truth that it doesn't matter how silly or stupid you make yourself look as long as there are people who will tune in to watch.)

So anyway, one chilly winter morning (not a Sunday - it was taped in advance) my parents dressed us up and trundled us down to the Metromedia Studios in Manhattan for my date with destiny.

I don't really remember that much about the day (with the large exceptions of the incidents recounted below). Sonny Fox was taller than he looked on TV, but seemed just as friendly. Robert Kennedy was a guest, but he was taped separately and only a small, select group of kids got to participate in that. My sisters—well, I guess they were there with me but my attention was focused on something much more important: The Loot.

You see, there were two major contests on "Wonderama": The Spelling Bee and Simon Says. The lucky boys or girls who won these were showered with an incredible amount of prizes. Think "The Price Is Right" showcases, but with Ideal toys instead of kitchen appliances. There were other ways to win stuff on "Wonderama," of course, but these two competitions were the Big Ones.

First came the Spelling Bee. I was a pretty good speller, so my confidence was high. I breezed through the first few rounds, and I believe it was down to me and one other contestant - a girl. But then came my Waterloo. My Gallipoli. My Dien Bien Phu. Sonny looked at the card in his hand and said to me the word which will haunt me until my dying day: "Eighth."

"Eighth." Easy, right? Especially for a precocious 7th Grader like me. I opened my mouth and began to spell: "E...I...G...H...T...H..."

If only I had stopped there! But somehow—I don't know if it was the bright lights, or the cameras, or the burning knowledge that everyone I knew at East View Junior High would eventually see this moment— somehow, I lost my place.

"E...I...G...H...T...H.......T...H...T." Finally, mercifully, my mouth and tongue stopped moving.

Sonny, his voice conveying what I now have no doubt was genuine sympathy but at the time seemed to me like bemused contempt, informed me that I was incorrect. I slunk back to my seat and slumped, head down, as my opponent correctly spelled "EIGHTH." Music played, lights flashed (at least that's how I remember it) and Sonny proceeded to tell her - as well as all of us in the studio and the kids at home—exactly what she'd won.

But I wasn't listening. I was too humiliated. And angry! I had spelled the damn word right! I'd just added a few extra letters AFTER spelling it right! Why hadn't Sonny stopped me? He could have stopped me. He should have stopped me! It wasn't fair!

It was this twisted 12-year-old logic which led directly to what happened next.

Simon Says. The other Big One. All the kids from the audience stood in columns, facing the Leader (who I don't think was Sonny—the man had far too much class to demean himself that way). The Leader would give a series of directions ("Simon says touch your head. Simon says touch your nose") which we had to follow—unless he neglected to precede his instruction with the words "Simon Says." If he didn't say "Simon Says" and we made any kind of move, we were out.

This was not my game. As a youngster, my physical co-ordination was such that I'd invariably be picked last whenever teams were chosen for any sporting activity. Seriously. I was picked after Ricky Reinman—and he had polio.

Sure enough, within the first 90 seconds of the competition I put my arm down when Simon hadn't said to put my arm down. That meant I was out.

But I was standing near the back, and the Leader hadn't seen me!

Now, everything I'd ever been taught about honesty, integrity and fair play indicated that the right thing to do at this moment was to sit down along with the other boys and girls who'd unlawfully moved. And I was a decent kid. I had been brought up right.

So why did I keep playing? Why did I feign innocence and continue touching my chin and clapping my hands and doing whatever the hell else Simon demanded of me?

And why, when (against all odds) I actually won the thing, and the music started playing and the lights started flashing and (as I only saw when I watched it on TV that Sunday) my smiling face was suddenly framed in a chyron diamond on the television screen, did I not speak up? Why did I blissfully accept the mountain of prizes offered me? The Snow Wing. The Milton Bradley Time Bomb. The Polynesian dinner for 5 at the Luau 400 restaurant in Midtown Manhattan. And more. So much more.

Why have I not spent the last 47 years tormented by pangs of guilt when thinking of my deception?

I'll tell you why: I may not have deserved to win Simon Says, but I was robbed of the Spelling Bee.

I knew how to spell "Eighth," damn it.

One day I was having lunch with an agent. She told me that another agent in her office had won a bicycle playing Simon Says on "Wonderama," but always felt guilty because he had cheated—moved when he shouldn't, and I did not spot it. I asked for his name—which had changed since that appearance from Weintraub to Wayne.

A couple of days later I called and asked for Lloyd Wayne. When asked who was calling I told her my name. A few seconds later a man's voice said "Hello"—with a hundred question marks.

"Mr. Wayne, we are doing a retrospective on a program I used to do called 'Wonderama'."

"Yes."

"And in researching our show archives we discovered an unsettling thing. It seems, sir, you won a bicycle on Simon Says and you cheated."

By now he is starting to chuckle.

"Mr. Wayne, we take this very seriously. We now find, not only did you move from N.Y. to L.A. to cover your tracks, but you even changed your name from Weintraub to Wayne."

By now he is laughing uproariously.

"I just want you to know, though you have lived your whole life as a lie, you can keep the F–ing Bike!"

That led to lunch and a greatly enjoyable reunion.

I don't get monetary residuals from all those episodes of Wonderama. What I do get is much better—the recognition and immediate connection from my "kids"—now in their fifties and sixties. Overall those decades, the relationships I built with them have lain dormant—and they spring into life upon contact today.

In the early 1980s, I was producing a series of programs with outstanding composers and lyricists. It was early January, and I was standing on the stage of the Henry Hudson Theater—the very stage where I had hosted "The Price Is Right" decades earlier. It was the site of a program I was producing, featuring Alan Jay Lerner. As I was standing, stage center, staring at the vacant seats in the theater, I was aware that the stage door had opened and someone had come in, but it was not until that someone abruptly halted, that my attention was drawn to him. There, in his buttoned-up coat stood a musician and his double bass.

"The toy you gave me, broke."

That's the way he started. Not, "Oh, it's you!" Or "Wow!"

"How old are you," I inquired.

"Thirty Five."

"By now, the toy I gave you should have broke."

The immediate regression to the child he/she was became a common result of such encounters. I have seen rather distinguished looking men and women, who, upon running into me, immediately start remembering the joke they told, or the word they missed on the spelling bee or the prize he or she had won.

About fifteen years ago, I started receiving e-mail from adults in their forties—and now their fifties—who had stumbled on my e-mail address. These were my "kids," now grown and with families and careers of their own. There followed, and still occurs on a weekly basis, a spontaneous flow of memories and recollections of their interaction with "Wonderama." Being remembered is flattering. The vividness of their recollections is remarkable. I will share a few of these with you.

When I was a kid growing up in Brooklyn, I used to watch you on "Wonderama" and "Just For Fun." One day you started talking about how kids could do something important by having a Carnival for MDA. I believed you, and had my first carnival—gathering my sister and all the neighborhood kids and working all summer. Not much money was raised that first year, but we continued for 10 years—each year getting more successful. In the meantime, I started Brooklyn's "Young Adults Against Muscular Dystrophy" and eventually was asked to join MDA's National Youth Board.

I learned valuable skills, learned to work hard, and knew the world was something much more than "all about me"—and that one kid can make a difference.

When I was in the 7th grade I performed the violin with my family on his show as part of the talented youth section and later went on to create a flourishing career in the music industry and have served for the last 10 years on the Board of Governors for the Grammys in New York. In looking back I can say with all certainty that preparing for this performance on his show, saved my life and the spirit of my family. That preceding July my younger brother was killed in front of our house by a car while on his bike. He was 6 and I was 12. It was the music and the rehearsals for the show that pulled us through and brought me back to consciousness.

I thought Mr. Fox would want to know.
—Claudia Koal

First off thank you! As someone who watched "Wonderama," as a kid, it is a honor to be able to communicate with you. Sunday's were my favorite times watching "Wonderama"! I think that you and your colleagues had a slight influence over me as a got older. It sparked an interest. An interest in broadcasting and communications. So, when you left "Wonderama", I never was able to say, "Thank You" for the

wonderful times! Your Sunday shows were a necessary respite from what was going on in the world at that time."
  –Marc Thorner

"I'm a 45 year old man who use to find so much joy from the "Wonderama" show which you hosted. I really wish that the kids of today had television like that. I thank You...I thank You...I thank You...for providing me with so many joyful memories that I still cherish some 35–40years ago. May GOD Bless You with Health, Wealth and Longevity. –Reverend Christopher V. Foster

I grew up without a father in my home and so I looked to people like yourself to learn how to live a caring and dignified life. I really believe that you'll never know how many of your "kids" you helped along the way. Maybe to you it was just a job, but to us it was magical to see an adult who really cared about kids.

I hosted the last episode of my version of "Wonderama" in August of 1967. We are looking at memories that go back more than forty years. These spontaneous recollections should remind us of the profound impact we have, and the opportunity, with some effort and imagination, to not only entertain, but to help each child grow.

While I think of TV's power over our kids, it is flattering to think of the role I played—but a bit frightening in a broad sense. Think of all the exposure, hour after hour, day after day that is pouring into the malleable minds of our young children through television, YouTube, Facebook, interactive games, and movies. Each of these, intentionally or not, is shaping attitudes and behavior. What is troublesome is that in a huge preponderance of these programs and events, very little thought is given to how all of this ramifies in a child's mind. This flood of stuff is made even more problematic by the changing family structure in this country. When I was performing and producing children's TV programs in the

1950s and 1960s, the model was a two-parent family, and the mother was more likely to be on duty at home full time. There was more apt to be a moderator present—one who could decide on the rate of maturation of each child. That parent could monitor language, friends, programs, and at least attempt to filter out that which was deemed unsuitable.

Today, we have more single parent families, or in the case of a two parent household, the mother also works. Therefore, it is more difficult to control what is impinging on these young people who are voracious in their intake and still in the process of becoming. It is difficult, in the absence of a moderator in the house, to control their rate of maturation.

In pondering the success and durability of those eight and a half years, I have concluded that it was largely due to my lack of talent. I know that sounds anomalous, but here is what I mean. I don't draw. I don't do puppets or voices. I don't do comedy sketches or work with second bananas. I don't sing. The list goes on. So I was left with but one asset—I did a very good Sonny Fox. I WAS intrigued by children and loved rooting around in their minds. I appreciated their uniqueness—and recognized their limitations.

There were three other major talents presenting kids shows on Channel 5. Sandy Becker, Chuck McCann and Soupy Sales had shows on weekday afternoons. Each of these performers was vastly more talented than I am, and each had his loyal audience. For the most part they were totally baffled by the success of "Wonderama" since, apparently, I did nothing. They created sketches and characters and props and worked hard to perfect their performances. But that was the critical difference— they were performers—the kids were the audience. On "Wonderama" the kids WERE the show.

Chatting with my kids on "Wonderama." Not a glamour shot, but the very heart and soul of what "Wonderama" was.

YOUR FULL NAME: Dedorah Schein

YOUR AGE: 7½

YOUR ADDRESS: 219-2021/ Ava

1. WHAT DO YOU THINK IS THE BIGGEST PROBLEM WITH GROWNUPS?

Yel Yel Yel !

YOUR FULL NAME: John Dominic Russo

YOUR AGE: 9

ADDRESS: 1908 Mulford Ave.

1. WHAT DO YOU THINK IS THE BIGGEST PROBLEM WITH GROWNUPS?

hit, hit, hit.

YOUR FULL NAME: Joseph Michid Leville

YOUR AGE: 9½

ADDRESS: 1878 Hotchinson River

1. WHAT DO YOU THINK IS THE BIGGEST PROBLEM WITH GROWNUPS?

talk talk talk

The audience fill out questionnaires as they waited in line to go into the studio. These were presented to me before I walked in so I had some idea of what strange and wonderful minds I might explore in the next four hours. In response to the first question, I was struck by the use of the three word mantra, written by three different children, months apart.

YOUR FULL NAME *Audrey Freollyn*

YOUR AGE *9*

YOUR ADDRESS *816 New York Avenue*

1. WHAT QUESTION WOULD YOU LIKE TO ASK SONNY?

   If it just a fake out about he likes kids

2. WHAT'S THE FUNNIEST THING THAT EVER HAPPEND TO YOU?

   When I went fishing and caught a shoe

3. IF YOU HAD ONE WISH, WHAT'S THE ONE THING IN THE WORLD YOU'D WANT MOST?

   have a million dollars

4. WHAT'S THE ONE THING THAT BOTHERS YOU MOST ABOUT GROWN-UPS?

   When ever something important happens my room gets messy

5. WHAT TROUBLES YOU MOST ABOUT THE WORLD?

   School

6. HOW DID YOUR PARENTS MEET?

   At a dance

answer as many questions as you like.....write quickly

Parents, if you think kids don't know what is REALLY going on, check the answer to question 4. They understand pretty much EVERYTHING!

139 Rockwell Ave
Middletown New York
January 3, 1965

Dear Sir,

I would like to attend the Presidents Inauguration becase, a Moose chased me in Alaska it scared me so hard I Got _shook_ so badly I had to go to a doctor for a long time. Then I was in the Alaskan Earthquake and was really _shook_ Iv never seen a President so I would like to attend the Inauguration and relly Get _shook_ with Joy For a change.

Thank you

Sincerely,
Stephen Price

A letter from a young man seeking to be the person selected to attend President Lyndon Johnson's 1965 inauguration. Writers, please note how succinctly this child tells a long and plaintive tale.

Jack O'Brian

ON THE AIR

A Beautiful Farewell

THE MOST BEAUTIFUL single TV farewell to Gen. MacArthur came yesterday on Ch. 5's "Wonderama," a children's show . . . Sonny Fox, a fine children's-show host, narrated a child's length, simplified TV story . . . Simplified, but not for a moment patronizingly as some TV shows unfortunately talk down to youngsters, in some primitive pidgin kidtalk as if soothing puppies; Fox merely cleared away all overly ornamented or so-called sophisticated verbiage and told his MacArthur story straight; the result was splendid . . . The narration was spoken quietly, seriously, without funereal solemnity, with filmed clips of the great soldier in his most triumphantly dramatic moments . . . It ended with Gen. MacArthur's magnificent final speech at West Point, dramatic when delivered, now a speech to be treasured and reprinted, respoken and remembered down through the history of inspiring language . . . It was a job quietly well done; Ch. 5 can be proud of Sonny Fox, who weaves an uncommon thread of responsibility and a lightly serious and healthy point of view between the cartoons and cheerful trivia of his all-morning Sun. show.

Jack O'Brian

Jack O'Brian used to scourge me every Monday in his column when I was on "The $64,000 Challenge." He subsequently became one of the most constant fans on "Wonderama." My mother marveled at how much smarter he had become in the intervening years.

A thank you note from Ethel Kennedy after the show she had asked me to arrange at their estate in McLean, VA, for the children of Embassy and Consular officials.

HICKORY HILL
1147 CHAIN BRIDGE ROAD
McLEAN, VIRGINIA

May 27, 1966

Dear Sonny —

Many happy thanks for everything you did to make the picnic yesterday the success that it was.

The show was terrific, and both Bobby and I think that you were great to take care of arranging for all those fabulous performers.

You not only charmed all of us, but all the hundreds of children that were here for the afternoon. Thank you again for the wonderful time that you gave to everyone.

With warm wishes from

A very grateful,

Mrs. Robert Kennedy

Mr. Sonny Fox
Sonny Fox Productions
59 East 54th Street
New York, New York

My big break in the big screen in "The Christmas That Almost Wasn't" filmed at Cine Citta in Rome. One day of shooting. One day of looping. Ten wonderful days in Rome. I turned down Rossanno Brazzi's offer to make me a cowboy star like "Clint Eastwood" and happily returned the far Weston, Connecticut.

Now THIS was a really big deal. Playing on a celebrity team against the fabled Harlem Globe Trotters at Madison Square Garden. Please note that the white guys are dashing around, but the Globetrotter is toying with the ball—and us. Nevertheless, I LOOKED like a basketball player!

From the office of . . . *Gertrude Fox* 4/3/64

Re: Wonderama —

Dear Sonny :—

Mrs Goldsmith, is a new a—
ccount with me but a good
one and has reccommended
another large group whom I
sold for the fall —
So whatever you can
do will be a help.
5 — Children ages are —
7 - 8 - 9 - 12.
mail to Mrs. Dorothy Goldsmith
221 Willard Drive
Hewlett, L. I.

CLARIDGE THEATRE PARTY SERVICE, INC.
156 West 44th Street • N. Y. 10036   JUdson 6-1408
. . . WE PUT THE FUN BACK INTO FUNd RAISING . . .

This is why it was so hard to get tickets to be on "Wonderama." Each
week, it seemed, one of these hand written notes would arrive from my
mother with a list of children—in this one letter five in one family—
whose receipt of invitations would clearly help her land another client
for her theater party business. I do believe she thought of "Wonderama"
as her sales agent.

In Nazare, Portugal. The dancers had something like 11 petticoats under their skirts.

With Jerry Lewis the day I reported in as an extra in one of his movies. The camera tracked me all day so my audience could begin to understand how complex it is to make a movie.

Park Litterer Faces Fine

By JOHN DERAVAL
World Journal Tribune Staff

Parks Commissioner Thomas P. F. Hoving is getting ready today to slap $25 fines on litterbugs who clutter up the park landscape—an offense that has gone unpunished for the last 19 years.

Hoving got the go-ahead from Mayor Lindsay after he and his wife, along with the Mayor and his children, took advantage of yesterday's Indian summer weather to join 4,000 youngsters and their parents in a clean-up of Central Park's North Meadow area.

In two hours the kids collected more than 1,000 shopping bags of assorted debris, enough to fill two large sanitation trucks.

"There must have been at least 10 tons of junk," Hoving said.

The Mayor stopped briefly with his two daughters Anne and Margie, then hurried on because he had other business in the park in the form of a touch-football game between the City Hall Regulars and the cast of off-Broadway's "Mad Show." The Regulars lost 13-2.

Informed later by Hoving of the extent of the clean-up, Mayor Lindsay okayed the issuance of littering summonses.

"Some people should be made to realize that our parks are a thing of beauty . . . maybe a $25 summons will help them realize this," Hoving declared.

The indignant commissioner pointed out that in addition to broken bottles, bear cans, hub caps and loads of paper, the children had found a 50-foot length of bridge cable two inches in diameter.

Hoving claimed a shortage of maintenance personnel made it impossible to keep the park clean. He said he only had 86 men to do the job where he should have a staff of 185.

The clean-up campaign was the idea of Sonny Fox, host of a children's program on WNEW-TV. Fox has been telling the children to bring their parents equipped with a shopping bag and pair of gloves to the park.

The story as reported in the Journal Tribune the day after we cleaned up Central Park. We did bring about a change, and the kids felt important and empowered!

Senator Robert Kennedy on one of his regular appearances on "Wonderama" and, later on, "The New Yorkers." I, of course, enjoyed hosting his interactions with the kids—and he, clearly, enjoyed his visits.

N500D2 2B PD   NEWYORK NY NFT JUN 7 1968

SONNY FOX (N)

DONT PHONE 59 E 54 ST NYK

YOU ARE INVITED TO ATTEND A REQUIEM MASS IN MEMORY OF
ROBERT FRANCIS KENNEDY AT ST. PATRICK'S CATHEDRAL IN
NEW YORK CITY ON SATURDAY, JUNE 8, 1968 AT 10:00 A.M.
PLEASE ENTER THROUGH THE FIFTH AVENUE ENTRANCE BY
9:30 A.M.

INTERMENT WILL BE AT ARLINGTON CEMETERY, ARLINGTON,
VIRGINIA, AT 5:30 P.M.

YOU ARE WELCOME TO TRAVEL ON THE FUNERAL TRAIN FROM
NEW YORK TO WASHINGTON. BUSES TO PENNSYLVANIA STATION
WILL LEAVE THE FIFTH AVENUE SIDE OF THE CATHEDRAL
IMMEDIATELY FOLLOWING THE MASS.

THIS TELEGRAM WILL ADMIT ONLY THE PERSON OR PERSONS
TO WHOM IT IS ADDRESSED AND MUST BE RETAINED AND
PRESENTED FOR IDENTIFICATION WHENEVER IT IS REQUESTED.
THE KENNEDY FAMILY

The telegram I received inviting me to attend the services for Robert Kennedy following his assassination. I shall never forget that day—the long trip on the train to Washington, the throngs at every station we passed and the burial at Arlington.

Dear Sonny,

Many thanks for your recent letter concerning Bobby's memorial.

I am so touched that you are interested. We have not yet decided what form this memorial will take but I will certainly let you know when there is something definite.

You know we would love to see you and your family anytime - anywhere. I'll be here 'til Sept. 16th - and then Hickory Hill.

Mr. Sonny Fox
Sonny Fox Productions Inc.
59 East 54th Street
New York

Perhaps you might be interested in helping Alan King in a special closed circuit program we are trying to set up for Bedford Stuyvesant. I'll have John Doar get in touch with you for a

The partly typed, partly handwritten note from the newly widowed Ethel Kennedy.

2

preliminary talk to see if you are at all interested or have any ideas.

Bobby's memorial requires such an incredible amount of preparation that it is just too early for anything but probing at this stage. Maxwell Taylor has a suggestion about including a public tv program which Bob McNamara is trying to include in the overall plan. If this should work out I hope you'll still be interested in helping out. - We'll keep in touch - Much love - and thanks for being Bobby's friend when he needed you and now

CHAPTER 16

Meanderings

One of the lovely dividends of high ratings and good notices is that the phone rings and people want to pay you to use your popularity on their projects. Most often it would be a school or a synagogue or a charitable event wanting me to do a PA—many of which I did. Then there interesting and ego-massaging invitations such as the PT Barnum Day Parade in Bridgeport Connecticut on the July 4th holiday. The parade lasted over two hours and about 250,000 people lined the route. I was paid to sit on the tonneau of a Cadillac convertible to wave at cheering throngs. Now that is pretty heady stuff. After the endless cheering and waving, I thought seriously about becoming a dictator. When I got home, my wife, Gloria, was sitting in the living room, reading the papers. I stood on the steps leading down, waved my arms and said, "Aren't you going to cheer?"

She studied me for a beat and, returning to her paper said, "Oh, go dump the garbage." My dreams of vainglory crumbled and were dumped along with the rest of our refuse.

Another phone call came from the manager of the New York Philharmonic. Coming up was the summer Promenade series and one of the pieces scheduled for three performances was Saint-Saen's "Carnival of the Animals," with introductory verses by Ogden Nash. Would I be available to be the narrator for those three programs? They could only pay me, he said somewhat apologetically, $1,500 dollars. What he didn't know was that I would have paid him that amount to appear at Lincoln Center with the New York Philharmonic. After the war we had season tickets to Carnegie Hall for the Sunday Philharmonic Concerts. That I would now have the opportunity to appear with this fabulous organization filled me with glee and a bit of trepidation. Of course I readily accepted the invitation.

Rehearsals came along and I was delighted to find that the piano duo playing along with the symphony was Jascha Zayde and Leonid Hambro. I knew Lee, and he had appeared on "Wonderama." Lee had been the staff pianist for 17 years with the Phil so he knew all of them. He was not only a gifted musician—in many ways he was a genius. He could sight read the most difficult scores and perform them better than many professional soloists could after rehearsing them. And therein lay one of his problems. The fact is for Lee it all came too easily. He and Jascha Zayde were a successful piano duo, but Lee never made it into the top ranks of performers. After ripping off a difficult score in his dazzling way, Lee did not enjoy going back and re-thinking the composition. The result was that although his virtuosity was unquestioned, Lee was perceived as missing that final depth of interpretation the highest standards demanded.

The conductor was Andre Kostelanetz, a figure of some glamour since he had appeared in movies with Deanna Durbin, as well as being a respected conductor. As the rehearsal progressed, Kostelanatz became more and more annoyed with the byplay between Lee and the orchestra after each animal segment. I guess he felt this sort of laughter was undignified. Finally he leaned toward me and sneered, "The great philharmonic. They are beasts, no?" I quickly nodded in agreement. After my army experience, I knew enough not to disagree with a higher-ranking officer.

The night of the first concert finally arrived. The hall was packed and included, of course, my Mom and Dad and my wife. Carnival was to close the first half of the concert. I listened to the beginning of the concert in my dressing room. As it got later I moved to the green room just off-stage. Finally it was my turn to walk out of that stage with the Maestro. I settled in my chair, opened the book with the Nash verses and we started. It was going well. The audience was laughing in the right places, the orchestra sounded divine and I was relaxed. We got to the Swan, which I introduced with the delicious Nash quatrain:

> The swan can swim while sitting down
> For pure conceit it takes the crown
> It looks in the mirror, over and over
> and claims to have never heard of Pavlova.

I leaned back to await the lovely cello solo. Nothing happened. I turned to the Maestro, who was leaning toward me with clenched teeth that were supposed to suggest a smile, but looking more as though he would gladly sink his teeth into me, he hissed, "Fossils! Not Swan. FOSSILS!"

I had turned two pages. Behind me the orchestra was in a state of disarray, not knowing whether to hold on the fossils or flip to the swan. I turned to the correct page and said to the by now puzzled audience, "but first..." and followed with the proper recitation leading into the Fossils. As the orchestra launched into that passage, I pondered on what would come next. Would Kostelanetz go directly into the swan or would he come back to me? I really did not want to repeat those four lines. It would sound foolish. The music ended. I watched as the Maestro laid down his baton and smiled at me. At which point I took a deep breath and launched into what the *New York Times* critic the next day termed, "limping verse":

> A moment ago you heard me goof
> I thought the Maestro would go through the roof

The show however must go on
So here, at last, is the Swan.

The cello solo at last was played. The rest of the piece spun out fault-lessly. When we left the stage, Kostelanetz grabbed me in a bear hug and exclaimed, "That was wonderful. How do you have so much poise?"

"Maestro, a life time of committing gaffes, tends to breed poise."

The next day I got half the *Times* review. After writing of the musical highlight, it then went on to discuss the 'literary highlight'—my quatrain. Poor Ogden Nash was upstaged by Irwin the Improviser.

Another wonderful call came in January 1962. It went like this…

"Hello. You don't know me. My name is Maurice Levine and we have never met."

I agreed to both statements.

"I am the director of the 92nd Street YMHA symphony, and on Mother's Day in May, we will be presenting two new musicals for kids at the Y. We would like you to narrate them. The composer, Hank Beebe is with me now. May we come over to play some of the songs for you?"

One of the properties Maurice and Hank played for me that day was a charming story of a little boy in Texas who yearned for his own horse, but was told he was too little. Undeterred, he walks to the place where they have everything, even horses for little boys—New York City! I was thoroughly charmed by the story and Hank's music and agreed to participate in the Mothers Day performances. Subsequently, an ad agency executive who had clients on "Wonderama," fell for the Cowboy and the Tiger, and in 1963, we were contracted by ABC-TV to produce this program for a Sunday afternoon.

Looking for the performer to play the role of the song and dance tiger, who was distraught that everyone thought of him as vicious instead of the cuddly pet he knew himself to be, I had the inspired notion to approach Jack Gilford. I knew of him from the Broadway production of " A Funny Thing happened on the Way to the Forum," as well as the

Shalom Aleichem tale of Braunsche Schweig, where he never said a word until the final line and brought the audience to tears. An actor with that range and with the innate sweetness in him seemed like the right talent. I sent Jack the script and he loved it! We got David Wayne, and two other wonderful performers, and all seemed to be moving ahead splendidly. Then I heard the profound noise of silence. Gilford's agent was supposed to have closed the deal, but I heard nothing regarding this—for about a week. I phoned Harold Cohen, my agent, and heard "You better start looking for someone else to play the tiger."

"What are you talking about?"

"ABC-TV won't clear Jack. It seems he is still under a contempt citation by the House Un-American Affairs Committee."

I could not believe what I was hearing. Jack had refused to name names in the fifties and, as a result, had been held in contempt by the committee and was blackballed from TV and motion pictures in this country for ten years. But this was 1963. Jack Kennedy was President. The era of Red Channels and the blacklists had long since gone away. Or so I thought. When I pointed out that Gilford was currently all over TV in a series of famous and delightful Crackerjack commercials, their answer was, "But we don't use his name." So, if we uttered those two words, Jack Gilford, the republic would crumble???

After the war, I had been president of the Press, Advertising and Radio Chapter of a new Veteran's organization that was designed to be the NOT American Legion. It was called the America Veterans Committee, and our line was "Citizens First, Veterans Second." The concept was not to see how much we could get from the government as vets, but rather how we could help make this a better country for all. It was a time of the Marshall Plan overseas and the GI Bill here. The communist party decided to infiltrate our organization and take it over as its mouthpiece to fight the Marshall Plan, since the Russians decided that as a U.S. initiative, it had to be anti-Soviet. While I had no sympathy for the HUAC witch hunt, I was not willing to allow our nascent organization to become the political adjunct to any party. When approached by the FBI to help them identify the "aparatchiks" of the party, I did cooperate. I also knew many of our members were being affected by the spreading influence of Red Channels. I was aware that some of our members were being denied access to their livelihoods by the blacklist that the networks created based on these all-too easily compiled lists. So when I was now, two years into the Kennedy era, confronted with this inanity, I was not prepared to continue to cave into the cowardice and stupidity of the network. I called my agent.

"You tell ABC there is no substitute for Gilford. They either clear him or there is no show!" I held my breath for a few days. The phone rang.

"ABC cleared Gilford. He's Kosher." A small victory for common sense.

We rehearsed the show in a space above Ratners, a famous purveyor of Jewish foods on 2nd Avenue. One day, on our lunch break, I was sitting next to Jack and suddenly became aware he was holding a conversation with the ceiling. As I listened closer, I realized his dialogue was with a place out of this world.

"Is it raining up there? Oh it never rains there."

"Are you married? Oh, not married. You know people will start to talk—maybe you should get married." And so on.

"So, Jack, you talk with him often?"

"All the time"

"Can I ask you to ask questions?"

"Sure." And anytime after that, I could turn to Jack and ask, "So how are things going up there?" and an immediate conversation with the invisible He would start up. It was then I determined I wanted to do a one-man show with Gilford some day. It took 18 years, but I produced it for CBS Cable in the early 1980s. I stayed friends with Jack, his wife Madeline and his son and daughter until he died of cancer. One of the sweetest, most talented performers I have ever known.

With some hitches that forced me to take a loan against my life insurance policy to complete the production, the show aired. It was the first day after the four-day hiatus by the networks to cover the assassination and funeral of JFK. "The Cowboy and the Tiger" was so successful that ABC repeated it ten days later. The *Daily News* called it the perfect program as the country recovered from the shock and sorrow of the assassination and termed it "a minor classic." I'll settle for that evaluation anytime.

CHAPTER 17

The New Yorkers

In the early summer of 1967, Channel 5 Station Manager, Larry Fraiberg, called me into his office to inform me that the station would be starting a new two-and-a-half hour, daily variety/talk show in the fall. They offered me the role of host. Ah, but there was a catch—I would have to leave "Wonderama." I had never contemplated leaving the show—at least not seriously. I asked why I could not do both, and Larry responded that to feature me as the star of an adult show of this dimension he wanted me divorced from the kid's show image. I suggested trying it out for thirteen weeks. "I have," I reminded him, "a wife, four kids and a mortgage." I wanted to make sure this new show would work before I cast aside my stable and proven program. Larry would not yield on that point. So, what to do? I figured this was another intervention. Did I want to end up being a fifty year old children's show host or was it time for me to move on to a new challenge? I finally agreed and in late August of 1967, after eight and a half years, I said goodbye to my friends and left "Wonderama" with regret—and a renewed sense of adventure.

A two-and-a-half hour daily show with our limited resources was probably doomed to fail, which it ultimately did. Our production staff was young and there were not enough of them. I was the only person who had kids. Every interview seemed to go on ten minutes too long in an effort to fill huge chunks of time. But there were some good things. My co-host, Penelope Coker, was a classy lady from Charleston, S.C. society. She had a soft southern accent that played well against my New York brashness. Stewart Klein was a witty theater and film critic and Gloria Okun filled out the on-the-air contingent. My greatest joy was discovering the enormously talented and sweet–natured Joe Raposo, who led a trio of musician that provided some variety. Joe, of course, went on to great acclaim and was the musical genius associated with Sesame Street, writing songs like "Rubber Ducky" and "It's Not Easy Being Green." Joe died much too soon and we lost troves of musical treasures he did not have time to write.

After many years of trying, Penelope became pregnant with her husband, Bill Wilson. She worked through her gestation. She finished the show on a Friday, and on Monday we came in to learn she had given birth during the weekend. Channel 5 decided that I should have a different female personality as my co-host each week. I got to work with some delightful ladies, including Ruby Dee and Julie Harris. The thought that one day I would not only meet Julie, but share the show with her for a week, both astonished and worried me. With a changing roster of co-hosts, there was a subtle change in how the show played. As the permanent (well, as it turned out, not exactly permanent) host of the show, I understood its dynamics and the process. On the other hand, you wanted to allow the talents and personality of the guest hope to have enough room to bring some new colors and perceptions to the show. Sometimes that did not exactly work out as one would have liked. The two hosts would be sitting with a guest. I had a line of questions that had continuity about them. My guest host would have her own take on the conversation and just as I was about to get to the payoff, she would jump in. I had to back off—though at time I really wanted to perhaps gag her for a bit. That was not the case, I hasten to add, with Julie.

One of the most interesting weeks stemmed from pairing me with Colleen Dewhurst. As it happened, the Sunday before Colleen was to start her stint was the night of the TONYS, Broadways big awards show. After the theater presentation, we repaired to the Rainbow Room atop the RCA building for the big post show party. Colleen sat next to me. She turned at one point and asked.

"Do you like this dress?"

Even if I didn't, I certainly wasn't going to start off our week together by telling her I thought it looked frumpy.

"It's lovely, Colleen."

"GC hates it. That's why I wore it."

Uh, oh. Storm clouds gathering. GC would be George C. Scott. They were working on their second marriage—to each other. Everyone knew that this was a tempestuous marriage of two highly emotional actors who loved each other, but spent a lot of time tearing away at each other. We had already worked out that GC, who was starring in a revival of "The Little Foxes," would be a guest on "The New Yorkers" on Thursday's show.

When the week started, I was having a lovely time sharing the show with this great actress. On Wednesday, I was off camera while Colleen was interviewing someone, when I noticed a delivery person enter the studio with large bouquet of flowers. I learned they were for Colleen and took them with me when I went up on the platform to rejoin Colleen. As I approached, I could tell she was preparing to thank me for my thoughtfulness. I quickly assured her I was not that thoughtful and gave them to her. I settled in my chair and leaned back far enough so I could read the card. It read, "I love you, GC." Clearly, at that moment, only Colleen and I knew what the card said. She looked into the camera with that beady-eyed stare that would freeze monsters in their tracks and said, "It won't help a bit." She then tossed the flowers aside. I loved the moment. It was live drama! It did, however, have dramatic consequences.

The next day, Colleen looked a wreck. Apparently when GC finished the matinee performance of Little Foxes he asked his assistant, who was assigned to watch the show when she got the flowers, about her reaction. The assistant told him of her few biting words. When Colleen got home, she received a call from the theater—GC did not show up for that evening's performance. Scott had decided this rejection was reason enough to go on a tear. Colleen got back into the car and drove from South Salem to NYC and checked all the usual spots until she found him. She dragged him to their N.Y. Pied-a-Terre and got him to bed. Two things were obvious. GC would not be appearing on the show, despite that fact we had been promoting it earlier in the week. The other was that I would have to be very supportive on Colleen in this matter. Trouper that she was, she went through Thursday's show as though nothing had happened. But when she came in on Friday, she was wearing dark glasses to hide her red and swollen eyes. George had missed yet another performance and Colleen, again, had been up much of the night. I told her to leave the glasses on and I told the audience she had a scratched retina. We stumbled through to the end of her guest-host stint.

It seemed to me that these two splendid actors had taken the drama of their relationship from the setting of their home into the outside world. Today, when so many plays are being situated in warehouses, empty hotels and other non-theatrical venues, perhaps that fact is not so startling, but I felt, for those three days, that I had been plucked from the audience to play an unscripted part in this unfolding drama. Heady stuff! Years later, in 1978, I had the delightful good fortune to have Colleen star in the production of my first TV movie for NBC, "And Baby Makes Six." Colleen was extraordinary.

Nine months into "The New Yorkers," I was called into Larry Fraiberg's office and was informed that they were not picking up my option. After nine and a half years with Channel 5, I was given four weeks' notice and then, out. I was stunned. I knew the show was getting disappointing ratings, but I honestly felt the shortcomings had to do more with our inadequate production staff. I did not have the presence to demand a separation commensurate with my contributions to Channel 5's success. In addition to "Wonderama" and "The New Yorkers," I had created and hosted a two-and–a-half hour Saturday morning kid's game show called "Just for Fun." I did that for five years as a way to make more money until the fee for "Wonderama" allowed me to let that show go. I also hosted a weekly teen-age bull session called "Speak Out" each Saturday for an hour. That lasted a year. All this from 1959 to 1969. And now, four week's notice and out the door. Ironically, at just about the same time, I was preparing to become Chairman of the Board of the National Academy of Television Arts and Sciences. But that prestigious position did nothing to pay my mortgage or feed my family. So, I was entering a new testing time for me. It had been a long time since I was not working on a show.

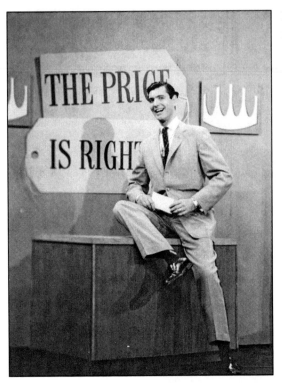

I was the guest host from time to time on the Goodson-Todman shows, including "I've Got a Secret," "Beat the Clock," "To Tell the Truth," and, in this photo, "The Price Is Right."

This was the "Movie Game." Army Archerd, standing to my left, was the powerful *Variety* columnist whose presence on the show insured that a superstar such as John Wayne would be on a syndicated daily half-hour game show of little distinction.

Boy Meets Tiger In Gay Fantasy

HOLLYWOOD (UPI) — For this viewer, it has been virtually impossible to watch the crassness of everyday television entertainment so soon after President Kennedy's assassination.

But of all places yesterday, it was a special children's show — a one hour musical fantasy called "The Cowboy and the Tiger" — that brought to the home screen the sorely needed qualities of civility and gentleness.

The ABC-TV Thanksgiving special was so disarming that despite the oppressive commercials aimed at children, and despitre the somber tone of the day, one could enjoy the good-natured whimsy about a 12-year-old Texas boy who wants a tiger in a New York zoo to become his horse.

The instincts of all concerned with project were so healthy and engaging that a gaiety and theatricality flowed naturally through the script, staging, music and dance — and earned the show, one hopes, many repeat airings.

The pivotal role was that of the tiger, and it was entrusted to Jack Gilford, who created one of the most delightful children's characterizations ever seen anywhere— faintly reminiscent of Bert Lahr's cowardly lion in the movie "The Wizard of Oz."

thing called "The Old Soft Paw, which is derived from "The Old Soft Shoe."

There were only four other parts, and all were filled to perfection. Paul O'Keefe, 12, played the boy who decides to go to New York to get a horse because no one will give him one at home. And not only was he a fine, sturdy and appealing youngster, but he sang with a voice that could fit equally well into a choir or a Broadway show. He is, in fact, the in the musical "Oliver!"

David Wayne was the narrator, and stepped into several cameo roles, and, of course, he is not capable of a bad performance. The two other parts belonged to the tiger's zoo mates, a lovable bear (Nathaniel Frey) and a primping peacock (Sue Lawless), and there hasn't been such a happy menagerie since Hollywood's golden days.

In the story, Gilford the tiger was extremely depressed at constantly being referred to as ferocious. He wanted to be loved for his gentler qualities. He wanted to be a pet. Frustrated with the unbending minds of people, he escapes, and soon is lassoed in Central Park by the boy cowboy, who also is lonely and insist that the tiger be his horse. In a fine line after being lassoed, the tiger, more insulted than angry, says: "Would you mind taking that rope off? I've had enough trouble for one day."

One of the many wonderful reviews for our production of "The Cowboy and the Tiger." I am not sure that headline would be used today in exactly the same way.

Paul O'Keefe played the part of the Cowboy who desperately wanted a horse of his own and found one at the zoo in New York, and never, ever knew it was a ferocious, man-eating TIGER!

Sixteen years after I decided, while working with Jack Gilford on "The Cowboy and the Tiger," that I wanted to do a Jack Gilford special, here we are in rehearsal. Director Tim Kiley, who went on after his first directorial job on "Let's Take a Trip" to direct the Ed Sullivan Show among many others, is on my right. David Eagle, who was the number two person at my production company, is on my right.

Actress Ruby Dee was one of my delightful co-hosts on "The New Yorkers."

Penelope Coker, the elegant lady from Charleston, SC, who was my co-host on "The New Yorkers" for six months. Her southern charm certainly helped balance my New York brashness.

Julie Harris, director Del Mann on set in the Wicklow Hills near Dublin for the shooting of "Bronte."

CHAPTER 18

The Tomorrow Show

By 1973, I was in a lot of trouble. My last job, hosting "The Movie Game," had ended in 1971. Being Chairman of the Board of NATAS kept me in a high profile, but put no food in the family larder. There were occasional projects, but they did not pay the mortgage and other expenses involved in our family of four children Chris, 16, Meredith, 14, Dana, 12, and Tracy, 9.

By 1973 I called on Mort Werner, an NBC Vice President, whom I knew from my activities in the International Council of the Television Academy. I finally had to admit that I needed a job. Until then, I had been trying to sell program packages or hook up with some studio in an executive capacity. I had a deep-seated fear of saying, "I am unemployed." I think that tapped into my lack of security that probably went back to adolescence. Or maybe it's a man thing. My wife clearly laid it out for me four months after I left Channel 5, when for the first time in our fifteen years of marriage the money wasn't coming in each week. "You are a failure," she announced one day in the kitchen. "Our deal is I take care of the children and you earn the money. You have failed as a husband and as a father!" I realize now that was panic taking over her rational being, but at the time it felt like a knife being twisted inside me. I could not admit in any way that

I was a "failure," so I would not admit that I was, to all purposes, out of a job.

Mort Werner listened sympathetically and said he would see what he could do. A few weeks later he called to offer me the position of associate producer on a new series NBC would be putting on the air in September 1973, called "The Tomorrow Show." This would open up the 1–2 AM time period and was designed to follow the Johnny Carson show that ran, at that time, from 11:30 PM to 1:00 AM. An L.A. newsman, Tom Snyder, would host it. The money wasn't great and it meant being away from our home in Connecticut at a time when our oldest child, Christopher, was having major difficulties. After discussing it with my wife, it was decided that I had little choice. If things worked out, perhaps they would increase my salary and I could move everyone out to the coast. Things were getting tense between Gloria and me and I thought that being away for a while wouldn't be all that bad. I was wary, however of the whole move and insisted on writing a contract where I could fire NBC every thirteen weeks. I did not want to be stuck out there if the money did not get better or I hated the show.

Thus began my seven-month stint with Tom Snyder and his wonderful nightly show. Our staff of six or seven was a motley group. One senior member was a hard-drinking affable veteran of *Life* magazine. Rudy Tellez was the producer and he had had experience of "The Tonight Show." He was very L.A. He talked the talk, owned racehorses, and was good at the care and feeding of a star's ego. Tom proved to be a fascinating and complex subject. He was good looking, tall and certainly had presence. When he walked into a room he filled the space. Women were attracted to him and men enjoyed his company. His mind was trained by the Jesuits. It was disciplined and coldly logical. He was also arrogant and was surprisingly limited in some ways. His hobbies were collecting old model train sets, and golf. As far as I could determine, he never read books. In all the time we gave him material to read for upcoming guests, I do not believe he ever read the book or report.

We always distilled the material in a two or three page backgrounder that included shaping the interview. He was not comfortable around those who disagreed with him and he expected his views to be final. And his attitude was not helped by the fact that a few years earlier I had hosted a talk variety show in New York. It would have been understandable for him to think I might be lurking as a substitute should he falter. I tried to make it clear to all that I was only interested in building my career as a producer.

I quickly determined that I would leave Tom to the tender care of Rudy while I got on with trying to define what we were—and were not—to be. Clearly, we wanted to define "The Tomorrow Show" as being something different from Carson. We were ably assisted in this effort by a small budget and the ukase that prohibited us from booking any talent which the Carson show had used, were using or might use in the future. The man in charge of protecting the valuable Carson carcass was Dave Tebbett, head of talent for the network and full time resident of the Beverly Hills Hotel. One of my tasks was to trudge over on occasion and try to convince Dave to relax so someone we wanted could be booked. I lost most of those fights, since the rewards for saying no were far more comfortable than the risk of saying yes.

We did give the continuity acceptance people some perplexing stuff as we pushed the envelope of what the network would allow on its airwave. I learned that there was a nudist colony in Topanga Canyon that was sort of "EST au natural." What would be more defining than originating an hour show from a nudist colony?

I visited the Elysian Fields and met with the honcho, Ed Lange. He was a large man who, in deference to his visitor, wore a loose fitting garment. All around the grounds were couples who were, as advertised, enjoying whatever they were doing totally unclothed. I discovered an interesting truth. When nudity becomes commonplace, nudity becomes invisible. Over a period of weeks I had to spend some hours there researching, meeting and preparing our program. I had gotten to the point of not being aware of the nakedness until one day I saw a couple heading toward the tennis court. They were naked except for their tennis socks and shoes. Suddenly, their nudity became vivid. The addition of one article of clothing suddenly made them seem very naked indeed. I was discovering what every stripper and burlesque producer already knew.

The prospect of originating from Elysian Fields was guaranteed to set NBC's teeth on edge. It led to a two-hour meeting around the refectory table in the conference room with the suits from standards and practices, the program mavens and assorted others. During the conversation, these highly paid executives discussed, with complete sobriety, such issues as how much of the asshole one could show and how much of a nipple on the breast would be allowable. This was all done with the gravity of the Sanhedrin discussing the Talmud. It was finally agreed that "The Tomorrow Show" could tape the hour on location, but we would be accompanied by two—count 'em—two censors.

The day of the taping, I made a speech to the crew regarding their conduct at the nudist site. "We are their guests. There will be no snide jokes and no leering. We are professionals doing our jobs. When you get home tonight, say anything you want to your wives or husbands. During the taping, keep your thoughts to yourselves." Okay, so it wasn't the "gipper" speech. But it worked. I have a picture somewhere of the lunch line for the crew and the Elysian Fields folks. On the line are two nude people followed by an NBC technician—fully clothed—followed by a couple of more nudes, etc. In each case, the eyes of the NBC crewmember were staring straight at the back of the head of the person in front.

The standards and practices people split their emplacement. One was with the cameras, the other in our truck. The first taping was to take place in the pool with one of the members of the group being held in the arms of the others in the best EST traditions of the day. Of course, they were all nude. As we viewed pictures of this setup, it was very clear that the anatomy of this scene was beyond acceptance—a point made loudly to me by our point censor. After letting him stew with this for a few minutes, I said quietly to one of the residents, "Okay, turn on the bubbles." I knew that there was a Jacuzzi in the pool and that, in all probability we would use that to mask the bodies. I just wanted to see if it would work without turning it on. With the bubbles burbling, we went on with the taping.

The day went on with talk about foreplay, tumescence and a lot of 1970s jargon. The two censors kept pointing out shots that were beyond the rules—too much nipple here, too much asshole there, but we managed to finish up the taping pretty much as planned. And the crew behaved well. The editing process went on with the constant attendance of the Standards and Practices people whose eagle eyes were ready to seize on any breach of whatever passed for propriety at 1:00 AM.

Mirabilis Dictum, the L.A. censors finally passed the show. NBC was about to present a full hour direct from a nudist colony. I didn't think anyone would confuse us with Johnny Carson after this. The show was slotted on the Monday of Thanksgiving week. It happened that date coincided with the annual International Emmy Awards banquet being held at a New York hotel. I was in New York for the event. During the afternoon, I called my office in L.A. just to check in.

"Oh, you heard," said the voice from Burbank.

"Heard what?"

"The shit hit the fan. They pulled the show."

New York had seen it and the peacock's feathers were clearly ruffled. As were mine. Herb Schlosser was president of NBC and that very night was scheduled to be a presenter of one of the awards. At the reception I spotted him across a crowded room. "What the hell is going on?" I sputtered.

"All I know is I was in the shower preparing for this evening when I got a call from Travi (Hermione Traviesas, the Vice President for Standards and Practices at NBC, who I knew of from NATAS). He told me we had a problem with the program. I had no time to screen it because

I had to be here at your gig, and I am not going to ignore the vice president of the division, so I told him to yank it. Come to the office tomorrow at ten and we'll take a look at it."

I was really miffed, having taken each step with the appropriate supervision, and having had it cleared by those responsible in L.A.. There was nothing to do until the morrow. Mort Werner, my direct boss at 30 Rock, suggested I come into his office at 9 AM. Upon arrival he suggested I sit at the typewriter and narrate the whole process we had gone through leading to this moment. Up on the sixth floor, the corporate inner temple, Herb, Travi and a bunch of other suits were gathered for a screening of the tape. Any NBC employee in the building could dial into the screening. It was probably the most watched close circuit screening ever held at NBC. Mort and I watched in his office. As the program played, I sank deeper into my chair. Now that I was seeing it through the eyes of the brass, I began to wonder how I could ever have been so brash as to think that I could get away with this. I began to calculate how much I would have to take out to make it useable. I finally settled on about twenty minutes. When the screening was over, the phone rang and Herb invited us to come up. I entered the sanctum like a man about to have the doctor tell him he had a fatal illness. Herb immediately sought to reassure me. "No one is blaming you, Sonny. You did everything by the book."

Some other people mumbled stuff and finally, taking my dilemma by the horns, I turned to Travi. "Okay, what is there in the show that is not acceptable?"

"You know that part by the house when he kisses the girl. He put his tongue in her mouth. You can't show that on TV!"

All of how to turn on your partner and delay orgasm…all the nudity…and he was concerned about a French kiss.

"So, Travi," Herb asked, "how much do you think we would have to take out?"

'Oh, about a minute and a half."

I started to breathe again. It was quickly decided to send the tape back to Los Angeles for the extra editing. Herb Schlosser decided I was to stay in New York until the tape returned. It would then be reviewed and, if it passed inspection, would be aired. As instructed, I hung around until I got a call on Wednesday, the day before Thanksgiving. "Tape room at five," said the voice. At the appointed hour I appeared in the tech part of the complex where most of the executives were rarely seen. Amidst all the banks of amps and the dozens of two inch tape machines, we found our place where the by now infamous nudist show was once again to be screened. With me were five designated executives all of whom, I am sure, were just aching to get out of there and start their Thanksgiving vacations.

The program started unreeling. I could not believe my eyes. In the pool sequence, while the others were cradling one of their numbers, amidst all the bubbles apparently the tip of the man's penis had briefly broken through the surface of the water. So briefly, mind you, that it had eluded the careful scrutiny of two censors during the editing sessions. To rectify this dangerous assault on the sensibilities of tender eyes that might be up a 1:15 AM, NBC had carefully crafted electronic black rectangles to place over the area. What had been practically invisible to the naked (no pun intended) eye, now visually screamed PENIS!

And so it went. Too much of the anal crack? Black box. Two much glimpse of a nipple? Black box. Meanwhile, the talk of how to turn on a woman and delay sexual gratification proceeded unimpeded. When the hour finally ended, I awaited the judgment of the jury. "They did a nice job."

"Yeah."

But no one would take the responsibility and say, "run it." Sizing up the situation, I took a step back behind this phalanx of indecision. Putting my head down and lowering the pitch of my voice I announced, "I think it's a go."

"Yes, so do I," came back the chorus, after which there was a hasty exodus as the stalwart defenders of decency headed for their trains and country homes.

That night, the visit to the nudist site was telecast across the United States. In the morning the republic still stood. NBC was still in business. I did some checking with our affiliates to see if there had been any negative reaction. The manager of the NBC station in St. Louis said he had gotten one call from a somewhat querulous older lady criticizing the station for broadcasting such a program.

"How did you respond?"

"I told her she should not have stayed up so late to watch it."

One day we received a letter from a woman challenging us to put her on. She wrote that she was ugly, that people avoided looking at her and that TV would never put someone like her on a show. That letter piqued my curiosity. It was certainly true that even "The Tomorrow Show," which put on some strange people, had never shown anyone who, at first glance, one would instinctively want to turn from. I got her on the phone and asked her if she would really appear if we invited her. She vowed that she would. We had a long chat and I was intrigued. I didn't know if Tom could do such an interview. Clearly he could not make fun of her, would have to treat her with respect while digging in and finding out the emotional and psychological depths that would make this a compelling story. To my surprise Tom agreed.

The night of the taping I suggested to Joel Tater, our director, that he start off on a fairly long shot and gradually close in. This would give our audience a chance to get to know her as a person before they got to view her close up. I don't know if ugly was the word to describe our guest. Strange and unusual would probably have been better words. She proved to be a bright and engaging woman and she spoke frankly about being inside a body that almost no one looked beyond. It was a touching and revealing piece. I was glad I had thought to present it.

Stories like that one sustained me through those months. There was the two-hour piece on the issue of choosing life or death for a Down's syndrome child. Because of an atresia of the colon, the child needed an operation or it would die. The parents withheld permission, electing to allow this child to die rather than raise a child doomed to a limited and short life. The issue raised by the family, the doctor in the case, the nurses in the ICU and others made for a compelling and thought provoking piece.

Then there was the evening we talked about dying. We were probably the first to present a man who knew that he had only months to live. His gallantry in the face of his imminent demise was both touching and inspirational. A few days after that program, we received a letter from a woman. She described how she was going through the preparations for her suicide that night.

"I was laying out my bedclothes and putting the pills by my bedside. The TV was on, at first as background noise which I paid no attention to. Gradually I heard this man speaking of his own death. I sat down and really started to listen. At the end, I concluded that if he could deal with his lot in life, I could deal with mine. This letter is to tell you that because of that program, I have decided not to go through with my plans."

The power of television writ large—and good.

One of the most complex situations arose the night I had booked the head of the Louisiana KKK, a young man named David Duke. At that time few knew him. I knew he was smooth and articulate. I figured matching him against Tom's cool, logical mind would allow us to hear the hate being ranted by the new generation of the Klan while watching Tom chew him up. I led off with Duke, figuring to give him the first half of the hour. I had another guest ready for the second half of the program. But soon into the program a strange thing happened. David backed Tom down. Whether Tom thought Duke would hang himself if he let him go on, or he just was not up to dealing with him that evening I do not know. He let Duke run the show. My mouth dropped open as I heard the anti-Negro bilge smoothly dripping from Duke's mouth. As we approached the end of his allotted time, Duke started on the Jews. I couldn't pull the plug on this. It was the first time that the unexpurgated hate was being heard on a network. Perhaps it was time to let others hear what was out there in our land. I blew off the second guest and allowed Tom to finish the hour with David Duke. Then I hustled into the storm cellar.

By the next day the cloudburst of reaction had already broken over my head. Predictably every Jewish and Black organization was on the phone to NBC demanding equal time. My position was to invite those representatives to appear with Duke and let them tear him apart. That, I thought, would be a widely watched show and be the stuff of fascinating TV. The demand, however, was that the other organizations get equal time with Duke. He got an hour. They wanted an hour. They did not want to share that time with David Duke. Although I understood their point, I tried to convince them that, without Duke, those who had not watched the original show would not understand the blatancy of the evil he was propagating nor how skillfully it was packaged. There would be no conflict. There would be an hour of right-thinking folks inveighing against Duke and his cohorts.

Some weeks later, while I was vacationing with my family, I watched the return engagement. It was as I had feared, dull. To this day, I still cannot fathom what happened to Tom Snyder. I could have worn an MIA bracelet with his name on it after that performance.

Things had also gotten progressively tenser between Tom and Rudy Tellez. Finally, in the spring of 1974, when I returned from a hiatus, I was told that Tom had attacked Rudy verbally on the air. It was clear Rudy's days were numbered. By then Tom was very close to Pam Burke, an attractive woman with a good story sense, who had been working her way up the production chain over the months. She visited me, clearly as an emissary from Tom, with the proposition that I take over the show.

"I don't think so."

"Why?"

"If I produce, there is one producer and one star. That is not what

Tom wants. He wants to be surrounded by people who will adore him and not say no. He wants sycophants. I cannot do a show under those circumstances." I called NBC and informed them I was going home at the end of the next cycle, after six months. They asked me to stay on for one more month until they could straighten things out. Before I left, Tom and I had a short conversation.

"Tom," I said, "In all the time I have been here, you and I have never had a conversation. Just two people chatting. Either you have been putting on a show, or you have been screaming. I have never had that experience before."

Tom replied. "I have never met anyone like you before. You are always two or three weeks down the road, ahead of where everyone else was."

Later I realized trying to locate the real Tom Snyder was like trying to find a Chameleon on a gingham bedspread.

Toward the end of my "Tomorrow Show" stint, the President of NBC, Herb Schlosser, and the head of programming, Bob Howard, hopped into the corporate jet and flew in from NYC to wait on Tom in order to convince him to move the show to NYC and also become the anchor for WNBC-TV nightly news, which was in trouble. Tom knew he had leverage and he used it. He told me that his aim, in 1974, was to become the first million-dollar-a-year newsman in TV. That was pure Tom. His success was to be measured in dollars. To sweeten the pot, they gave him some specials and the anchor spot for the weekend version of the evening news on the network. The head of NBC News, Dick Wald, was in Europe when all this happened. When he returned and heard of the deal done without his participation Wald was livid. I knew that with that kind of hostility from the top of NBC News, a general distrust of Tom as a newsman after watching him hobnobbing with the cross-dressers, hermaphrodites and the other strange assortment of outliers that found a home on "The Tomorrow Show," Tom would not last long in N.Y. as the savior of NBC News. He never went beyond the original thirteen-week commitment as the night time weekend anchor. He did one or two documentaries. The million-dollar baby was selling at a large discount, and eventually, the show returned to California.

I recently checked in with Dick Wald, currently Emeritus at the Columbia School of Journalism, to check my memories on this. While Dick confirmed the events, he had an interestingly different take on Tom. Here, with his permission, is what he wrote:

Tom was probably the best television news natural I ever worked with. He could read a script as though he were just thinking of it now; he could keep two trains of thought going at once; he had a built-in sense of timing. The problem was that every once in a while, he slipped the reins of good behavior and acted like a fool. I wasn't ready to take a chance on him as one of the three main news anchors of those days and so I chose Tom Brokaw as the anchor. The NBC management of the time was, to say the least, very annoyed. They liked him. They saw his strengths. They were used to dealing with entertainment people with his weaknesses. They were sure I was nuts. (As you may remember, I was ultimately fired for several annoyances to management).

At the time he was wooed to come to New York what they wanted was a place for him in network news as a sweetener. They promised it to him, but not in writing. He would probably not have come if there was not some sort of promise. I was, indeed, pissed—not so much about using him in the network, as about making promises they had no right to make. As it turned out, he helped the ratings and made a lot of money.

We had known each other for a long while (I was instrumental in bringing him to L.A. as an anchor in the days I was also running owned-station news), but it wasn't until I had to sit down with him and deal with the situation the other folks had set up that we became friends. I found him to be honest, funny, outrageous, bitter and very sensible to deal with. And, by the way, I thought "The Tomorrow

Show" was the best use of his talents anyone had found. If he could have been around in the present world of cable shows, he would have been king of the heap and nobody would give a damn when he acted outrageously.

When they moved the program to 30 Rock, the staff invited me to come down to the studio and visit the program. One evening I did go down for the taping. It was a program examining the heritage of the Kennedy years as recalled by Ted Sorensen, Dean Rusk and others, exactly the kind of show I would not have done at 1:00 AM. At one point in the program, Tom turned to Dean Rusk, former Secretary of State and now President of the Ford Foundation, and asked, "We hear all kinds of things about the 'Eastern Establishment.' Is there such a thing?"

"No," answered the epitome of the Eastern Establishment.

"I didn't think so," said Tom.

I was happy to be out. So it was back to Connecticut and more problems—both financial and marital.

CHAPTER 19

The Slow Road to VP-dom

It was clear soon after I returned that any attempt to get our marriage back on track was not going to work. Two people ideally suited to each other as they were starting out may end up needing things from each other that aren't there. People grow in different ways and at a different pace and the couple that was ideal in their twenties gets to their forties and life can seem to have built a chasm where there had been a deep love. Gloria had not signed up to be the wife of a TV personality, nor had she reckoned on the fact that someday the merry-go-round might stop and the money might not come in each week.

At the same time, I was having a lot of problems dealing honestly with my financial woes, sinking deeper into debt. We had sold our lovely house on the river and were now renting a house in Weston that was charming and adequate, but a large step down from where we had been. From 1974 to 1976 things grew increasingly tense. In 1976, my friend Paul Klein became Program Director at NBC. Noting that there was no Vice President of Children's Programs, and that NBC was in last place in the Saturday morning competition, I raised the prospect of NBC hiring me for that position. CBS and ABC each had such a position. There seemed to be interest which, as it percolated through the executive structure at 30 Rock, seemed to ebb and flow in some mysterious pattern. As the winter became spring the prospects for this position looked good one week, hazy the next.

About this time the phone rang and Jerry Golod, the Vice President of CBS Children's Programming, was inquiring about my availability to host a new CBS series called "Way Out Games." It would shoot in L.A. during the summer and it was set for a firm 26 weeks starting in September. My dilemma was taking the gig—and the dough, which I needed—and maybe missing out on the NBC position, or saying no and finding out that NBC was not, after all, going to open that position. So I went to Paul Klein and urged him to give me a decision now. He explained that there was a hiring freeze, that he could not hire me until another person left. I told him I was going to take the CBS gig and if he got the okay and hired anyone but me I would lay a curse on him—something like "may you live in a mansion with a thousand rooms and may you have a toothache in each one!"

With that I was off to the Oakwood apartments (I had lived there during my "Tomorrow Show" stretch) and a series to be produced by Dan Enright. Dan had been the producer, along with Jack Barry, of the quiz show "Twenty-One." In the 1950s, I had worked with Dan on a couple of game show pilots, so I did know him. We also had the connection of both having been involved with big money quiz shows. When the scandal broke, most of the culprits, be they advertisers or network moguls, were able to walk away from this seedy experience undamaged but it was "Twenty-One" which led the downfall, so Jack and Dan had to walk the plank. They were effectively exiled and spent time in Mexico and Canada producing as best they could. Now they were back in this country and enough time had passed that they were acceptable again. During the six months we spent shooting the series, I spent some Sundays with Dan, the family and friends. We would start talking about the scandals and, inevitably, Dan would deny having done anything wrong. His point was it was "only entertainment and what was the big deal of rigging it to make it more dramatic and compelling?"

"Dan, you committed fraud. You told everyone it was legit. They believed it was. It was corrupt and it was dishonest."

We finally agreed just not to talk about it. Years later, when I was a consultant to Granada TV of England helping them put together a history of television. I approached Dan about talking with them regarding the show fixing. He refused. I was really surprised when a documentary, "The Quiz Show Scandals," produced for PBS by Julian Krainan, presented Dan talking honestly and straightforwardly about how he had rigged the show. Shortly after the program aired, Dan died. Later, I spoke with the woman with whom he had been living and asked her what had changed his mind. "Maybe he knew it was time," was her reply.

"Way Out Games," a sprawling, weekly affair involving three teams of ten to twelve year-olds gathered from across America, was taped outside Six Flags in Valencia. It was brutally hot and we were shooting four shows a week. Dan was producing. The director was Richard Klein, a frenetic game show director who had never done a remote before. The spaces were large, the contests were large and the problems were VERY large. There was a moment that seems to have captured the chaos of the production. Dan was arguing with the coach of one of the teams, an African-American gentleman. Without thinking, he started waving his starters pistol around and ended up aiming it squarely at the coach. This, mind you, in the turbulent period of the civil rights drive. I watched thinking; we are one blank shot away from a new race riot.

We finally wrapped the 26 shows and I scurried back to New York to pursue my berth at NBC. They were still stuck in the bureaucratic quagmire. I finally became a bit more proactive. I told them I did not want a contract—that I would be worth much more now in a year than they were prepared to pay now. In effect I showed up one day and said, "Okay where is my office?" It worked. The letter announcing my appointment as Vice President of NBC Children's Programming went forth to my new confreres throughout 30 Rock. I walked through the marbled lobby, under the Sert murals, and experienced a special frisson of joy. These were the very places I had visited as a kid in Brooklyn, sitting in the audience of radio shows. At the end of a broadcast I would go as a supplicant to the stage and ask for a page of the script. Now here I was, a Vice President at the network.

The first day on the job I dropped in on Bob Howard, the president of the network. "Okay, Bob, I'm starting today. I'm here for my mission statement." I settled back waiting for my charge. Bob stared at me for a moment.

"Just don't do anything to embarrass us."

Not quite Henry V's speech at Agincourt.

Half my staff was in N.Y., the rest at NBC in Burbank. It was time to meet the man who had been running the department as director of children's programming, Bill Hogan, and his two assistants, Margaret Loesch and Jeanne McCurdy. My first task was to inform my inherited staff that I knew absolutely nothing about the production of animated programs. I had a lot of experience dealing with a kid's audience, but I had never seen a story board nor dealt with the Hanna-Barbera's and Scheimer-Prescott's of the network children's world. Further, I was taking over a number three schedule. The more I watched the shows and looked at the ratings, the more convinced I became that none of the eight extant series was ever going to become a winner. The fall schedule was already in place and being presented, so I had some breathing space to figure out how to deal with this situation. A complicating factor was that Bill Hogan did not want to continue with me replacing him as senior in this department. Although Bill did not have the VP title, he was Director of Children's TV, and had been in charge. I tried to convince him that, given my lack of solid experience in this area, he would continue to play a critical role. He insisted on resigning. I then moved the rest of my staff, Margaret Loesch and Jeanne McCurdy, up one notch in title and pay. For better or worse, we were it.

As this was playing out, I was beginning another crash course on life inside a network. For years I had dealt with networks, mostly as friends and acquaintances in the same business. I had known the top executives in my role as Chairman of the Academy of Television Arts and Sciences. What I did not understand was how a huge bureaucratic structure such as NBC differed from my freelance experience. The first time I looked at the form for memos, I puzzled over the dozen or so names at the bottom of the page to which copies of my memos would go. "Who," I asked, "were all these people and what do they do?" They all had titles— sales, continuity acceptance, station relations, production executives, and so on. The good news was my area of children's programming was deemed a backwater of the network schedule and of little interest to these moguls, mini–moguls and mogul-ettes. When I had lunch one day with Paul Klein, head of entertainment, he asked,

"To whom do you report? Oh that's right," he said, answering his own question, "you don't report to anyone."

This was fine with me. When I first opened business at NBC, I was assigned a suite of offices on the 6th Ave. side of the NBC building. All the other program mavens were on the fourth floor, some overlooking the Channel Gardens and the skating rink. I was very happy to be away from there. No one examined my visitors or knew what was going on. As an independent performer/producer for many years, this felt fine to me. Bob Howard kept asking why I was up there and I kept responding, "It's fine, Bob. Don't bother yourself about it."

I discovered that being on the buying rather than the selling side made a whole lot of difference, especially when I was in charge of 13 million dollars for programming. When producers were taking a pitch meeting with me, they were sometimes kept waiting for twenty minutes. When I finally came out and apologized for the delay, every one of them said, "No problem." I guess I said the same thing when I was waiting to sell a show. When I first came out to meet the possible production houses in L.A., I traveled to each company. Later, I realized, they were very pleased to come to my office or my hotel.

When, eventually, we were moved down to the fourth floor, I had a lovely office with a rare extra, my own bathroom. My status did not merit such a prestigious addition, but that was the suite they gave me. That turned out to be a questionable plus. When I was on the phone I would swivel my chair to face the outside. I would speak openly and freely about programs, personalities and other matters in the privacy of my office. Then I would hear the toilet flush and realize that one of my fellow executives had slithered into my private privy. I immediately had to review my conversation while it was still going on. What had I said? Who had I possibility insulted? Who was going to emerge from the john? A network is a perilous workplace!

It is also, as indicated, a curiously convoluted one with its own peculiar personality. In the halcyon days of the '70s, when even a second place network was rolling in dough, a person at my level was entitled to fly First Class anywhere. I was delighted to take advantage of the frequent transcontinental flights in first. I was also delighted to stay at the Bel Air or the Beverly Hills hotels on the NBC tab.

As time went on, the ratings for our programs remained firmly fixed in last place. I finally decided that we would dump all eight series and start with a totally new slate. There were certainly risks involved. At least these ongoing shows had a following—albeit inadequate. Starting a new show meant getting kids to at least sample the shows and compare them against the ones they seemed to prefer on the other two networks. On the other hand, I reasoned, it was more likely that I would get a couple of hits out of eight than out of, say, four. If I could get two or three shows that worked, I could use those as the building blocks for season two, and so on. That decision raised some eyebrows around the program department. No one had ever tried anything like that. It was bold enough to merit a separate piece in Variety.

Although I only had eight slots to fill, I met with a multiple of potential suppliers. I wanted to break out of animation only on my schedule. When I grew up, my world was filled with radio serials, codes and secret rings. Why wouldn't that work again? At my urging a producer created a "gang" adventure show where the kids became the detectives. The idea would be to run the story lines in three or four week units so that the end of each of the programs would leave the kids in a perilous plight, to be resolved next week. That's what lured us back every week to the movie houses—to see how the hero of the weekly adventure serial dramas got out of the last plight. Aha, but we were in a new age. I had inherited a panel of academic advisors from Yale and Harvard and Stamford. They, and our continuity acceptance people, were concerned that we might be putting some of our audience into stressful psychological traumas. When I tried to argue the going that most of my audience would be perfectly fine with this format, they alluded to the, perhaps, 5% who were not emotionally stable. This set up a continuing concern for me. Was I programming to protect that 5% or was I programming for the 95%? It was a dilemma I never successfully resolved in my time as Veep. I slotted the gang show, but had to soften the cliff-hanger endings. The show did not catch on in its one-season run, but I still think it was a good idea.

The advisory panel, which I really bristled at, I later came to value. They used a light hand and their observations were usually well taken. I had taken pains to pass the word to my producers, that if a woman was a character, I wanted her to be more than just a mother. I wanted, if possible, to have her be a professional with a career. When Scheimer-Prescott created a super hero animated show, I suggested that they add a woman superhero. I wanted to use these images to allow our young girls in the audience to have role models as they were being entertained. When I got a note from one of my advisors that he had a problem concerning the depiction of women, I was pissed before we talked. After all, I had already been out there promulgating good things—how could they even question me? When we spoke he informed me that it was not with the lead characters they had a problem, but the background characters that peopled each episode. Their research, he said, showed that 90% of these characters were male. I realized I had paid no attention to these characters in terms of their sexual identity.

"For instance," he continued, "in the scene where the principals walk into the hardware store, why can't the owner be a woman?"

"No reason at all," I admitted.

So that got me thinking. How was it that across the entire spectrum of my shows, this held true. I went upstream to check on the source. It did not take long to find that 90% of the writers were men. No one set out to make 90% of the characters men, it was just that the guy writers lived in a guy world and that's what came to hand. I took it one step further and realized that 100% of the production companies with which I was dealing were owned and run by men. I passed word to my staff that the next year, I wanted 50% of the writers to be female and, if possible, I wanted to find at least one company that was either run by a woman or at least had women in senior positions. Alas, as it turns out, I never did get to that second year.

I was proud of the interstitial 90-second pieces we created for the series called "The Junior Hall of Fame." It featured young people who had done something noteworthy. We had several categories: overcoming a handicap, service to the community, heroism, etc. We hired Alan Landsburg, an intelligent and successful producer in Los Angeles, to produce the series. We asked our affiliate stations to nominate kids in their area and we reached out to the Boys and Girl Clubs. Then Alan sent a crew on the road for three months to tape the stories.

The other innovation was to carve out time and money for four specials. One was on pro football with some wonderful sidebar and feature bits, including a poem about mud, showing football players sliding, wallowing and slipping during games played under horrible conditions. This particular show started when I had made my first presentation to the affiliates, an annual even each network conducted to let their stations get a preview of what they would be carrying—and selling—in the following season. When I was finished with the presentation, Don Ohlmeyer who was a young man running NBC sports, came up to me and said, "I'd like to work with you." Bingo. Next thing, he is agreeing to produce a one-hour sports special for kids for $75,000. For years to come, any-time I ran into Don, the first thing he would say, with a shake of his head, was "I can't believe I did that for $75,000." Don became President of NBC sports and a very important part of that corporation.

Oh, and after my presentation, Herb Schlosser, President of NBC, shook my hand and said, "Why don't you show the Prime Time people how to do it." I reminded Herb that I hadn't even gotten my first sched-ule started and maybe it might be a good idea to let me figure out my new job first. I was struck by the casual way I was invited to butt into the experienced hands dealing with the nighttime schedule by Herb—who primarily was a financial expert.

Other anomalies of life inside a network began to surface. I was in-formed that all our proposals for program series were being "concept tested" by NBC's research department—on children between the ages of 8 and 12. And it was coming out of my budget. Really? I found out that they were showing young kids storyboards, telling them something of the story, and asking them if they would watch. Then with their magi-cally and mysterious mathematical skills they would come up with three classifications reflecting the probability of success or failure. Research was apparently quite convinced that I had but to follow their predictions and we would rule the kid's world. I pointed out to them that kids of 8 or 9 do not conceptualize—that without the voices and sound effects and music and animation, there is no way for a kid to know the impact or watchability of a program. I was unwilling to even consider that re-searchers using this methodology, with no insight into how children's mind work and no experience in working with them were deigning to tell me what to do.

I set my staff to reviewing the past five years of their high, medium and low ratings against how shows actually performed and found, to my delight, zero—ZERO—correlation. It all came to a head with a meeting involving the head of NBC research and two of his merry band, myself and two of my staff and Bob Howard, the NBC head of entertainment.

As the meeting progressed, I had the impression of the research trio as the three witches in "Macbeth." They kept stirring the cauldron and pulling out numbers. Margaret Loesch had been around for while and knew the numbers and the history of each show. Each time we shot down one of their theories, they would reach into their cauldron and pull out another set of statistics. It went on for about an hour, at which point Bob Howard turned to me with a hint of a smile and said, "Do what you want." I had won this battle—but I had burned a few more bridges.

I ran into another bureaucratic roadblock trying to help my schedule. I checked on how our affiliates were clearing the Saturday time periods—8 AM to 1 PM—for my schedule of half-hour and one-hour live and animated shows. I found that some of the markets were cutting away from the network in the middle of the morning to carry other shows—primarily stuff on their shelves they had bought and wanted to burn off before they lost their investment in the properties. I called affiliate relations—I was getting somewhat more sophisticated about working within the system—and asked if they could help me reach the right person at the various stations. They did give me the leads and so I proceeded to call some of the larger markets. I tried to persuade them to carry the entire schedule, but if they had to shorten the Saturday schedule to please do it at the first or last hour. I started having some success with my powers of persuasion. That is until I got a call from one of my counterparts in the sports department. Turns out, some of the shows being shoved into the Saturday schedule were sports features and that department was taking umbrage at my success. I suggested if they were that concerned, they might try the same strategy I was using, instead of calling me. Another moment of scoring a moral victory.

Another bridge burned.

When we finally decided to make a deal with a producer, I turned the negotiations over to the business affairs folks. I wanted the deals closed as quickly as possible so we would have maximum time for the development and production of the series. In almost every case, the negotiations went on too long. I would call business affairs to find out what was happening and find NBC was low-balling the production company. Since by FCC law all rights for subsequent distribution remained with the production company, NBC would only pay 90% of what the production would cost the producers. The result would be that for the triumph of getting a show on the network, the production company would be guaranteed to lose money—unless the show was a hit for five years and could create enough product for subsequent distribution.

I knew exactly what would happen, since I had been an independent producer. I tried to explain to the business affairs people that all those wonderful scenes on the story boards would start being eliminated to bring the production companies' costs into line with what they would be receiving. I told the NBC money people that I was on the side of the producers. It still took too long and, in many cases, was too little. In the end we were cheating the kids out of the better quality productions they deserved. Knowing this would be the case I was still appalled when I started getting the programs from the producer of "I Am the Greatest," the half hour adventure show featuring the animated version of Mohammed Ali, who at this time, was undoubtedly, the best known man in the world. I had gone out on a limb on this one—Ali doing his own audio dialogue and using a new producer located in Hawaii. When I screened the shows I knew they were not putting their production budget on the screen. I showed the product to a few people in the business, without revealing the name of the production company, and received the same judgment. After pushing for corrections and better production, I finally decided to cut off any further funding for the series until they redid those shows already produced and agreed to raise the standard for the rest.

When I went to my bosses with this plan, they looked at me as though I was an alien from another weird planet. One did not do that in mid-production. I suggested that maybe that's why there was so much bad product on TV. Business affairs wondered if I could do this and the lawyers were nervous—but then lawyers were always nervous. I finally got the kind of go-ahead that implied I was out there by myself on this one. I sent out the requisite notices cutting off further payments until they satisfied our standards. It did not take long for the phone to ring and a very angry voice—that of the producer's lawyer, Dixon Dern—to start screaming that I had no right to do this and that he was going to sue me and NBC-TV for 50 million dollars. I don't think he actually said that I would never work in this town again, but that was clearly implicit in the threats that were being hurled at me. I took a breath and quietly explained my reasons and how this impasse could be solved. After a few days, the producer agreed to fly in to meet with me and go over the storyboards and the produced shows. I ended up practically re-directing some of the sequences. Considering how little I knew about animation when I started this job some months earlier, I was either a quick study or an arrogant SOB. We did finally improve the production from awful to almost adequate.

Working with Ali did give me a chance to know this complex person. I traveled with him and his family in their van. I was at his training camp. And I rode with him the morning after a fight, which, when he had been in his prime, he would have finished in two or three rounds at the most. It took a decision, once the fight took 12 rounds, for him to retain his title. It was clear that he was slipping with each fight. When I picked him up at his hotel, it was early in the day and we were on the way to an audio record session. He slumped in the passenger seat, all the sass and bravado we associated with him absent. In this intimate moment I asked him, "Champ, why do you do it? Why do you keep fighting?"

In a quiet and subdued voice he began to speak of his fear of ending up like so many of the boxers he knew—broken physically and broke financially. By now he had made a lot of money, but in his mind, being surrounded by these broken men, the ghastly possibilities that haunted him were forcing him to continue fighting. He spoke of getting a 'Jew' financial adviser—the use of that word was one implying a really smart person. He spoke of how he was buying real estate and so on. It was a revealing and poignant conversation. I had seen the other sides of Ali; the mischievous side; the ego-maniacal side. This was the side very few had experienced.

I recall a wonderful moment when Ali, and the others who were involved in the production of a TV Special we were creating to introduce our schedule. We were walking along Central Park South in NYC on the way to lunch. As part of the production we were using celebrity look-alikes. One looked remarkably like Telly Savalas who at that time had the lead on a very popular detective series, "Kojak." Ali insisted that the Kojak look-alike walk a few paces ahead of him so that Ali could see how people rushed up to him, and he, Ali, could enjoy how they were fooled. The trouble was, all the oncoming people saw was the self-proclaimed most famous man in the world, Mohammed Ali. They rushed past the ersatz Savalas screaming Ali's name. Ali was getting more and more pissed. His ploy didn't working because, of course, he WAS the most famous man in the world!

When the 1977–78 schedules were revealed by all three networks, I was looking at a most unusual configuration. There in the middle of the CBS Saturday morning schedule was "Way Out Games," starring your congenial host, Sonny Fox. Against it was an NBC show, picked and scheduled by your congenial NBC VP, Sonny Fox. Who was I going to root for? As we approached the start of the season, I couldn't stand being around when my go-for-broke gamble was finally put to the test. A week before we went on the air, I flew to England and to Bristol where, in partnership with a British production company, we were filming a live action adventure series. The Saturday we premiered, I was in a pub in Bristol eating lunch and idling away at a slot machine trying to line up three cherries. Finally, I could not stand it any longer. I phoned Margaret back in New York and was given the news that we had come in last in every time slot. Eight out of eight. When I returned to my group they asked how it had turned out. "How come," I lamented, "here I cannot get three cherries, but in the United State I got eight lemons." And, I later found out, at the time when I occupied two network slots, one as the VP on NBC and one as a performer on CBS, ABC beat us both. I lost two network slots at the same time. That is not easy to do!

I never had a chance to fix my schedule. A few months later, in the need to reduce staff by 300 bodies, NBC decided it really did not need a Children's TV VP. They found me totally resistible and gave me six-week notice and a three-movie development deal, what *Variety* would call "a multi pic-pac." About three weeks into that period I remember looking up at my schedule board that had the Saturday schedules of all three networks, and thinking, jeez, is this what my entire life has been about for the past 18 months? Suddenly it all seemed insane. It wasn't just the challenge of producing and scheduling. It was how the whole culture of the network drew you in. Your friends and co-workers were by now NBC or other network people. Everything tended to be turned in on itself. TV was a powerful force in those days and the networks were at the center of that power. I was wined and dined. I was old enough to understand that so much of this was attached to my office and was not about me. Nevertheless it could be pleasant and heady as well as intense and tiring.

CHAPTER 20

Go West,
Middle-Aged Man

When word got out that my time was ending at NBC, I got a strange call from Lou Scheimer and Norman Prescott, who owned the animation studio that produced an hour-and-a half of my five hour schedule. They both were on the phone to commiserate with me regarding my impending departure, but assured me there was *no* place for me at their shop. I had not approached them, and smiled wryly at their preemptive strike.

One call that did interest me was from Alan Landsburg. Alan had been producing the "Junior Hall of Fame" interstitial pieces for me and we had gotten to know each other socially. He was smart and had produced a large number of highly regarded documentaries before expanding into features and movies-of-the-week. He had assembled a group of able producers such as Paul Freeman and Mel Stuart, from whom I learned a great deal about producing MOWs. He invited me to join his company to develop and produce TV programming. Although I did not get the title I wanted, the money was fair, plus having an office and the support that came with being part of an established presence in West Coast TV. It also seemed like a good idea to make a fresh start, personally as well as professionally.

I was now a full-time producer. After four months in L.A., I returned to Weston and decided the time had come for a formal separation. I wanted there to be a written agreement with Gloria that would guarantee her a monthly income. She countered with her decision that if we were not going to live together, she preferred a divorce. I agreed and the terms we worked out included alimony that would only cease if she remarried. The FCC suit, which Gloria had characterized as childish nonsense, was included with Gloria to get 15% of any benefits. I was to pay for all the children's college costs.

Now came the hard part. That night, at dinner, I told my four children about the separation. The fact that I was not leaving for a woman, or Gloria for another man, and that they would be assured of our continuing love for them, I think helped. It also helped that Tracy, our youngest, was 15. Meredith was already working in L.A. and Dana had one year left of high school. They all seemed to handle it well—and, of course, it was no news to them that there had been a lot of stress and tension in our marriage. Our separation, at this point, was so affable that we agreed to hire our friend, Ron King, to represent the both of us in the Connecticut court proceedings.

So, I was now not only a Hollywood producer, but for the first time in my life, I would actually have a bachelor pad—at age 53.

While I made seven development deals with networks that first year, the project of which I was proudest was a movie-of-the-week called, "And Baby Makes Six."

Many years earlier, I had gotten to know Shelley List, who lived in Westport with her ophthalmologist husband. She had written a book about her mother that had been well received. Shelley shocked the community in the early 1970s by walking out on her marriage to carve a career for herself in Los Angeles. Sometime in 1978, Shelley and I ran into each other and she mentioned she had some ideas for a Movie of the Week, (MOW), the two-hour long form that had become a staple of network television. When she sent them to me, I told her she was still writing for reading—not for filming. She had to make that transition where events and the power of the close-up took the place of many words. She kept on working and, one day, showed me a six page treatment about a woman of 46, content in her marriage and with three children, the youngest being 16, who unexpectedly finds herself pregnant once more. The question then is whether to abort this late-in-life surprise or go through the process of raising another child at a much older age. I was intrigued since abortion was becoming much more of an issue in America, and I found Shelley's sensitivity to this dilemma really interesting. I took it to the number two executive in the MOW department at NBC and she loved it. Now came my great coup—not only selling this, but, in conspiracy with my ally at NBC, I got Shelley approved to write the screenplay. Networks were seldom inclined to risk a couple of million bucks on a neophyte writer—especially one with no screen credits of any kind.

I received less than an enthusiastic reception from Alan. I think his version of my job would have required me to check with him each step of the way. I was still operating in my usual independent mode and, although I was bringing him a really good property with a network deal to be negotiated, it was clear he was somewhat irritated. Nevertheless the deal was consummated and Alan and I were to share EP credits.

My co-host friend from "The New Yorkers," Colleen Dewhurst, was the first choice to play the lead and I was enormously delighted to be involved with her again. Warren Oates, known mainly for western themed movies, was to play her husband who, in the film, was ready to now have time to be with his wife since the kids were now grown. His character was pressing for the abortion while his wife tried to sort out her conflicting emotions. Timothy Hutton, just then known only as a young actor starting a career, was hired to play her youngest child.

Shelley wrote an astonishingly good script. I did make one suggestion that I think made an important contribution to the movie. In a scene where Colleen's daughter is trying on dresses in a store, and her daughter is upset with her mother's reluctance to abort this pregnancy.

"But Mom, you supported the movement. You baked cookies."

And Colleen responds, "But that was for the right of a woman to have a choice. One can choose to have an abortion, but also one can choose NOT to have an abortion."

I did not want to be carried of on the shoulders of the Right to Lifers.

Production started, and despite my EP credit, I was relegated to a back seat. I did not mind since I was a novice in this part of production and was grateful having a hand in the scripting and in making my comments heard after screening the dailies. When NBC looked at the rough cut, they understood that this was a special production. Word came back that they wanted to have everyone signed to a series and that they might order this for their next prime time schedule. Wow! My first production—a series—and I had a 25% interest in the property. I think I started practicing preening. But first I had to head out to South Salem, N.Y. to convince Colleen that she should commit to something she had never agreed to before. She agreed. When the movie was played on NBC-TV it won the night and sterling reviews. When the following May came around and NBC was getting ready to announce its schedule, word came back to us that our show was scheduled for Thursdays at 10 PM. I double checked with N.Y. on the Friday before the Monday announcement and, yes, we were still in there on Thursday nights.

A funny thing happened on the way to fame and fortune. On Monday, NBC announced that a Universal TV show, "Mrs. Columbo," a spin-off of Peter Falk's lovable character, was to be their 10 PM Thursday show. What happened? There was a notorious connection between Universal TV and NBC involving Bob Kinter, NBC chief, and Lew Wasserman, head of Universal. Whether it was based on the leverage Wasserman had to give NBC shows it needed to buttress its schedule, or other reasons, clearly people in the know were not surprised at this switch. "Mrs. Columbo" disappeared quickly, but Colleen never made it on with this series.

Later, after I had left Landsburg, CBS picked up the story for a sequel called, "And Baby Comes Home." The script was again written by Shelley List and, since I still retained an interest in the property, I was sent a copy of the script. My heart sank. A major plot line was the post-partum depression of Colleen's character, which clinically can be an outcome. However, to put Colleen Dewhurst's energy into that black hole was, it seemed to me, the worst use of her indomitable spirit. Indeed it worked out that way, and was the end of the line for this promising adventure.

Alan Landsburg came to me one day and said, "NBC wants to work with a particular writer-director. Can we use one of your three slots on your NBC deal to produce this—you will be the Co-Executive Producer."

Someone at NBC had decided the writer-director was a genius on the order of Orson Welles. I agreed, and entered into a really weird adventure. First of all the movie, "The Mysterious Two," was based on one of those news stories no one was ever able to pin down, telling of strange extra terrestrial goings-on in the Nevada Desert. According to this story, numbers of people were selected to leave behind all their possessions and families and embark on an expedition to meet up with a mysterious rocket ship, and were never heard from again. The foggy, ill-defined story line created a lot of headaches for me. I began to understand why Alan had turned this one over to me. I never did understand it as we worked on the story and script for five months. John Forsythe was cast as the male lead. As I sat in on readings for the other parts, I would read the part that was not being auditioned. After several days of this, the director said to me, "you are a performer, why don't you play this part. We can save some money and you will be great." Ego is a terrible thing to have lurking around. At moments like this, logic is totally swamped by the prospect of dazzling the audience. When I pointed out I was not a member of the Screen Actors Guild, he assured me the show would pay my $2200 initiation fee and then pay me scale for my efforts. So for the good of the movie, I reluctantly agreed.

What I had totally overlooked regarding my acting debut in a Movie of the Week was that most of my scenes were to be shot at night. For a week my call was from 6 PM to 6 AM. My make up was a large puff filled with dirt. And what made this even more a problem was that a couple of months earlier I had come to the end of my year contract with Alan's company.

We both came to the conclusion that I was not a comfortable fit for working within his company. I could make deals, but when it came to producing the movies I became more of an onlooker than a producer. Fair enough—he and his principal production staff had far more experience than I did in the actual hands-on work of getting a movie cast, filmed edited and delivered on budget. On the other hand, I chafed at not being in control of the way the script was revised and some of the casting decisions. After 25 years in the business I really was itching to have my own company and take my chances. Alan offered to put up the money for that company in return for first look at any projects, but I really wanted to start clean. I had a couple of people who were willing to put up some substantial money to start me off—the kind of backers who would allow me to be in control.

So I had rented an office and was in the process of becoming Sonny Fox Productions at exactly the time this production of "The Mysterious Two" was underway in 1979. When I came off the set at 6 AM, I went straight to my new office. I was the grubbiest looking, worst smelling independent producer in Los Angeles.

I never understood what the movie was about as it took shape. I did not understand it as it was being filmed. I left Alan's Landsburg before it was edited. Surely, I thought, after careful editing, I will discover the deeper, hidden message. Landsburg sent me a DVD. I watched it and discovered it was still incomprehensible. And I was wildly over-acting. How bad was it? It was so bad that NBC put in on the shelf for nearly three years. Almost two million bucks sitting on a shelf, until one day, reading the TV schedule, I noted that NBC was actually going to play it that night. I suppose the accountants had pointed out they were coming to the end of their time to screen it under their contract, and had pushed to burn it off. I made a silent bet that it would win the night. The premise was intriguing and people would not understand that they would not understand it, until too late. It won the night. Worse, it was re-aired at three or four in the morning for a while. Each time I would get a call from a friend announcing that he/she had been unable to sleep, flipped on the set and, "there you were in the film. I tuned in the middle. What was it about?"

"It was about two hours. I have no idea what it was about!"

I seldom heard of reruns of "And Baby Makes Six." Only "The Mysterious *damn* Two." For many years, I would hold it over John Forsythe's head if I needed him to do me a favor.

"John, if you don't do this gig for me, I will remind people you starred in 'The Mysterious Two'." A very effective form of blackmail!

CHAPTER 21

Sonny Fox Productions

I hired my former teaching assistant at Stony Brook, David Eagle, to be my number two at Sonny Fox Productions and, over some months, ended up with a small staff of five.

Although I tried for a while to make development deals for Movie of the Week properties or sit-com pilots, I came to realize the thinness of my bona fides in those areas. In series development, the network was not only looking at your pilot episode, but for some assurance that you could keep delivering 22 reasonable high quality episodes year after year. With no experience to offer that would assure a network maven, I realized my chances of breaking through in these areas were slim. So SFP evolved into a small shop dedicated to creating specialized programs that the bigger companies would not want to spend their time on, but for which there were markets.

In 1980, I was approached by a young man named Jim Cross, who told me he had been in conversation with Carol Serling, Rod Serling's widow, seeking her cooperation to obtain the rights to replay Rod's 1957 production of Requiem for a Heavyweight, the second production of CBS' Television Playhouse 90 series. I recognized at once that a TV series bringing back those remarkable dramas of the 1953–1958 era we often referred to as the Golden Age of Television would, if possible, make for an important contribution to the history of our medium, as well as being eminently watchable. In recognition of the fact that Jim had brought the idea in, I hired him as an associate producer on the series. We decided to use Requiem as a pilot for the series and pitched it to the PBS stations. They found the idea entirely resistible.

I was approached by a company in Boston that distributed programs individually to PBS stations. They had heard the pitch and wanted to try it. The budget they gave us was so small I had to deficit finance the pilot. Now came the really interesting part. First I had to find the best kinescope. In the 1950s there were no videotape machines. When live programs were aired at 9 PM in New York, it would, of course be 3 hours earlier on the West Coast. In order to delay the program, a means of recording the feed off the air had to be developed. Engineers adapted a 16 MM black and white film camera to the 30 frames a second TV timing from the normal 24 frames per second of a film camera. They then filmed the program off the face of a TV tube and "hot" developed it so that it would be ready to be aired at 9 PM PST.

Since these programs were to be broadcast live, and seen only once, the kines were regarded as having little or no value after they were aired. Twenty-five years later, when we started asking the networks for their copies, we were dismayed to learn that many had been discarded or lost. We found some in archives, such as the UCLA one, and even in private hands. Fortunately, there were a few of "Requiem for a Heavyweight." We put the best ones through an ultra-sound cleaning process. Actually, I was amazed that after such careless handling of such a primitive recording device, we were able to come up with versions acceptable to the stations.

Now came the really hard part. My first stop was at CBS to ask them their position on the use of the kinescope. The underlying rights had long since passed on to Serling as the author, but that spoke only to a new production. CBS claimed ownership of the property. On the basis of their claim I agreed to share profits with them. Subsequently NBC would also claim ownership. ABC said they had no ownership interest in these properties. "Don't forget to run our copyright at the end of the credits," said the CBS person. I did not remember seeing such, so I ran the end credits again. There was no copyright notice. We checked lawyers in DC who specialized in copyright notices. There appeared to be no copyrights on these productions. The premise of the networks at that time was that there was no ongoing property right involved since at the end of the program, that performance would disappear forever. Thus before 1959, there was no such thing as residuals—payments for subsequent use of a program—since the unions were dealing with live TV.

Since I did want to play fair with the writers and directors and performers, and since there was no template for how to proceed, I had to visit each union and guild to figure out how to make this work. My first stop was AFTRA actor's union, of which I had been a member for decades. They had no idea how to handle this either, so we sat around the table and invented a format that recognized the modest amount of money this series would spin off and, appreciating the fact that I had approached them to create a fair way to deal with this, we arrived at a very workable deal. I was to pay 75% of the then day rate. This figured out to be $187.50 for each principal—less for under five lines.

Ah, but then came the kicker. Since the performers had not agreed to this deal—it having just been invented—we would have to get "current consent." This meant finding every actor of every show we used—or their estate—and get a signed release accepting this deal. Getting the performers to agree was not the problem—finding them all after 25 years was the problem. We agreed to make "best efforts" and, indeed, were to spend a large amount of time finding the approximately twenty-two performers times nine shows. It turned out that in all our dealings, only one actor demanded a substantially larger amount—Mickey Rooney. He was still angry that all those movies he made at MGM—all the Andy Hardy movies and all the "My dad has a barn, let's put on a show" musicals that had made so much money for the studio, but none of the performers got residual payments. Rooney had been at war over this fact for decades and now, he'd decided, this was going to be his get-even time. As I dealt with his lawyer and explained that his price just about matched the entire budget for the project, I got the lawyer's sympathy, but no agreement from Mickey. I really wanted to include his remarkable performance as an ego-maniacal star of a comic variety show, "The Comedian," directed by a young John Frankenheimer. Finally, after months of persuasion and, I think, whining, we came to terms and the "most favored nation" agreement, where no performer got more than anyone else, was maintained.

The crazy quilt of how to treat these kines continued as I moved on to other guilds and unions. The Writer's Guild decided they had no rights in the matter since there were no pre-agreements; I was free to make any deal I wanted with the writers. The Director's Guild, likewise, said nothing was due to the directors for a PBS showing.

So, finally we were able to get on with the series. We made up lists of possible dramas from the era and hunted down the kinescopes. In some cases, alas, there seemed to be none available. I got a call one day from Reginald Rose, one of the most formidable writers of that time, wanting to be included in the series with one of his shows. I wanted to use the original "Twelve Angry Men." We kept finding only one of the two reels of film. I finally called Reggie and asked, in view of the fact we only had that one reel, would it be alright to present "Six Pissed-Off Jurors." Reggie didn't think that was funny either.

One truth I discovered as we screened more than 60 possible programs; not everything in the Golden Age was golden. And even those I remembered as compelling when I viewed them 25 years prior turned out not to have worn well. That was especially true of stories that were anchored to specific events of the period. The programs that had lasting power were about a fat, little man trying to get a date (Marty), or two people who love each other and then end up loving the bottle more than each other (Days of Wine and Roses). Even today those plays and those characters are affecting. They are of timeless personal struggles with which we are still dealing.

There were no sound stages or back lots in New York then. We had radio studios and small theaters that had been converted for TV shows. The result is that the shooting spaces were small. Crowd three or four cameras, lights, mike booms, crew and actors, and it got REALLY small. Imagine the ballet of cameras weaving around to set up for their next shot and actors scurrying to the next set with a change of costume en-route and you understand the constrictions placed on the directors. Partly because of these space limitations, a scene would be staged so that for minutes at a time the camera would hold on a two shot, while an in-tense emotional interchange played out. The result was an intensity that made "Marty" or "The Comedian" or "Patterns" the immediate hits they became and, when watching it today, still pack an emotional wallop. All that emotion could not escape into a larger space.

The second critical factor I was reminded of was that the writers were coming out of drama schools. Nobody got his or her skills by attending a TV academy or taking a college course, on writing for television. There could be no car crashes or transformations into aliens or other hallmarks of today's movies and TV. There were pages of dialogue. They were lit-erate and intimate. Today if a scene runs more than half a page, produc-ers get nervous that the audience will be bored. So words were important. If you were to play a Chayefsky character, for instance, you didn't have to work hard on becoming that character; all you had to do was say the lines. He built the characterizations into his writing. In "Marty" there is a scene where Marty's Italian mother is pointing out the inadequacy of the place her sister is sharing by saying "Whatta you got here? Three skinny rooms." Skinny! Not small or tiny. After all what is the worst thing an Italian mother can say about someone—skinny!

We finally picked nine of the best productions for which there were ac-ceptable kines and, after "Requiem" was well received, plunged ahead. To make room for the prologues we planned, we dumped the commercials and promos from the original airings. That opened up anywhere from 8 to 15 minutes. Then we found the actors, directors, writers and producers who made those plays happen 25 years earlier and invited them to talk of what it was like in live TV. What we tapped into was not just a recitation of events, but a deep well of emotional connections back to when the medium was new, and live TV production was full of hazards—but also filled with the emerging creative energies that would shape our motion pictures and theater for years. When you watch these prologues, you hear Jack Klugman and Johnny Frankenheimer, Jack Palance and Keenan Wynn, Julie Harris and Mel Torme, Chris Plummer, Jason Robards, Del Mann, PJ Miller, Cliff Robertson, Piper Laurie and, yes, even Mickey Rooney, recreating that period when every night was opening night and every night was closing night, too.

To get to meet all of these people—to hear their stories—to become friends with Del Mann and to work with him on a movie with Julie Harris and a "Celebration of the Golden Age for a TV" special that garnered an EMMY, surely I had far surpassed anything I ever dreamed of as that kid in Brooklyn. The reception of our series was enormously satisfying. *Time* magazine devoted an entire page to the series. The title of the article was "There Really Was Gold in the Golden Age."

About the time the Golden age series was in distribution, I received a call from WCAU TV in Philadelphia informing me that they were going to be celebrating the station's 40th anniversary and had decided to make a new production of "The Days of Wine and Roses" as a highlight of this celebration, and could I put them in touch with the writer of that property. I was impressed with their concept, but asked them if a local TV station had the budget for such an ambitious undertaking.

"Oh," the caller replied, "we have a very good amateur acting group here that will perform it."

"Aha—I see. I will certainly send you the contact information for JP Miller, the author, but I am not sure how thrilled he will be to have the first new TV production of this classic performed by an amateur group."

I then went on to remind them that those rights were probably tied up with the company that had produced the film version.

"So what would you suggest?" was the question finally presented to me.

As always, when invited in, I will accept.

"I would pick some scenes from a classic such as Petrified Forest, I would follow the entire process of putting on a live drama production as had not been done in decades on national—no less—local TV and, finally, end with a live performance of two or three scenes."

Which is exactly how it came to pass and how I won an EMMY.

In 1955, NBC had presented a live two-hour version of this stage play. It starred Humphrey Bogart in the role that had made him a star in the Broadway production and, subsequently, in the movie. Now here he was, a year before he died, performing it —live—on TV. He undertook this exhausting work as a favor to his wife, Lauren Bacall, who, having retired from acting to have their family was now itching to get back to being an actress. This was her calling card, even though she was too old for the part of the teen-age character.

In that 1956 version there were three hoods, one of whom was played by a young actor named Jack Klugman. In looking for the programs I wanted to present on "the Golden Age of TV," I had desperately tried to find a copy of that tape, but was unsuccessful until I was told casually by a friend, "Oh Betty has one." That would be Ms. Bacall. I had called her agent and they finally agreed to screen it for me. They invited someone from NBC to sit in, since the copy had originally come from them.

After the screening, I decided this would be a great addition to my series and so informed her. NBC responded by saying it was their property and I could not have it—even though they had not looked for it or known it existed until I unearthed it. I called Bacall's agent and said, "It was 'lost' before I called you. As far as I am concerned, you can 'lose' it again!"

So I had the back-story on that property when the WCAU phone call came in. WCAU called back and said they wanted me to produce the show I had invented in our first phone conversation. I now had to start the work to deliver. My first call was to Jack Klugman.

"Jack, 20 years ago you were in the Bogart TV production of 'Petrified Forest.' You played the part of the hood, Jackie. How would you like to play Duke [the Bogart role]?"

There was a quick intake of breath. The deal was done right there.

I then called his agent. When I mentioned the project—and the price—he responded, "He gets more than that in the silences of the commercials he does." He paused, and then added, "You already called him, didn't you."

"Of course. If I started with you I would have been DOA."

With Klugman in hand, I the sought out the writer Tad Mosel, who had adapted the piece for TV, and whose rights I would have to acquire. Tad was one of those wonderfully talented creators of the Golden Age and he was delighted to make the rights available. He also agreed to attend the week of shooting and would write and speak the narrative for the three live scenes.

As the narrator for the live sequences we brought EG Marshall aboard.

Finally, I went to the director of that 1955 production, Del Mann, and asked him to repeat the way live drama happened in the 1950s—and to direct the final 20 minutes of the live drama telecast. At first the thought of going through those anxiety ridden times yet again spooked Del. However, the idea of being reunited with EG, Jack and Tad, won him over.

So we embarked on the casting, in New York and Philadelphia. We could not afford any 'name' players, but the casting went well. So here we were, at WCAU TV, where the usual experience for the cameramen and boom operators was doing the news or cooking shows or remotes. In a week they had to learn how to move without getting in the way of the performer—or each other. The boom operator had to accept the concept that there were no lavaliere or wireless mikes—it was all on him.

As the week progressed, there were the memories recalled by Klugman and Marshall and Mosel—how it used to be, along with working under the direction of the director who had all those years ago, directed Bogart and Bacall in these same scenes—and on the same set reproduced from the original designs.

We taped all of this day after day, right until dress rehearsal. We kept editing right until the show started. We were able to track the entire process for 40 minutes and then go live with the three scenes.

And we got an EMMY!

THE SONGWRITERS

One of the most delightful productions of that period was "The Songwriters," a series that ended up largely on CBS Cable, a new, and short-lived, cable network in the early 1980s.

Based on Maurice Levine's long running Lyrics and Lyricists series at the 92nd Street Y in New York, we produced eight one-hour shows that presented some of the greatest composers and lyricists of what has become known as "The American Songbook."

Alan Jay Lerner, librettist and lyricist for "My Fair Lady," "Camelot" and "Gigi," among others; Kander and Ebb, the team that gave us "Chicago" and "Cabaret"; EY "Yip" Harburg, who wrote lyrics for Broadway scores and for "The Wizard of Oz," as well as a trunkful of some our most memorable songs; Burton Lane, the composer who worked with Harburg on "Finian's Rainbow" and with Lerner on the movie "Easter Parade"; Charles Strouse, composer for "Bye-Bye Birdie," "Annie," "Golden Boy," "Applause" and the theme for the TV series, "All in the Family"; Arthur Schwartz, composer for many movie scores and songs such as "Dancing in the Dark," and "That's Entertainment"; Mitch Parish, a true Tin Pan Alley lyric writer whose catalog contains "Deep Purple," "Stars Fell on Alabama" and "Stardust"; Sheldon Harnick, lyricist for "Fiorello" and "Fiddler on the Roof."

The chance to get to know these remarkably talented men, to work with them and, later, have them as friends made this project a reward beyond the professional satisfaction it gave me. Although the format remained the same from show to show—each featured a composer/lyricist hosting the hour, sharing anecdotes, insights and singing his sons, assisted by two or three other singers and a backup quartet (with the exception of Kander and Ebb—more of this later)—each of the hours took on a different personality deriving from that of the personality of the host and his unique musical talent.

Edward "Yip" Harburg, who was in his eighties when I met him, had an elfin charm about him. His narratives and his energy reflected this. Although his voice was quavery and his meter somewhat difficult for the backup group to follow, when he sang/recited the lyric to "Over the Rainbow," it was as if I was hearing it for the first time. This proved to be true of so many of the performances—especially by the lyricists. They wrote the words. When they performed them, it was not about elaborate musical arrangements, or soaring lovely voices. Yip had written "Brother Can You Spare a Dime" in the 1930s. It was the anthem of the depression, but over the years had lost its significance. When, in 1980, Yip performed those words in our studio in Toronto, I understood the toll the depression had taken. The song was about bewilderment. Yip wrote this song with his partner, Jay Gorney, in 1931. Subsequently, Jay's wife Edie divorced him and married Yip Harburg. Edie used to declare, "I never marry a man unless he wrote 'Brother Can You Spare a Dime'."

The words were so significant in each of our shows, that I instructed our director to stay on the performer so as to not dislocate the attention of the viewer from the words. If you ever get to view any of these shows, I think consciously or not, you will get to hear lyrics as you have seldom heard them before. We put our guests through a pretty tough schedule in producing these shows. Yip arrived in Toronto the night before his taping. We had rehearsed with him in New York and his pianist was on hand for the recording. We rehearsed on camera the next morning and in the afternoon we taped the show before an audience. We took a dinner break, brought in another audience and did the show again. This way we had some editing choices in compiling the better of the two performances. Thus it was, at the second taping about 11 PM, when, after a break to put on a new reel of tape, we could not find Yip. The man was in his mid eighties. It had been a tough grind. I flashed on him laid out somewhere, drained by the rigors of the taping. After a few minutes of searching word came back that they had found Yip jogging around the area outside the studio. When we finally wrapped the show, Yip wanted to know who was prepared to show him around town— preferably some comely young women. He went out on the town. I went to bed.

Not too much later, on March 5 1981, I had a lunch date with Yip at the Beverly Hills Hotel. I arrived, waited for 40 minutes and Yip never showed up. I returned home and called the friend at whose home he had been staying. He confirmed that Yip had left to join me. He got into his car and traced the route Yip would have taken and found no trace of him. He drove to my apartment and we sat and chatted with growing apprehension. At 3:30 the phone rang. It was the coroner's office. They had the body of an older gentleman and in his pocket was my phone number. We drove to the location and identified the body. Yip had apparently had a heart attack. His car had drifted across lanes and hit another car. No one in the other car was hurt and there were no injuries to Yip to change our assumption that he was dead before the cars hit. I have always been grateful to have known and worked with this remarkable person. It was just too short a time.

Alan Jay Lerner wanted his show with everyone dressed in formal attire. By now we had moved the tapings to New York at the Henry Hudson Theater, where 30 years earlier I had hosted "The Price Is Right." Instead of adding the other instruments to the piano in post production, Alan wanted all the instruments there for the tapings. And on hand, as one of the performers, was a lovely English singer, Liz Robertson, Alan's eighth wife. You read that right! Alan was obviously not only a gifted lyricist and a wonderful raconteur, he was a serial husband. The cost to him was considerable. Having to settle with seven previous divorces—and his third was a French lawyer who apparently did quite well for herself—Alan could no longer live in the United States. There were so many tax liens against him here that, as he told me at one of our subsequent encounters, any money coming in from the licensing of his compositions went to the Isle of Man, an English tax haven. Once a month, a man traveled to London with a carpet bag filled with Alan's monthly allocation of cash. Alan was also a gambler. One evening after dinner, Alan took me to the lovely casino at the Ritz Hotel. While I enjoyed a bit of blackjack, Alan was off playing some other game of chance while Liz hovered over him, anxious that he not repeat his expensive experiences of the past.

I also learned an interesting lesson about how husbands deal with their performer-wives on location. In programming the material for the hour program, Alan put in a song from a show that was under development—"1600 Pennsylvania Ave."—for Liz to sing. In the song were two very high and very exposed soprano notes. During each of the tapings, Liz could not make it to those notes. She missed them by a full tone. When the audience left after the second taping, we stayed for pickups—to correct any shortfall during the tapings. I watched for Alan to point out this problem. He said nothing. Clearly he had heard it, and just as clearly he was not up to mentioning it. A week later we brought Liz back to do some looping, singing to the recorded articulation on the tape, which she did very well.

Liz was a wonderful performer and quite a bit younger than Alan. One day I was in New York on business and knew the Alan was at a hotel in town. I called him and asked if he wanted to have lunch. He couldn't, he explained, because of a previous commitment.

"But I can" came the voice of Liz on and extension. So she and I made a date to meet at the hotel for lunch. Alan, on his way out for his appointment, stopped off to say hello—but I know it was to assure himself that his much younger wife really was having lunch.

Alan was delightful to know and a brilliant book writer. Just as with every composer or lyricist, Alan had a property that gnawed at him. Yip hated the movie version of "Finian's Rainbow" with Gene Kelley and Fred Astaire, two brilliant performers too old for the parts. Richard Rodgers used to speak to me of the show that followed "Oklahoma," "Allegro," that failed. For Alan it was the movie version of the first Lerner and Lowe Broadway success, "Paint Your Wagon." The film version starred a young Clint Eastwood in a singing role. You don't have to rush out a get a copy. Take my word for it—it was a classic bit of miscasting.

Alan told me that Kirk Douglas wanted to star in a new version of this property. According to Lerner, Douglas had flown himself to London to sing a couple of the songs to assure Alan that he could handle the part. This sounded interesting, so I got in touch with Douglas' agent to explore this idea. I worked out a deal with the Houston Grand Opera to produce a stage version with Douglas that he would perform for three weeks, to get comfortable in the role before taping. I pursued this for six months before I came to the realization that, though Kirk Douglas was tempted, he realized that performing eight times a week before a live audience was like having unprotected sex. There is no post production to protect you—no second takes if one needed it. There is nothing more naked and exposed than taking on the leading role of an expensive Broadway show. Broadway critics wait for a Hollywood star to try to revive a fading career by crashing the sacred precincts of the theater. So, after all that time, I reluctantly abandoned that interesting venture.

John Kander and Fred Ebb represented a rare opportunity to present the entire package—composer and lyricist—in one show. John, the composer, was at the piano. Fred, the lyricist, performed most of the songs. Liza Minnelli, introducing them, described John as quiet and modest; Fred as brash and outgoing. Her description was accurate. Fred channeled the original Broadway performers as he sang "All that Jazz," "New York, New York," and "Cabaret." After editing the show, I called Fred to tell him how pleased I was with the result and added, "If you and John ever want to quit songwriting, I would like to take you on the road. You could be one of the great cabaret acts." Fred's response was, "I have four words for you. Don't hold your breath!"

Of all the programs, the Kander and Ebb show is the only one that has no backup musicians—that was one proviso for them signing on. The other was once the taping started, we were not to stop. As the show progresses, beads of perspiration are very apparent on Fred's face. We never had the chance to have him refreshed as he carried on. John later explained to me that his stage fright was so intense that if he lifted his fingers from the piano he wasn't sure he could ever get them down again.

I asked each of the performers to include an illustration of the pain that is sometimes associated with composing. There was an initial resistance to doing this since the pain tended to come from a more personal place, but eventually we did get poignant stories that added texture to the program. Fred told a story about an up-tempo song they were writing, about a bar in a small town and the people that inhabited it. While they were at work they got a call from a friend who informed them that another friend had just committed suicide. As Fred recalled, "We sat around for a couple of hours talking about it, as people do, and then went back to writing the song. It took a different turn as a result of how we felt." On the show, they then perform the song. I know where that dramatic transformation of the song happens, and I still get a chill every time I hear it change from an affable look at some of life's losers to a searing cry of despair.

Sheldon Harnick recalled being at a rehearsal of "Fiddler on the Roof" listening to a run through of the song between Tevya and his wife, "Do You Love Me?"

"Unaccountably," he recalled, "I started to sob. I finally had to leave the theater and as I walked the streets realized that I was writing about my Mother and Father's marriage—what they had and what they didn't have."

Sheldon, another giant among the theater lyricists, also had an astonishing range to his output. From his early days, writing brilliantly satiric songs reflecting the influence of Gilbert and Sullivan on his early efforts, to the lyrics on "Fiddler" that captured the culture and emotional life of a Shtetl, Sheldon brought an acute wit and sensibility to his shows. Most of his best work was in collaboration with Jerry Bock. "Fiddler" was a hit around the world. It was the longest running musical in the history of Japan. The music was specific but the humanity was universal. After Fiddler, Sheldon and Jerry had a falling out and never worked together again, which brings me to the mysterious alchemy of creative partnerships.

Alan Jay Lerner had his greatest success partnered with Frederick Lowe. When "Fritz" decided to retire to Palm Springs, Alan worked with Burton Lane and others with only modest—or no—success. Surely his creative juices still flowed, but the synergies that paired the elegant Viennese talents of Lowe with Lerner's sophisticated wit did not work nearly as well with anyone else. Richard Rodgers had a long career writing smart and sassy lyrics to the music of Larry Hart. When Hart died, Rodgers paired with the much more sentimental and elegant Oscar Hammerstein II and, mirabilis dictum, created a second career writing "Sound of Music" and "Pacific" and "Carousel"—almost operatic compositions. To be able to have two such different partners and produce two different oeuvres of such memorable quality is surely a miracle. After Hammerstein died, Rodgers still wanted desperately to get at least one more musical composed. He had cancer of the jaw by then; part of his jawbone had been removed. Clearly he heard the clock ticking as he told me of his frustration waiting for Alan Jay Lerner to produce some lyrics for him to score.

In the following years, I got to know Dick Rodgers well enough to spend time at his home in Fairfield, CT. This was a rather special place that was the dream of his wife, Dorothy, who wrote a book about it, "The House in my Head." Dorothy was a special woman in her own right having written many decorating books (and was the inventor of the "Jonny Mop"). When Rodgers took us on a tour of this home, I marveled at the spotless multi-car garage. In the basement all the equipment, air conditioning, heating etc. was redundant—two of each system, each color coded. It looked like I imagined an atomic submarine would look. Outside was a perfect croquet pitch where killer games of croquet took place.

The delightful experience of getting to know and work with these remarkable men—yes, they were all men—kept delighting and educating me. Each program reflected the persona of the featured talent. Charles Strouse was filled with the energy of a younger composer. His songs from "Bye Bye Birdie" and "Annie" were presented with verve and bounce, abetted by his composer on "Annie," Martin Charnin. His lyricist on "Birdie" and "Applause" and others was Lee Adams. After a couple of decades of success—and Lee and Charles had made a lot of money just from writing the theme for All in the Family—Lee did the same thing Fritz Lowe had done. He quit and took his family back to Ohio. It took Charles a while to find Charnin and generate his most lucrative hit, "Annie."

Mitch Parrish was the outlier in the series. Actually he was a last minute replacement for Jerry Herman who had fallen ill just before the taping of our first three shows. Maurice had done a Lyric and Lyricist show with him at the Y, so had a pretty good idea of how to quickly assemble a show built around his catalog. Mitch was the only true Tin Pan alley song writer in the series. He had written his first lyric when he was 16 and over the years had worked with a roster of the best known composers of popular music. But Mitch was not comfortable in his role as the host/performer. We did not help his feeling of security when, by scheduling him into Toronto the night of the Kander and Ebb taping, he watched them and said, "I can't do that." Their smooth and splendid hour really spooked Mitch. Of all the shows, I think I worked hardest on this one. I had to sit in the front row making eye contact with him to keep his confidence level up. In the end, his songs, "Stars Fell on Alabama," "Volare," "Deep Purple" carried the day, and when Mitch, in his hoarse tones, sang "Stardust," the song took on a personal poignancy that moved us all.

As of this writing only John Kander, Sheldon Harnick, and Charles Strouse are still alive. What a special treasure it was to have known these remarkable artists. I consider these experiences to be high among the reasons I have so enjoyed my career. It would be hard to overestimate the extraordinary work of these talents, who created whole worlds in the theater and in the motion pictures over a period of years.

PRODUCING BRONTE

This 1984 production actually had its roots in 1968. While being paired with a different co-host on "The New Yorkers," the daily two-and-a-half-hour variety show on Channel 5, I had the great pleasure of working for a week with Julie Harris, arguably the premiere American actress. I had first seen Julie as the 12 year-old Frankie in "Member of the Wedding" in the theater. I had enjoyed her deepening talents as she undertook roles such as Joan of Arc, Sally Bowles in "I Am a Camera" (later to become the musical, "Cabaret"), and in "East of Eden" with James Dean.

I had co-hosted "The New Yorkers" with her for a week, and I also dealt with Julie when we chose the Golden Age drama she had starred in; "A Doll's House" with Christopher Plummer and Jason Robards. Julie was the host of one of these shows on our "Golden Age" series, and we also taped her memories of working on "A Doll's House." I found her a most gentle and caring person. Although somewhat shy and certainly not assertive, when she was reciting poetry or performing she could be luminous and intense. As our friendship developed beyond the week on the show, I asked Julie if there was some role she had always wanted to play.

"Peter Pan. Not the musical, but the darker Peter Pan of the book."

The prospect of being involved with Julie Harris and making it possible for her to create another extraordinary role excited the latent producer in me. I knew that the underlying rights to that property resided with the Ormond St. Children's Hospital in London, Since the property had been produced as the famous musical, I had to find out if the rights were available for a straight production. I went to London to meet with the attorneys for Ormond Street and, in New York, dealt with NBC, which had produced the musical version on its network. Finally, after perhaps 18 months of work, I felt that it could be done. I triumphantly informed Julie. Alas, she informed me, she had just signed to star in a new television series.

I felt, I suppose, like a jilted suitor. Poor Julie must have felt even worse when, after only three weeks, the series was canceled. Meanwhile she was touring her wonderful one-woman show based on the poetry and life of Emily Dickinson, "The Belle of Amherst," written by Bill Luce. The artistry involved in filling a stage with a cast of characters who existed for the audience only as Julie created them by her speeches and by her reactions to their responses, some of which she recapitulated for the audience, was audacious and brilliant. She brought this American poet to life, and made us reckon with her wonderful poetry; made us marvel that a mid-19th century, single woman could have emerged as such an important voice.

A couple of years after the failure of "Operation Peter Pan," I received a call from Julie telling me that Bill Luce had written another one woman show she wanted to perform. This time it was an even more remote single woman of that period—Emily Bronte. Would I be interested in looking at it? Her thought was to stage it as a one-woman theater piece, and tour it, much as she had been doing with Belle.

I read the script and, indeed, Bill had done another superb job of bringing to life not only Charlotte Bronte, but her two sisters, Anne and Emily and their father, the Parson Bronte. The entire feeling of living in the stern Bronte household, where strictures joined with scripture, and death was never far off, created a much darker world than that of the Emily Dickinson's New England. Dickinson and the Bronte sisters demonstrated the ability to live through the isolation and create. Emily Bronte wrote, "Jane Eyre." Charlotte wrote "Wuthering Heights" and Anne "The Tenant of Wildfell Hall." A single woman living in the moors would probably have been ignored by the publishers at that time, so each sister took on male names—*Currer, Ellis,* and *Acton Bell*—to get their works published.

After reading the script, I told Julie that the similarities with "Belle" were so strong that if we put it on stage it would be like playing Belle sideways. Instead, I suggested, why not produce it as a TV special or even an art house film. Julie agreed to give it a try. I went into a frenzy of action—I did not want to let this one waft away and find Julie doing another gig again. Through my activities with the International Council of the Television Academy, I had met the head of RTE Television in Ireland. I approached them about co-producing this in Ireland in exchange for the Irish TV rights. They agreed. I turned to my sometime associates, Dick Seader and Maurice Levine, to come on board and help raise the budget. They did and they did. I was able to complete the deal to acquire the rights from Bill Luce, who agreed to join us in Ireland in case we needed any last minute changes.

Then a real stroke of luck. I had become friends with Del Mann, an OSCAR winning director, and one evening when we were chatting, I asked him if he would be interested in directing Julie Harris in a movie about Charlotte Bronte to be shot in Ireland. His eyes widened.

"You just hit the jackpot," he said. "I adore Julie, I love Jane Eyre and I am crazy about Ireland." Jackpot!

Del and I were working in Dublin with the scene designers on making a home they found in the Wicklow Mountains outside of Dublin look like the Bronte parish home in Haworth, England. Nearby were the moors that would help set the mood.

We finally got to the first day of shooting. I arrived at the location and found that, due to the jurisdictional RTE dispute, some of the crew refused to report. Included in that group was wardrobe. This meant, when we unpacked the boxers of costumes and wigs, we discovered that nothing had been done. The hairpieces had not been combed out and the dresses had not been pressed. My first reaction was one of acute embarrassment. Here I had engaged this great actress and this award-winning director to work in Ireland, and the most basic preparation, for which I was responsible, was askew. I sat there stunned and feeling quite helpless in the face of this unexpected situation over which I had no control. When I finally was ready to face Julie I was told she was in the kitchen of the house. I walked in and there was this celebrated and important actress—pressing her costume. Somehow she had gotten hold of an ironing board and an iron and was going about the business of getting her own costume into shape. Her friend, whom I had flown over with her as a courtesy, was busy combing out the wig. I could not say a word. I just took in the whole scene and retreated to check on the rest of the crew. Fortunately the camera crew was all there. We were missing a stage manager and a few others, but Del felt we could make do.

A couple of hours late, we began shooting Bronte on schedule. The production was to last just a week. We were able to make it so tight because, for one, Julie was a stage actress. She was used to long, extended periods of performing unlike most movie actors who shoot in very short takes, so Del was able to plan on extended scenes. Secondly, since there was only one performer, he did not need to repeat every shot for coverage. With more performers a thirty-second scene can sometimes take half a day, especially if one has to change camera position and do major re-lighting. The other asset we had was Julie's uncanny ability to match her emotional level of any scene, the completion of which might not be shot until a couple of days later. With only one performer, we had no one else to cut away to for reaction shots. When Julie swept out of a door in a highly emotional state, there might be a break of a couple of hours before Del was ready to shoot the sequence of her sweeping through the door on the other side. On screen that would be one continuous sequence where she had to look as emotionally distraught as she had two hours earlier. That is not easy. Nor is it easy to know that when you are the only performer, there is no place to hide. That they brought it off was due to the combination of Julie's talent and experience coupled with Del's calm and efficient way of making it all work.

Five days later, we celebrated the end of the production. It has always been one of the highlights of my career to have had a hand in producing this extraordinary film. And I do not think I will ever forget the sight of Julie at the ironing board.

Some years later, Julie was co-starring in a revival of "The Gin Game," with Charles Durning. Contemplating her successes with "Bronte" and "Belle of Amherst," I called her and reminded her not to start talking to an empty chair—that she did have another actor on stage. Many years later, Julie was celebrated as a recipient of the Kennedy Honors. She had had a stroke in her later years and was shunning contact with the outside world. To see her there, standing in her box, taking the salute of the audience, including the President of the United States, filled me with tears.

Cliff Robertson sharing his stories as one of those who were part of the Golden Age of Television. In 1957, Cliff was the lead in the original production of "Days of Wine and Roses" on Playhouse 90, but was passed over for the movie version in favor of Jack Lemon. Twenty-five years later, Cliff was still bitter about that.

Carl Reiner, now a friend with whom I often lunch, is now 90 years old—and still acting, writing, and vital!

Rudy Bond, Director Dan Petrie, George Peppard, and Albert Salmi who were part of the original production in 1956 on the US Steel Hour of "Bang the Drum Slowly," which starred a young Paul Newman.

With Eva Marie Saint, who was part of Sonny Fox Productions' "Golden Age of Television" series.

CHAPTER 22

A Different World

So how did I go from producing TV shows to using the power of story-telling to change the world, which is what I have been doing for the past twenty years? As with all the unpredictable events in my professional life, it started with a phone call, this one back in 1972.

"Hello. My name is David Poindexter and you don't know me."

True—on both accounts. He continued…

"We have a growing problem in the world, a population bomb that, if we do not deal with it now, can create huge problems for mankind. We have to get your people to make people aware of this new phenomenon."

"My people" referred to the television community, and David was calling me because I was the Chair of the TV Academy. My first reaction, knowing "my people," was a healthy skepticism that being Paul Revere to this group of commercial-minded talents would awaken nothing but shrugs. However, I invited him to drop by and chat.

Poindexter had emerged from the Methodist clergy first as an advocate for women's rights and family planning. He had the fire of the preacher on a mission. In 1968, a book, "The Population Bomb," by Paul Erlich, had been published. It focused on the little known phenomenon of a sharp spike in the world population caused not so much by a rise in fertility rates, but a considerable drop in mortality rates. It warned of the mass starvation of humans in the 1970s and 1980s due to overpopulation, as well as other major societal upheavals, and advocated immediate action to limit population growth.

This was the message Poindexter wanted to get before the TV community. I recognized the urgency of the reality and the projections of this phenomenon and, although retaining a healthy reserve of doubt that the TV community would respond, agreed to work with David to produce a conference to sound the clarion call. To my surprise, abetted by David's influence and whatever prestige accrued to me by my office, we presented an all day conference at the Plaza Hotel that fall. The morning was dedicated to presentations by people like the Erlich's, and other experts who filled in the data for the audience. The lunch was the lynchpin. I wanted to send a signal to my TV brethren that dealing with "birth control" and such was "kosher." Frank Stanton, the president of CBS-TV, and the most prestigious of the TV executives at that time, was our principal speaker. I made sure that the triple risers at the head table contained the CEOs of the largest ad agencies and executives from the other networks.

It was, I must say, a dazzling array. Norman Lear was in the audience, as were 500 other writers, program executives, performers and, I would guess, a reasonable number of unemployed professionals enjoying the food. That they came truly surprised me. That storylines, such as Maude's abortion on Lear's popular TV show would have its origins in this conference, showed me that it really was possible to use the power of TV to deal with these issues.

The party ended, but Poindexter lingered on. Anytime he was in town we would get together and he would keep me briefed on his activities. In 1985, David left Population Options, the organization he had been working with, and started Population Communications International (PCI) for the express purpose of using the power of storytelling to change attitudes and behavior.

In the 1960s, a young psychologist at Stanford, Albert Bandura, started conducting some experiments with young children as to how actions influenced behavior. He conducted a seminal experiment known as the Bobo doll experiment. From this and other research emerged Bandura's Social Learning Theory. What Bandura showed was that children who watched dolls being pounded aggressively would then behave more aggressively than children who had been made to watch less aggressive behavior. This led to Bandura's Social Learning theories; that behavior is not deterministic, but rather a compound of social interchanges and experiences. After being dominated by Skinner's deterministic theories for decades, Bandura had managed to restore the human factor into behavior theories.

In the 1970s in Mexico, a young Researcher named Miguel Sabido, working for the largest Mexican TV network, Televisa, learned of Bandura's studies and wondered if this could relate to the powerful medium of television. He flew up to Stanford, spent time with Bandura, and returned to Mexico with an improbable idea. Since the Latino version of soap operas, Telenovelas, were proving to be a powerful draw for audiences around the world, if social issues with which Mexican society was dealing could be dramatically presented in a serial drama, could this have an influence on these large audiences in shaping their behavior?

At the time, the Mexican government was pushing a major campaign to enroll people in a program designed to erase illiteracy. Not many Mexicans were signing up to this program. Sabido decided a telenovela creating characters similar to the very ones not participating might influence their behavior. When he approached his bosses at Televisa with his idea for a new telenovela that would entertain and achieve a desired end, he was given the go-ahead with the proviso that he was not to lose any ratings for the network.

To prepare for his series, Sabido did extensive research into what was holding back participation in the program. He discovered that some thought they were "too old" to learn; others could not bring themselves to believe that such a program was really meant for them. With this in

mind, his writers created characters to reflect these psychological pre-
sets. In the course of the episodes the viewers watched as these characters, who were finally convinced to enroll, could actually succeed. The
final scene of the last episode featured the oldest character shambling up
to get this graduation certificate, creating a moment of tremendous emotion and triumph. In that scene, Sabido demonstrated the power of
story-telling to change behavior. As the series played out on the Televisa
network, enrolment in the program started to increase. By the end of the
series, over a million new participants had signed up. The series was fully
sponsored and the ratings were high enough to please Sabido's hard-bit-
ten bosses.

Watching all this was David Poindexter. He quickly grasped the extraordinary significance of this proof that Bandura's Theory of Social
Learning was correct and that hooking it into the reach and power of
mass communications through story telling could create an important
new tool for improving social and health outcomes. David became, then,
the third ingredient in this methodology. Bandura was the originator.
Sabido was the transfer from psychological concept to operating system.
Poindexter was poised to become the multiplier. His first stop was India.
In 1985 the only national television network there was Doordarshan, run
by the government. Poindexter's was able to convince them to try this
methodology. The outcome was "Hum Log," the first soap opera ever
produced in India. It was not only a resounding success; it really kicked
national television viewing into a huge audience. With this affirmation
that the Sabido model could be used, Poindexter decided to use it elsewhere and thus started PCI, a not-for-profit designed to become the pioneer organization in convincing foundations and countries that he was
pushing a new concept that could become a major new weapon for dealing with social and health issues.

All through these periods, David kept me in the loop and in 1988
David invited me to join his board of international directors. And so
began yet another phase of my professional life—a phase that had

started with a phone call in 1972 and now was about to become the dominant part of my professional and, as it turned out, personal life. Through my activities with PCI, I entered into the world of foundations, the United Nations, the Centers for Disease Control and Prevention, and other persons and institutions. In 1992 I became Chairman of the Board of PCI.

I had entered a world where HIV/AIDS was becoming a frightening scourge, where women were powerless and abused, where girl children seldom went to schools and were often married off at 13 or 14 years old. The TV dramas, to be successful, required the creation of a reality that looked and sounded like that of the culture with which we were interacting. The characters had to reflect the character of those in the audience you wanted to influence. This required formative research, the kind one does before pen is set to paper, that would identify those at risk whose attitudes and behavior we wanted to modify. We had to find the producers, writers and actors in that culture who could actually create the programs, and then train them in the methodology. It necessitated working with the governmental agencies to agree on the issues to be embedded in the story lines. In countries like Brazil and the Philippines, it required some delicacy in dealing with the Catholic Church.

The members of the board came from Europe, Africa and Asia as well as the U.S. PCI was involved in the production of radio and TV serial dramas in Kenya and Tanzania, the Caribbean and China.

In 1992, when I became Chairman of the Board, I had two major goals in mind. One was to institutionalize the ideas and accomplishments of its Founder/President. David Poindexter spoke with the cadence of the minister he once was, and with the passion of a prophet. He was enormously effective in making converts of non-believers. However, if David were to disappear one morning, I saw no way for this institution to survive. I wanted to build the staff, budget and board so that the important work of PCI would carry on after David retired.

The other mission I took on was based on the fact that all our good works were going in distant places but all our fundraising was taking place in the United States. I felt it important to raise the profile of PCI in this country. When challenged by David to figure out how to do this, I suggested getting togetherall the writers and actors and programming executives involved in the eleven daily American soap operas when they would all be in New York for the Daytime EMMYs, the awards that featured the soaps. In addition, I suggested flying in their counterparts from Brazil and India and other countries where we were involved in programs that were designed to change behavior. David readily agreed.

That summer of 1992, we presented Soaps Meet Soaps, a two-hour session at the smartest boite in N.Y., the evening before the Daytime EMMY show. In addition to the large numbers of American actors, producers and network folks, we had on hand key players from Brazil, Pakistan, India, and Kenya. Celeste Holm co-hosted along with A Martinez, a leading actor in one of our soaps. During the evening, as the talent from each overseas soap took the podium, we showed a clip from their drama that illustrated how they were dealing with an issue in a dramatic and compelling fashion. For most of the audience, this was their first awareness that telenovelas were being produced all over the world and they were dealing with issues not normally engaged in by American series. One American actor turned to his companion after watching a sequence from a Globo telenovela saying, "Why can't we do stories like that?!"

Sometime after that I was meeting in Washington with the head of the Pew Foundation effort on population issues. I knew she had a good-sized allocation of money and I was urging her to consider some of our programs overseas. "This funding is only for U.S. projects," she declared.

"Ah, then what about our forthcoming Soap Summit that will bring together the people who control the story lines of the U.S. soaps?" I walked out of there with the assurance of a commitment.

As we left the office, my associate could not wait to ask me, "What Soap Summit"? Determined not to walk out of that office without a grant, I had just invented an annual event that continued for more than twenty years. With support from a number of foundations over the years, we presented full day conferences, involving the people who controlled the content of the daytime serial dramas in this country. The first "Soap Summit" was presented in L.A. in 1993. We brought in the U.S. Surgeon General from DC, Joycelyn Elders, representatives from the Centers for Disease Control in Atlanta as well as Jane Fonda. Here were these significant players taking the time and making the effort because they saw how soaps—this often dismissed and derided part of the television spectrum—could be of great importance to the country. And the creative community began taking themselves more seriously. We did not invite the actors from the soap world since they had little to do with the shape of the storylines. Those in the audience—producers and writers and network executives—heard what an important part they played, or could play, in changing behavior that would affect outcomes in critical and social health issues. The creative community response was that they began taking themselves more seriously.

We also changed the culture of the Center for Disease Control regarding communications Although there were always folks at the CDC who could not understand why this august body of scientists, epidemiologists and many other "ists," would be associated with something as frivolous as "soap operas," most of the people I dealt with at the CDC were on board. I was asked to work with a former newspaper person who worked in their communications sector, Vicky Beck. Over the years we built up a modus that worked like this.

"Vicky, I am preparing this year's Summit. I will be in Atlanta for one day in September to find out what's hot at the CDC. Will you set up as many meetings with your people as possible between 8:30 AM and 4 PM so I can begin to figure out what will be on our forthcoming program?"

Vicky would get to work and, on the appointed day, from morning to late afternoon, every 15 to 30 minutes, another disease would audition to get a part in the show. By now word had spread at the CDC that one could actually get story lines started or information imparted through these dramas that collectively reach 20 million American women—including many at highest risk. I would sit there, listening to the concerns of the CDC across a spectrum of medical issues. One morning I realized the pitch was about headaches in the work place. I interrupted the earnest presenter.

"Excuse me, but that will never become a storyline on a soap, so there is no use in continuing this presentation."

"Look, the people who are on this issue wanted to come down from Washington and we told them we would make this pitch for them, so please let us finish."

I agreed and heard them through.

After the exciting feedback from the first summit, we decided to address the newly exploding format of talk shows. Established for years in the persons of Oprah and Merv Griffin, talk shows had recently exploded into versions that exploited sexuality, focused on dysfunctional relationships and encouraged displays of hostility—sometimes acted out physically. By this time, in the early 1990s, there were twenty such programs on TV every day. They featured people rarely seen on television, and they did reach a large number of viewers, mostly women, who were at greatest risk.

We made a date for the first Talk Show Summit and I was pleased to have confirmation that Donna Shalala, Secretary of Health and Human Resources (HHS) would be our keynote speaker on that Friday night. I was not pleased to get a call from Senator Joe Lieberman's office two weeks before the event saying that the Senator would like to be part of this presentation. I was aware that Lieberman, along with Bill Bennett, former Secretary of Education under George W Bush, had been attacking these talk shows as the cause of the decline of Western Civilization.

If you are going to ask someone for his/her assistance, it does not help to beat them on the side of the head. Our approach was that these shows had impact on their audiences and we needed their help. I already knew that Lieberman would take this opportunity to don his garments of righteous wrath and flail away—not a helpful tactic. On the other hand, I was not going to summarily dismiss him.

"The problem is I have the program already in place," I told his office, which was true, but, I continued, "if he would introduce Secretary Shalala and spend five minutes talking about what a good thing it is for them to come together, that would work."

The next day, his office called back and said that would work for the Senator. He then asked me for the details of place and time. When I got to Friday night I heard, "Oh, oh." Then it hit me. The Senator was an observant Jew and would not travel or work after Sundown on Friday. This was indeed the case, and the Senator was, alas, unavailable.

Thank you, God.

Ah, but the drama was not over. The week before the Talk Show Summit, I received another call from one of the Senator's staff informing me that Bill Bennett and he were going to hold a press conference attacking the talk shows on Thursday, the day before our conference.

"Is the Senator going to blow me out of the water?"

"No. He likes you."

When I read the reports of the conference, Bennett and Lieberman ascribed most of our country's ills to these programs and suggested we would be much better off as a society if all of these shows were to be removed from the airwaves. After that blast, the press went to its day book for up-coming events and what did they see—Donna Shalala would be keynoting a conference with these very nefarious destroyers of all we hold dear. Suddenly I became the go-to guy for reactions to Lieberman and Bennett's conference. I quickly developed my political two-step response; "they want to get rid of these shows. My take is as long as these shows are on, we want them to do better."

As a result of all this stirring of the waters, 14 news camera crews arrived to cover our proceedings. In the history of not-for-profit panel discussions, I will guess this is a record. It was made even more so by Shalala's keynote address, which was the sine qua non of all keynote speeches. She was funny, direct and forceful. When she finished her remarks, I invited questions. When I gave the Secretary the microphone to answer a question, she decided to start her own talk show. She began an exchange with Jerry Springer, former Mayor of Cincinnati and one of the more notorious of the new talk show hosts. When I approached to regain control of the event, Ms. Shalala said,

"No, Sonny, I am enjoying this. You can sit down."

For the rest of the evening, I pretty much became a guest on my own show.

Perhaps the most remarkable part of entering this new world was to meet the writers and actors and others working in Africa and India on creating these radio and television series'. When we were on the island of St. Lucia, in the Caribbean, we found that the actors were recording the shows using a microphone, and recording on an antiquated audio tape machine. All the performers held regular day jobs. The idea that one could be a professional actor was not in that culture. But more pertinent, the culture of St Lucia was summed up by their own saying, "We are 83% Catholic and 87% illegitimate." St. Lucian men wore children like so many medals that attested to their male virility, but marriage was not deemed cool.

Trying to change behavior is tough, and that's the business PCI was in. It was relatively easy to raise the profile of a problem. The difficult part was to pierce the decades—or centuries—of custom and make a difference. In St. Lucia, the job was made even more difficult when the writers were told they could not use the word 'condom' due to the sensitivity of the church. Our writers decided to use the word 'catapult' each time condom would have occurred. The person would ask, "Are you getting a lubricated catapult?" Or a woman would say, "Not without using a catapult." As the series continued, listeners started to use the term 'catapult' to show they were 'in the know'. Eventually, an organization on the island decided to market condoms using the brand name "Catapult." It soon became the biggest selling brand in St. Lucia. In the ad business, this is known as a tracer—the thread one can follow from its origin on the program into society. This would have to go down as a unique tracer in the annals of research!

It took PCI nine years to get a television series on in China. Much of that delay was due to the bureaucracy of the Chinese government. David had signed an agreement with the Chinese family planning ministry to create a series that would deal with issues being faced by young Chinese women as they emerged from traditional roles into the wider educational and work places of China. The series would also deal with son preference, a big issue in Asia but most egregious in China, a culture which one way or another was disposing of girl children. As the ability to determine the sex of a child in the womb developed, Chinese families were increasingly aborting females and, any girls in orphanages were placed there by parents who, under the one child rule, did not want that one child to be a girl.

Finally, in the mid '90s, "Bao Xing" appeared on the CCTV network. It was brilliantly produced and directed. PCI supplied the funds for the training of the writers and producers and for the production. Any money that came from commercials would go to CCTV, since we were getting the air time free. The first series was followed by two more for a three-year run. The young woman lead became a movie star in China and the program won their equivalent of an EMMY. Anytime anyone wants to know why I became so involved with using the power of storytelling to purpose, I will refer them to this and show them some of the program. To have been associated with this series and the ones in Tanzania, Kenya and India put me in a position not only to feel I was making a difference but to be exposed to large numbers of remarkable people working, sometimes, under difficult circumstances, who were making a difference.

Over the years, as the research being conducted proved the effectiveness of this methodology, other organizations began to enter the fray. The BBC World Trust, a spinoff of the BBC that could accept outside financial aid to create serial programming to change behavior, became a valuable asset in this effort. They began with radio programs in the Balkans, and moved to Afghanistan while the Taliban was still in power. They produced the program in Pakistan and short-waved it into Afghanistan. When I asked the director of the BBC Trust how they knew people were listening, I discovered that on occasion British "newsmen" would visit Afghanistan and, in conversations, discovered not only were people listening but that the program was popular with the Taliban. Of course there was not a lot of entertainment going on in Afghanistan under the Taliban, so I suppose I shouldn't have been surprised that even a drama that was subtly undercutting their creed was entertaining enough to grab their attention.

All of this was confirmed when a couple of these "correspondents" were tailed by a carload of Taliban, who finally caught up with them. The Brits were understandably nervous until they understood that they were being asked what was going to happen to a character in the series in future episodes. Now the Brits understood the Taliban knew who they were, and they understood that the Taliban were really hooked on the series.

In a similar fashion, when the BBC World Trust wanted to do a television series for the Burmese, they, of course, were not allowed into the country. Instead they built a Burmese Village near its Western border, hired Burmese actors who had left Myanmar (Burma) and pumped the signal into Burma.

TELLING STORIES— THE STATE DEPARTMENT WAY

While I was becoming more involved in this exciting new world, I was going through a parallel change of life. While I was chair of PCI, presenting the annual summits, flying off to speak at a World Health Conference in Indonesia and dealing with my chair duties, I was still trying to keep my small production company active enough to keep my rent paid. This was getting more difficult as my hair grayed and the disparity in the age between me and the young TV executives became a larger factor. Ageism is not unique to television, but it is probably a larger factor than in most other business. As the ad agencies and their clients became more interested in the younger demographics of the audience, the trend at the networks was to hire programming people who reflected those demos. I was now walking into an office and behind the desk would be sitting a 27-year-old VP who, of course, would have no idea who I was. He saw his grandfather coming in, and who wants to negotiate with ones grandfather?

I would occasionally call my lovely daughter/producer, Meredith, to ask her to walk in with me so the network person would feel more comfortable. I cannot say that changed things, but I enjoyed being with Meredith. When urged by David Poindexter to continue my efforts on PCI's behalf, I explained to him that if I didn't sit at my Sonny Fox Productions desk and put stuff into the pipeline, six months later the cupboard would be bare.

"Than do this full time," was his startling response.

I had never actually considered moving from being a TV producer, something I had been involved in for so many decades, to working full time on developing this methodology—using the impact of storytelling to make a difference I realized then that I had l lost the fire-in-the-belly energy it took to make it as an independent producer in a rapidly changing production environment. I had done pretty much anything I wanted to do—or could do—in the TV world.

So in 1995 I closed Sonny Fox Consultants and became Senior VP for PCI. I opened an office in L.A. and soon had a staff of three working with me. It felt strange to get a check regularly. Suddenly I was relieved of the pressures that came from the Sisyphean labors of developing and selling programs.

CHAPTER 23

The Profit from Not-for-Profit

At the first PCI meeting I chaired in 1992, six new directors joined the board. One of them, Celestine Arndt from McLean Virginia, a comely, blonde lady, had a presence about her that automatically singled her out. When I first met Cely, the name she chose to go by, I was certainly not looking for a relationship. I had finally terminated a nine-year, on-off relationship and after a bit more dating had finally decided that part of my life was over. I was tired of it. I spent more time playing poker. Nobody cared who I was. You arrived and left these 24/7 establishments at any time and none of the other players was hurt if you did not call the next day. People would ask why I played so much poker. I would answer, "Think of it as safe sex."

I did sense that Cely was someone I would like to know better at some point. I appointed her co-chair of the Long Range Planning Committee. At this point I usually add, "without telling her what my long range plans were." Actually I had no 'long range plans' in that direction. After returning home I received a lovely two page letter from Ms. Arndt telling me how much she was looking forward to serving on the board and working with me. That did, I admit, encourage my personal interest in her.

A couple of months later I called Cely to say I was coming to N.Y. shortly and would she come up from McLean to meet with me and Jill Sheffield, her co-chair, so I could get them started on some issues. She readily agreed. About fifteen minutes later I picked up the phone and called Cely again, this time to invite her on the night of our afternoon meeting, to join me as my guest for a 'Salute to Taiwan Television' at Lincoln Center. She readily agreed. I then made one more call and blew off the lady I had already invited.

On the appointed day in 1992, Cely, Jill, and I met to discuss PCI matters and that evening I picked Cely up for the formal event. Cely told me she had been married for more than twenty years to a man in the U.S. Foreign Service. They had lived in India and Sri Lanka. They also had spent three years in Taiwan. I did not know this when I had invited her to this salute to Taiwanese TV. The planets had certainly aligned well for this evening. After the presentation was finished, a number of American and Taiwanese guests retired to a lovely club for a late dinner. We were seated at large round table Chinese and Americans interspersed. I was on the opposite side of our table, and at one point I looked over at her. She was chattering away with a Chinese gentleman—in Mandarin! My instinct had been right—this was one interesting woman.

After the dinner, I suggested we walk for a while before hopping in a cab. As we were walking eastward on 52nd Street, I suddenly stopped, swept her into my arms and impetuously planted and ardent kiss on her lovely lips. When I felt her knees buckle, I knew I had entered into new phase of my life.

Over the next six months, I met her four remarkable sons, whom, after her husband Tom's untimely death at 47, she was left to raise on her own. Our passion grew into the most unexpected loving relationship. On December 13th, 1993, Celestine abandoned her beautiful, five bedroom home on five acres abutting the Potomac and moved in with me in my two bedroom bachelor pad in the Oakwood Apartments in Burbank California.

Three weeks after arriving in our crowded quarters, the Northridge earthquake roared through about 4:30 AM, shaking us rudely and nosily awake. Our building was damaged and another 10 seconds might have wreaked total havoc. As it was our apartment was a mess. As the days went on we were feeling frequent aftershocks. When each started, you wondered is this going to be the "Big ONE?"

After three days of this rocking and rolling, Cely appeared in the living room, bags packed, and announced she was going to her mother's Hacienda in Mexico. I was left wondering if this had been one of the shortest co-habitations ever, and speculated on getting postcards from her saying, "Having a wonderful time. Glad I am not there." However, after ten days, her nerves somewhat repaired, she returned to me.

This December we will be celebrating our 19th year together. When asked about our status, I declare that I am her Prince Escort. Every man in a long-term relationship will understand that in the relationship he is, in some way, servile. By using that elegant terminology, I have, I believe, defined the position with a gloss of regality.

CHAPTER 24

Telling Stories, Saving Lives

In 1997, David retired as founder-president of PCI in 1998. In 2002 I resigned as Senior Vice President to open a new chapter in my life as a consultant dealing with the use of mass communications to improve social and health outcomes. In 2003, I was approached by Norman Pattiz, the Chair of the Near East Committee of the United States Broadcasting Board of Governors. This panel had been created by Clinton and Congress to beef up our public diplomacy. After the end of the Cold War, the Clinton administration had dismantled the public diplomacy arsenal as a dividend from the collapse of the Soviet Empire. The United States Information Service, which operated libraries and distributed films all over, the world was disbanded and folded into the state Department—a marriage of cultures, which never did work. Budgets for tours and student exchanges were drastically reduced. After 9/11, when Washington turned to the tools at hand to respond in ways other than military, the cupboard was bare. It had all been disassembled.

In 2000, the creation of the Broadcasting of Governors was one response. All American overseas broadcasting operations—The Voice of

America, Radio Free Europe—everything except military broadcasting—was put under this bureau run to be administered by eight appointees, four Democrats and four Republicans, with the Secretary of State having an ex-officio presence. Pattiz, a radio station mogul in the United States, was in charge of the Near East operations, including a 24/7 satellite television feed called Alhurra, which covered covering all the Arab countries. Competing against the national signals plus the two newly semi-independent networks, Al Jazeera and Al Arabiya, our signal was having a tough time getting viewers. Everyone understood this was an American operation and therefore tended to discount any news we presented as being slanted.

When Norman Pattiz and I met for lunch it was to discuss a matter he had raised with me.

"Could you produce a soap opera for Al Hurra?" My answer that afternoon went something like this.

"Norman, we could do a soap opera provided you accepted two important paradigm shifts. One, if you expect that through our dramas we can make the Arabs love us, I do not think we have writers brilliant enough to make that happen. Maybe if we changed some of our policies that would help. We have troops killing Arabs in two countries and we are friends with a whole bunch of authoritarian rulers. However, if our goal is to deal with the issues in these countries, customs and cultural biases that have to change in order for a pluralistic society to emerge, we might be able to help. We can deal with the status of women. We can deal with corruption. All that is the stuff of drama."

"The second shift is that after you have had your chances to approve the scripts, when production starts, there should not be an America within 20 miles of the studio in Cairo. This has to look like and smell like an Arab soap. Only then, if the stories are compelling and the production good, will we be able to lure those eyeballs away from the competing attractions."

Pattiz was enthusiastic in his response and asked me to write a proposal with a budget that he could take to his board. I left that meeting energized by this challenge. If the carriage was not ideal, it was a unique opportunity to try our methodology in a culture we had not heretofore tackled. I spent the next few weeks working on a proposal that broke the process down into a series of steps; research, development, writing and, finally five episodes to be tested. At each step the Broadcasting Board of Governors could drop the project. It would not have to commit the large sums needed for production until it was satisfied that the project was solid.

When I brought the proposal into Norman Pattiz he looked through it and said, "Great. This is just what I need." Many months later, after hearing nothing from Mr. Pattiz, I did ask him about it and he said, "Oh, it was never going to happen."

Your interpretation of that will be just as valid as mine.

Around this time, I was invited to join an interesting group in DC seeking to create a not-for-profit entity that would receive money from State and DOD as well as from private sources to underwrite co-production of serial dramas and other programming in the service of "soft" diplomacy. The host for this undertaking was Ambassador David Abshire. David was one of the old-line Republicans who, it turned out, was appalled by President George W. Bush. Abshire had been our Ambassador to NATO under Reagan and was a throwback to Republicans like Vanderbilt or Dirksen—men who took governing seriously and expected to work across the aisles. He had, in his later years, created The Office of the Study of the Presidency. With his contacts, he seemed able to get a continual stream of funding for one project or another from Congress, and had established his organization as a place to house various study groups that need a safe and responsible haven.

Around the table would assemble some people who were already engaged in the kind of programming with which I was familiar. Others included DOD reps, State Department types and the usual coterie of DC insiders. I attended several of these sessions for several years, but nothing ever seemed to get done. The problem, I suppose endemic to projects there, is that bringing in so many voices led to interesting, but unfocused outcomes. Abshire wanted to have the assurance of a lot of money in the pipeline before they could move ahead. One person in Abshire's group whom I met, Greg Franklin, had been at USIA and now, after the dissolution of that agency, was one of the misfits at State. He was interested in the use of serial dramas to achieve results and soon was introducing me to high level people at State in the Public Diplomacy area. There seemed to be receptivity to employing the serial drama methodology to impact in South Asia and Eastern Europe.

All of this culminated in early 2009, when I entered a new world as a consultant to the State Department Public Diplomacy sector. Although I had dipped in and out of this area, meeting on occasion with some of its members, I was not prepared for how unprepared I was for this peculiar culture. My experience turned out to be, by turns, enormously challenging, fascinating, troublesome and, ultimately, frustrating. That was due in part to the way the system worked but also, in some ways, to my lack of tactical prowess in working in this important, but strange, world.

Congress, in a fit of imaginative use of its resources, had neatly bypassed the Broadcasting Board of Governors, and slipped four million dollars to the Public Diplomacy Department and instructed it to find three co-production deals to create television programming for the Middle East. One of these turned out to be a proposed drama series to be produced in Cairo in partnership with a company headed by Dr. Ahmed Abou-Bakr. He had built a reputation as a producer who would not only risk his own money to produce highly charged, dramatic television series, but was also astute in selling these programs to other Arab countries. He was married to a well known TV and film actress, Tayseer.

Having entered into this arrangement, it apparently occurred to the people in charge that they had no idea how to manage this unique project. Greg Franklin, who was going to work on the development, suggested them getting in touch with me. So the phone rang one more time and I was off on this new adventure. The person at P.D. in charge was a lovely young woman named Seema Matin. Seema was an American

Muslim who, much to her father's dismay, had elected to wear a scarf head covering to denote her religious affiliation. We met, and the combination of Greg's experience working within the system and Seema's eagerness to include the methodology, seemed to promise a nice synergy.

My first indication of problems ahead was the contract they had already signed. State was to contribute $1,450,000 to a thirty-episode, hour-long drama series. This represented, according to the contract, 45% of the budget. Dr. Abou-Bakr's company was to put up the other 55%. The payout was 50% on signing and the remaining 50% on approval of cast and outline of the show. This meant that any leverage PD had was gone before the first episode was taped. Having approved the stories, State had no way of influencing the outcome once cameras started to roll. If the story or characters changed at that time, there would be no way of holding back money until "satisfactory completion." When I pointed this out to Greg and Seema, they agreed it was too late to change that since the deal was signed and the first money already committed.

The second problem was that there was no provision in the budget for research and evaluation. When one is setting out to modify attitudes and change behavior, it is essential to discover whether one has achieved that goal. In this case it was reasonable to assume that Congress was going to want to know if we moved the needle—if attitudes had changed. Seema and Greg agreed that was important, but since the contract allocating the entire amount to Abou-Bakr's company for the production had been signed, it would be difficult to claw back some of the funding for research.

Indeed, when Dr. Abou-Bakr was informed about the new wrinkle, he reacted as I knew he would. He had negotiated the contract in good faith and they were now, in his mind, grabbing a sizable chunk of his budget back. So I spoke to Dr. Abou-Bakr, and I told him how much I identified with his anger since, when I had been an NBC, I had a running war with our research department. I also explained that if the

State Department received proper evaluation the series would have the chance to go on for a few years. Without it, no way. Grudgingly, he agreed to give us $200,000 out of his budget, with the understanding that if we were able to get the research done for less, the difference would be restored to his budget.

In early May, 2009, Greg Franklin, Seema Matin and I flew into Cairo to meet with Bakr. When he responded to the request for proposal (RFP) put out by State, he offered a continuation of his successful series called "Fugitive," shot partly in the United States, dealing with an Egyptian woman who witnesses a shooting by an Egyptian assassin in this country. She is helped in this series by an FBI agent and, eventually, enters the witness protection programs. The continuation of the series would be her adventures, in Cairo; "Fugitive Two." This proposal, plus his willingness to invest $1,850.000 of his money into the series resulted in the contract. So when we arrived in Cairo, we pressed him to share with us his story line for the Fugitive Two. A meeting was set up in Seema's hotel room for our first encounter, at which he was to start the process by telling us his ideas. After our greetings we were startled by his declaration.

"I have decided not to do Fugitive Two—I have a better idea for a whole new story line."

I turned to my two State Department cohorts and asked if this presented a problem. Seema was mute—Greg said he saw no problem. With that assurance, Dr. Abou-Bakr left to write his version of the new story line. A day later we received his two page proposal on our computers. I read it with a sinking feeling, and sent a note to Seema telling her I had read it and was concerned. I still treasure her response to me. Here is the e-mail, in its entirety, I received from this Muslim-American woman.

"Oy Vey."

So we began to work with Ahmed, who clearly had friends who had lost property in Egypt, and he was going to use this series to settle old scores. I suggested we not use the wealthy and enabled as our models, since any successes they might have would result from their resources and contacts, not able to be duplicated by most of our viewers. We needed characters in the series with whom the younger and less connected citizens of Egypt, and the other Arab lands where this would be seen, could identify.

While we dealt with this, I received an E-mail from Greg Sullivan, who handled communications for the State Department South Asia Bureau (Afghanistan and Pakistan), now under the direction of Richard Holbrooke, the President's Special Envoy to South Asia.

He wanted me to go to Afghanistan, Pakistan, and/or India to explore the storylines that would work in a Pashtun language drama, and find the people and operations in South Asia that could assist in such a venture.

There was a sense of urgency in Greg's message. I responded that I had to finish my business in Cairo first, and when I returned home, we could discuss this further. I then turned my attention back to the dismal prospect for the second storyline. Over the next few days I tried to convey to Abou the underlying purpose of this collaboration. His contribution to the collaboration was his knowledge of the audiences and how to construct a drama series that would attract and hold large ratings. We now had the job of adding to the mix our desire to reach strata of his audience who were not the wealthy and the connected, and how to create characters that reflected their realities. But the methodology that had attracted the Public Diplomacy folks to this undertaking was, to Ahmed, a complication with which he was not yet comfortable.

I also realized, as we went through this exercise that the PD folks had no real grasp of why the use of TV serial drama was effective or what their expectations should be. It was no accident that an evaluation had been left out of the contract. I think their impression of the power of storytelling was, you just told a compelling story and, presto, the culture would change.

When Seema, Greg and I returned home, we continued to get the outlines for the 30 episodes on which the series would be based. The corruption of the judicial system and the plight of women in that society were interwoven with the drama and cliffhangers known to the fans of the soap opera world. Finally it was agreed that the script writing would move forward. I now confronted an issue that had been mishandled in the original contract. Each script for the hour shows would be at least 50 pages long. In the contract, Ahmed had to deliver an English translation of just one page per script. I explained to Seema why this would be a major problem; one page would touch on the action points and story development but could not include dialogue and a sense of how characters were developed. When we raised the issue with Ahmed he claimed that translating all of the script into English would cost $50,000. I asked Seema if State had the facilities to do the translation at no—or much less—cost.

Apparently not. Seema, I realized, was not comfortable arguing with Ahmed; perhaps because he was a Muslim male, perhaps because it was not in her comfort zone to be confrontational. I felt that since State was an investing partner in this series, it had a right to read, and agree with, the final scripts.

It all came to a climax at a meeting held in DC when Ahmed was going to be in town. It became increasingly clear to me that Seema was not going to insist on these translations. I therefore confronted Ahmed directly, telling him, "Ahmed you have no choice. Either you get them translated, or we will and take the payment out of the budget."

I had clearly exceeded my role as a consultant, and by filling what I perceived to be a vacuum, had co-opted Seema's authority. I received a memo from Seema instructing me not to speak with Ahmed directly any more—that he felt more comfortable dealing with her.

"But as far as this Project" she wrote, "I hope you have felt that I have been direct and clear. I asked that you not directly speak to Ahmad b/c I saw the situation works better this way. Ahmed has been asking from day one that he deal directly with State and I think it's fair since State—not Ahmed—hired the dramatic expert. I believe I see your role as advising us on the content of the scripts, budgets and any other way you can advise us."

I was told that Ahmed was explaining my 'hostility' by informing people that I had an "Israeli" brother (I don't). The flow of information slowed to a trickle and my involvement effectively ended. When months later, I inquired about the translations, I was told that Seema had found someone at State who would read the scripts and tell her whether he liked them. This was a young man who, aside from his knowledge of Arabic, had no other discernible qualification to evaluate these scripts as to their effectiveness to accomplish the original purposes.

So after all this time, I had a sense of great disappointment. It turns out that State wasn't so different from NBC after all. I suppose that when any organization grows to a certain size, the bureaucracy that forms begins to shape the culture that does not favor boldness or creativity or risk. Not imperiling one's position in the bureaucracy is more important than rocking the boat.

All the above was underscored by the follow-up to the South Asia section of State and its request for me to hurry up and go to Kabul—where I would be living in a "hooch," I was informed. It turns out a hooch is a metal cargo container of the sort one sees on the deck of container ships. They placed those in the "safe" zone of the "Golden Triangle," put in air conditioning and, I would hope, some sort of bathroom and declared it habitable.

I had made it clear to my friends at State that I would be willing to meet the producers in both Pakistan and Afghanistan and explore the difficulties as well as the opportunities, but I had no interest in moving there for any length of time. I was already 84 years old, and while I still considered all of these prospects exciting, I also knew that my energy levels were not sustainable for a long period of time.

While itineraries were being made and unmade, I asked the Pakistan desk folks what they sought from a serial drama, if one could be created. What were, for them, the critical issues? Who, in that complex of cultures, were they trying to reach? "That's why we are sending you there" was the only response I was to receive to my ongoing, detailed questions.

As spring moved into summer and the number of travel dates and itineraries multiplied, I began to understand that I was getting glints from the frenetic world that was the South Asia Bureau. Not only were relations with Pakistan deteriorating, but decisions were pending regarding our presence in Afghanistan. Overlying this was the turmoil created in the wake of Holbrooke's takeover of the department with many personnel changes and, seemingly, new policy ventures every other day. Hence the receipt one day, from an officer in Islamabad, of a form to be filled out for my "upcoming trip to Islamabad" that was followed the next day by this email:

> *Hi Sonny, just want to avoid any confusion. This form was sent to you in case we can move forward with a visit sometime. But for now, unfortunately we are not able to go forward with this visit as I explained last week.*

In the end, the trip never happened. It too trailed off in a cloud of dust and confusion. It was never actually cancelled—it just faded away. I decided the best thing I could leave behind was a deeper understanding of the methodology underlying all of these efforts. I would try to get the staffs at State, DOD, USIA and the White House Communications Office, to at least understand how to tap into the power of storytelling. Clearly those with whom I was dealing, well-intentioned as they were, did not have the depth of knowledge that underlies the effective use of serial drama to change behavior. So I offered to set up a series of seminars for all those who were now dealing with this communications sector. I felt it would be helpful to have all the departments together for presentations from Professor Bandura, and the prime researcher in this area, Arvind Singhal, as well as some of our producers and experts involved around the world who could explain why this methodology works, and what their expectations should be.

I met with members of these sectors and, while each meeting seemed to evoke interest, nothing happened. I finally realized, working from Los Angeles, there was no way I was going to change those cultures. But I still value the large numbers of well-intentioned, smart people I met along the way. Just as I could not, in a relatively short period of time, change NBC, I could not leave my imprint on the Public Diplomacy sector of State.

Perhaps it was a case of hubris on my part—but that's the way I am. I am goal oriented, and when I work from a sense of conviction, I can be effective. However, as every president has discovered, changing the deeply entrenched ways in all those agencies is like turning a large oil tanker around—by hand!

Epilogue

So, here I am, in the words of Abraham Lincoln, Four Score Years and Seven.

My professional life has spanned the start of "Candid Microphone" on radio in 1947 to, now, a digital drama series that can be downloaded onto I-Pads or Cell phones. My personal life has spanned the great Depression, WWII, the baby boom (to which I happily contributed my four), the Cold, Korean and Vietnamese wars, the A bomb, the H bomb, the Cuban Missile Crisis, an attempt at a presidential impeachment unsuccessful), two attempted assassinations (Roosevelt and Reagan) and one tragically successful, JFK. In my lifetime we have wiped out Infantile Paralysis, Small Pox and Measles, learned how to replace body parts like knees, hips and hearts and increased life expectancy for American males by more than ten years. I have seen the United States grow from 48 to 50 states, from 119 million to 320 million people and from an isolationist country to a world leader. I was born when Calvin Coolidge was president, cast my first vote for the 4th term of Franklin D Roosevelt and now live under the 15th president of my life.

I have lived more than one third of the history of this country.

At 87 years of age I should be able to reflect on this textured life with the wisdom of many sages and philosophers who have shared their thoughts over many centuries.

Alas, I confess that looking back at the peregrinations—the ziggurats of my life—I am filled not with wisdom but with a mixture of wonder and amusement—like watching a magician who has pulled off a great trick. I think, ultimately, it is about the journey. As I have written about the highs and lows of the improbable paths my life has taken, it occurs to me that the most exciting aspect has been my willingness to go through doors that suddenly opened, without knowing what really lay inside. Changing my life by switching from textiles to radio was such a choice. Flying off to St. Louis to audition for the job of host and producer of a children's TV series when I had never performed in front of a camera, never had produced a TV show and had no experience in dealing with a young audience, certainly contained a large dose of chutzpah. Sometimes I walked in and found it was a trap door. "$64,000 Challenge" was such a choice. However, one can learn even from failure. I learned about the limitations of my talent and the brutal amorality of our business. I learned from being a POW about my resources and how not to surrender control of one's life even when, externally, you have no control.

So, taking the journey, taking risks and accepting failures, are all part of an unfolding adventure. I was once asked, in a magazine interview, what my fantasies were. I thought about that for a minute and answered, "My life has so far exceeded my expectations that I don't have fantasies—I just have my life."

Three of my four children have found their calling and have produced seven wonderful grandchildren. They are now spinning off into the world—two have graduated college two are in college, two are just starting college and one is in her senior year of high school.

And then there is my heroic son, Christopher, who is 56 and has been trapped in his Schizophrenia for 40 of those years. I have come to know hospitals, half-way houses, psychotropic drugs, strait-jackets, social workers, section-8 housing and conservatorships through all these years. I have also come to understand how a brain that misfires can create alternate realities that are as vividly real as our real realities. It can create a frightening and dark world that sucks the victim in. Those who love him become outsiders trying to tear down this cage of paranoia. I have also come to know the wonderful world of professionals who spend their days and nights working with people like Chris. Finally we have all come to appreciate Chris' bravery; his willingness over the decades to fight his way back after so many collapses. Along the way, we have heard of many suicides—those who have given up. That Chris is now probably as un-sick as he has been since falling ill at fifteen, is a minor miracle. Yet, as we appreciate having him back in our homes, we all understand the cyclical nature of this tragic ailment. I sometimes feel that Chris' purpose is to keep me grounded. No matter how exotic parts of my life have been, this stark and sad reality had always been just off camera.

I realize my life has been surfeit with adventures both good and bad. My proposal from Tokyo to Gloria to fly to Japan to get married was done without any consultations—it just felt right. Declaring I was Jew-ish while standing in the snow outside a German prison camp was a gut call. Quitting the UN TV series, accepting "The New Yorkers" show and leaving "Wonderama," moving to Los Angeles—all were decisions made with a willingness to deal with the consequences if the decision turned out to have been wrong. The role of a victim—being passive—is a terri-bly negative role to embrace. It shifts the responsibility of your fate onto others. I never have wanted to give up what I finally developed in Stalag 9A; being in control of my life regardless of the circumstances.

And I plan to be in control through the end. This week I am signing the paperwork supplied by the Neptune society. I have decided to have my body cremated when I die. By making the contract now, when I am finally cured of the temporary condition from which we all suffer called life, Cely will just have to pick up the phone and they will handle the rest. And even now, my smart ass, Brooklyn based, ironic take on life is working. I told Cely the society is offering a two-fer; if she throws her-self on the pyre she won't have to pay extra!

Acknowledgments

When I look at the title of this page, my mind fills with the names of people who made the book possible. They would include those few teachers who really did help shape me, the mentor in the POW camp, the producer at the TV station in St Louis who took a wild gamble on a totally unqualified supplicant, the phone calls that changed my life; so many people whose intercessions brought me to the point where I have a life, perhaps, worth writing about.

OK, down to the business at hand.

First, and foremost, my beloved Celestine Arndt who made me feel important enough to even consider writing this book, and whose constant encouragement and love kept me going.

Linda Schreyer who played an important part at the start, a decade ago, by organizing a welter of letters, pictures, articles, and other memorabilia in chronological order and encouraging me to go for it.

My literary agent, Carol Mann, who took on the book and made me feel that there might really be a future for it.

Gary Grossman, whose friendship and experience promoting his own novels using new information technologies were of great value.

Estelle Margolis, who sharpened her proofing skills by poring over all her husband Emanuel Margolis' copious writings—especially on the first amendment cases he so often and effectively argued—and who used those skills to good effect on my words.

ACKNOWLEDGMENTS

Finally, all my "kids," now in their fifties and sixties who grew up watching my childrens shows in the '50s and '60s and who constantly encompass those experiences into their lives today. They have encouraged me to believe there are important areas to explore about that unique class of humanity we call children.

Index

CPSIA information can be obtained
at www.ICGtesting.com
Printed in the USA
LVOW12s0742160816

500535LV00003B/159/P